MW00353366

Rev. Jessica Asbell has long been one of my go-to people for guidance on ministering to children and families, and this wonderful collection of family devotions showcases the many reasons she is a trusted voice to bring alongside your family's faith journey. These devotions lead families not only into deeper relationship with God and richer understanding of the Bible but also into deeper relationship with each other and richer understanding of the things that shape us. The framework of intertwining the stories of Scripture with the shared stories of our lives and the invitation to ask questions and reflect together provides a beautiful opportunity for families to connect more deeply on this wondrous journey of life and faith.

—*John Carroll*
*Pastor, First Baptist Church*
*Danville, Virginia*

How refreshing it is to have a devotional resource for families that provides a thoughtful reflection of the Scriptures. Jessica, out of her love for family ministry, has written beautifully about the lectionary text, bringing it to life in a way that is practical and reflective. Parents will find this resource useful as a springboard for telling their own stories to their children and for reinforcing the church's journey through the seasons of our faith.

—*Ruth Sprayberry DuCharme*
*Associate Pastor of Faith Formations for Families*
*Highland Hills Baptist Church*
*Macon, Georgia*

The two words that immediately come to mind as I read Jessica Asbell's book are *personal* and *practical*. Jessica has a passion for teaching children the essence of the Christian faith. This passion resonates in every word of this great resource. I don't know of a better book for growing Christian faith through family devotions than *Where Faith & Family Meet*.

—*R. Kevin Head*
*Senior Pastor, First Baptist Roswell, Georgia*

Smyth & Helwys Publishing, Inc.
6316 Peake Road
Macon, Georgia 31210-3960
1-800-747-3016
©2019 by Jessica Asbell
All rights reserved.

*Library of Congress Cataloging-in-Publication Data*

Names: Asbell, Jessica, author.
Title: Where faith & family meet : a weekly devotion book / Jessica Asbell.
Other titles: Where faith and family meet
Description: Macon, GA : Smyth & Helwys, 2019. | Includes bibliographical
    references.
Identifiers: LCCN 2019031085 (print) | LCCN 2019031086 (ebook) | ISBN
    9781641731232 (paperback) | ISBN 9781641731607 (epub)
Subjects: LCSH: Families--Prayers and devotions. | Common lectionary (1992)
Classification: LCC BV255 .A75 2019  (print) | LCC BV255  (ebook) | DDC
    249--dc23
LC record available at https://lccn.loc.gov/2019031085
LC ebook record available at https://lccn.loc.gov/2019031086

# Where Faith & Family Meet

A BOOK OF WEEKLY DEVOTIONS

Jessica Asbell

# Dedication

This book is dedicated to my big, sometimes loud family, whose unwavering support has guided me through good times and through bad ones and who have been my biggest cheerleaders in my call to ministry. I am especially grateful for my mom, who has always been my rock, for my grandparents, Granny Rose and Granddaddy, and for Shug. I would not be who I am today without them.

I also dedicate this book to Jonathan, my partner on this journey called life. I am grateful for his encouragement and his understanding, and for the ways in which he has helped me see this project through. I am blessed!

*I hope this devotion book helps your family's faith grow!*

*Blessings,*
*Jessica*

*Jessica Abell*

# Acknowledgments

These devotions wouldn't exist without the families of First Baptist Roswell, for whom I began writing these. I am especially grateful to Kevin Head, who began writing devotions with me when I first began at First Baptist, and who encouraged me to continue writing them. And of course, this book would not have happened without the encouragement and support I received from Jonathan, my now husband. I am so lucky to have him as my cheerleader!

# Contents

# March

# April

# May

# June

# July

# August

# Year B

## January

## February

## March

## April

# Year C

# February

# March

# April

# May

# June

# July

# August

# September

# October

## November

## Extra Devotions

## About the Author

# Introduction

Dear Reader,

Thank you for choosing this book of family devotions! This is a three-year, weekly family devotion book based on the Revised Common Lectionary for 2017, 2018, and 2019. Some of the readings in later lectionaries may change slightly, but they should be similar. The lectionary is a resource for churches that cycles through most of the Bible in a three-year period. Liturgical churches generally use the lectionary to plan their worship services. It is based on the church year, which begins with Advent and ends with Thanksgiving. You can either begin with Year A of the devotions, or, if you are in a liturgical congregation and would like to follow along with your church, the church years are as follows:

- Year C: Advent 2018–Thanksgiving 2019
- Year A: Advent 2019–Thanksgiving 2020
- Year B: Advent 2020–Thanksgiving 2021
- Year C: Advent 2021–Thanksgiving 2022

Since the dates for Lent (the six weeks before Easter), Easter, and Thanksgiving vary, and there are times when some months have five weeks instead of four, you may need to adjust the devotion schedule accordingly.

Use the Scripture translation and format (digital or print) that works best for your family. Some of the more familiar stories may even be found in illustrated Bible storybooks.

These devotions are designed to help you and your family see how stories from the Bible intersect with stories from your own lives. Each devotion is divided into three sections: "Your Story," "My Story and the Bible Story," and "Discussion and Prayer." By telling your own stories to your family, you can help them see how God has touched your life and how these Bible stories are still relevant for us today. I've included several questions to help your family think about the ways in which God and the stories of the Bible affect your lives. You are welcome to use my story, or you can feel free to add more of your own.

As you go through these devotions together, I hope you will feel comfortable changing the wording as needed for your specific family situation. Many of the devotions mention parents, moms, dads, and other aspects of the family unit. My prayer is that no matter what your family looks like or what each person has experienced, you will be able to use these devotions in a way that works for you and your children.

It is my hope and prayer that this resource will help your family see how the Bible intersects with your lives and how God impacts us in important and meaningful ways. Thank you for joining me on this journey through the Bible!

Blessings,
Jessica

# Year A

# December

## First Week of Advent
### First Week of December
### Isaiah 2:1-5—"Hope"

### Your Story

Talk about what you think heaven will be like. Tell your family several things that you are looking forward to about heaven (such as seeing loved ones again, asking God questions, etc.).

### My Story and the Bible Story

When I was a kid, I loved reading about heaven. My mom would read the part in Revelation 21 that talked about heaven. I loved hearing about the pure gold of the New Jerusalem and the gems (jasper, sapphire, chalcedony, emerald, sardonyx, carnelian, chrysolite, beryl, topaz, chrysoprase, jacinth, and amethyst) in the walls. I enjoyed hearing about the pearly gates and how the Lord would be there in the middle of it all. I'm so glad the Bible paints a picture of heaven for us, but the most important thing in heaven is the Lord's presence. God will be there and will wipe away our tears. God will be the light, and we will never walk in darkness again. We can have hope because we know that one day we will be with God.

The book of Isaiah talks a lot about hope. In Isaiah 9, Isaiah prophesies about Jesus, saying that "the people walking in darkness have seen a great light; on those living in the land of the shadow of death a light has dawned" (9:2). That light, of course, is Jesus. The prophet said a child would be born and bring light to the world, and with that child would come hope.

Read Isaiah 2:1-5.

The Lord gives us hope that eventually we will be in God's house. God will judge between nations, and instead of fighting, nations will work together. "They will beat their swords into plowshares and their spears into pruning hooks" (Isa 2:4). Weapons of war will be turned into farming equipment. God reminds us of our hope that one day there will be peace. As we begin this Advent season, we light the candle of Hope and remember the hope that Jesus brings. Isaiah reminds us that the fighting and chaos in our world won't happen forever. Someday we will be with God and experience true peace. Jesus came so we could have hope. When you look around you and worry about what's happening, remember the hope that Jesus brought, and remember that God is always there.

## Discussion and Prayer

1. Ask your children what they think heaven will be like. Ask them what they are most looking forward to about heaven.

2. As a family, talk about what you can do when you feel afraid or worried. Talk about what hope means and how you can remember the hope that Jesus brings.

3. Discuss ways you can share God's hope with others this week.

4. Pray, thanking God for the hope Jesus brings to us and asking for help in feeling hopeful amid chaos.

# Second Week of Advent
## Second Week of December
## Isaiah 11:1-10—"Peace"

### Your Story

Talk about a time when you saw an animal that made you afraid. What happened?

### My Story and the Bible Story

When I was a teenager, my family and I went tubing down a river. Before we got in our rafts, the guide warned us to watch for bears. I knew that bears were dangerous and didn't want to get close to one, so as we started floating down the river, I was looking around me to make sure I didn't see any bears. I was in the lead, with my mom, sister, and aunt behind me.

When I came around a bend in the river, suddenly I saw a big black thing on the other side and I was headed right for it! I was sure it was a bear. I was terrified because I thought if I got close to it, it would attack me. I started trying to paddle away, and my mom was trying her best to get to me. As we got closer to it, though, we realized that it was a cow and started laughing with relief. I wasn't in much trouble with that cow, but if it had been a bear, it would have been very dangerous. I could have been hurt. We learn what animals to fear. We learn not to get close to lions, tigers, and bears (oh my!). We learn that snakes and wolves can be dangerous. But one day, we won't have to worry about which animal is safe and which one is dangerous. We won't worry when we get close to a bear or a lion. One day, all of creation will be at peace.

Read Isaiah 11:1-10.

Can you imagine a day when all animals are safe for humans to approach, when the wolf and the lamb are side by side, when children can play near snakes and not worry about being bitten? Can you picture the day when the Earth is at peace? Jesus, who is a descendant of Jesse and is the shoot that came up from the stump of Jesse, brought with him hope, and he also brought peace. He brought hope that one day there will be peace on Earth. One day, as we learned last week, the nations will be at peace and there will be no more war. And one day, all creation will be at peace too. One day, we will not need to fear any animal because we will all be at peace. What a beautiful picture of heaven (known as the mountain of the Lord in Isaiah): all creation will be at peace with one another! We can look forward to the day when there will be peace forever between humans and creatures. Jesus came so we could have hope and peace. As we light the candle of Peace on the second Sunday of Advent, we remember the peace that Jesus brings.

## Discussion and Prayer

1. Ask your children if they have been afraid of any animals. If so, talk about how one day they will be at peace with them. (If your child is afraid of a specific kind of animal that they pass frequently, like dogs, talk to them about how Jesus can give them peace and help them not be afraid. Talk about ways to stay safe around animals who may be dangerous.)

2. Talk about which animals you'd like to see up close if they weren't dangerous. (You might even plan a trip to a zoo or aquarium.)

3. As a family, find ways to share Jesus' peace this week with those around you.

4. Pray, thanking God that one day all of creation will be at peace and asking God for peace for any situations in your life that need peace.

# Third Week of Advent
## Third Week of December
## Isaiah 35:1-10—"Joy"

## Your Story

Talk about a time when you felt joy during a difficult circumstance.

## My Story and the Bible Story

There's a catchy song on the radio about how God makes diamonds out of dust (Hawk Nelson, "Diamonds," 2015). God takes the dustiness of our lives—the mistakes and the bad things that happen to us—and uses them to make diamonds. In order for coal to turn into diamonds, it must undergo a lot of pressure. But then it turns into something beautiful! Something like this can happen to us. In our lives, the pressure may be hard situations or circumstances, sad things that happen, or even just the ordinary time when things are not very exciting. There are times when we are happy or sad, times when we want to sing, and times when we are mad. But whatever happens, God can make something beautiful, and the joy of the Lord can be our strength. God helps us get through everything that happens. Even though we may not feel happy, we choose to have joy because we know that God is there, and God is bigger than anything that happens to us. Joy is the emotion of great delight or happiness, but it's deeper than just being happy. We take delight in God because God saves us. We trust that God delights in us and loves us, and we bring God joy as well. Have you ever thought about that? You bring God joy.

Read Isaiah 35:1-10.

What a picture! Everything will burst into bloom. The wilderness will shout for joy. God will come! The blind will see and the deaf will hear. The physically disabled will leap and those who cannot speak will shout for joy. The burning sand will become a pool. And the redeemed will have everlasting joy crowning their heads. "Gladness and joy will overtake them, and sorrow and sighing will flee away." Right now, we have joy because of God. We can delight in knowing that God saves us and that someday we will always be with God. But there are times when it's hard to have joy. There are times when terrible things happen and it's hard to be joyful. But Jesus came and brought hope of a new tomorrow, peace, and joy. We have been redeemed! We can have joy because of Jesus and because we know that God is always there, will give us strength when we need it, and loves us no matter what happens. Remember that the joy of the Lord is your strength. God is always there for you. As we light the Advent candle of Joy, we remember the joy that God gives us.

## Discussion and Prayer

1. Ask your children to talk about a tough situation they have faced. Talk about ways we can choose joy when difficult things happen (for example, we can pray and ask God for help, we can try to find something good in a situation, and we can remind ourselves of how much God loves us).

2. Talk about how happiness is a feeling we get when something good happens to us and how we choose to have joy no matter what happens.

3. How can you share God's joy with someone this week?

4. Pray, asking God to help you be joyful in every situation and to remind you of God's presence.

# Fourth Week of Advent
## Fourth Week of December
## Matthew 1:18-25—"Love"

## Your Story

Talk about a time when you felt love.

## My Story and the Bible Story

In the book *Love You Forever*, both the mother and the son sing these words to each other at different times in their lives: "I'll love you forever, I'll like you for always, as long as I'm living my baby you'll be."[1] There are different kinds of love. We love our friends and we love our families. But there's no stronger love on Earth than a parent's love for a child. Parents love their children no matter what. Your parents will love you always, and no matter how old you get, you will still be their child. God's love is like that for us. God is our heavenly parent, and God's love is stronger than anything else. God created us and loves us no matter what. And God is forever. God never dies. As long as God is there, we are God's children. This means we are God's children forever!

One night, when nobody was expecting it, God's love came down to Earth in the form of a baby.

### Read Matthew 1:18-25.

On that dark night in Bethlehem, Jesus was born. His name was also Immanuel, which means "God with us." God had come to Earth to save God's people. This happened in the only way possible—the only way that was strong enough. God saved us through love. When Jesus lived on Earth, he taught about God's love. He showed the people what God's love looked like. Then, when he died and came back to life, he showed everyone that God's love is more powerful than anything else. Nothing, not sin and not death, can ever separate us from God's love. This week, we light the candle of Love. Soon we will celebrate Jesus' birth, and with Jesus came hope, joy, peace, and love. The greatest of these is love! God showed love for us by coming to Earth, by dying for us, and by defeating sin and death. God

---

1. Robert Munsch, *Love You Forever* (Buffalo NY: Firefly Books, 1995).

was willing to go through the worst thing we can imagine to share this love with us.

God also wants us to share love with others. Love is a feeling, but it's also a choice. We can choose to share it with others, or we can choose to ignore them. We can choose to forgive others when they are mean to us, or we can choose to hurt them back. We can choose to love people when they seem unlovable, or we can turn away from them. God chooses to love us even when we are unlovable. God chooses to love us no matter what. We have a choice too. We can choose to share God's love, or we can choose to spread hate. Which will you choose?

## Discussion and Prayer

1. Talk to your kids about the reasons you love them. Share with them that you love them when they do the right thing and when they mess up, that you love them when they get As and when they get Cs, that you love them no matter what.

2. Talk about ways you can show love to others this week.

3. As appropriate, discuss what to do when people are mean to us. Sometimes simply showing love only brings us more pain. Help your children know who to talk to when they are experiencing cruelty from someone else. Explain that we can show God's love by finding help for people who are bullies.

4. Pray, thanking God for loving us no matter what. Ask for help sharing God's love with others.

### Note

Some children are aware of situations in which parents don't show love in the way that they should. If your children raise questions, be willing to talk about their concerns. Share how God's love can be shown to kids in those situations through other people who care about them.

# Christmas
## Isaiah 9:2-7—"A Child is Born"

## Your Story

Talk about how Jesus has changed your life.

## My Story and the Bible Story

When we go through tough times, when it feels like we are walking in darkness, waiting for the light to come, where do we turn? There are times when it's all I can do to push through, trying to make it to the next day. In those times, I find myself turning to God, asking for help. As I read this passage in Isaiah, I think the Israelites would agree with me. Over and over again, they turned to God, asking for help. Because God promised them a Messiah, they continued walking in darkness, waiting for the light. Trusting in God, they continued believing that the Messiah was coming. Finally, at just the right time, he came. When I go through difficult times, I remember that the child who was born changed the world. I remember that the Messiah has come, and that no matter what I go through, God is with me. I don't have to walk in darkness alone. The light is there with me.

### Read Isaiah 9:2-7.

Can you imagine the joy Mary and Joseph felt on that first Christmas morning? The people had been waiting for a Messiah for a long, long time. They had been walking in darkness, waiting for the light to come. They were clinging to the promise that God would send a Messiah who would get rid of their oppressors. Isaiah reminds us that the Messiah would be called "Wonderful Counselor, Mighty God, Everlasting Father, Prince of Peace." On that first Christmas morning, the Messiah was here! A light had dawned for the people. We know, of course, that Jesus wasn't the military leader they were expecting, but he shattered the yoke—death—that burdens us.

When it feels as if you are walking in darkness, when the world seems like a scary place and you aren't sure where to turn, remember that the light has come. And the light is with you. God is there in the midst of the darkness. There's no need to fear. The good news of Christmas is that God's light has broken through the darkness. A new day has dawned. The Messiah has come!

## Discussion and Prayer

1. Have each family member share a bit about how Jesus has changed them. Help your children find concrete ways that Jesus has changed/helped them.

2. Find a dark room in your home and a flashlight. Take everyone into that dark room and let them feel how dark it is. Then, turn on the flashlight and show them how it lights up the room. Talk about how a small light in the darkness can change everything.

3. Sing a Christmas carol in praise to God

4. Pray, thanking God for sending Jesus on that first Christmas morning. Thank God that God promises to always be with us.

# Last Week of December
# Matthew 2:13-23—"Listening to God"

## Your Story

Talk about a time when you listened to God and God kept you safe, helped you, or showed you what to do.

## My Story and the Bible Story

Have you ever felt like God was telling you to do something? There have been times when I felt like God wanted me to call someone on the phone. When I did, I learned that the person was having a tough time and I could help just by listening. After I listened and offered my help, the person usually said, "God knew just what I needed." There are times when we know that God is talking to us. There are times when it feels like God is giving us directions. When we follow, amazing things can happen. For us, most of the time God's directions don't deal with danger and safety. But for Mary, Joseph, and Jesus, following God's directions meant that Jesus stayed safe.

Read Matthew 2:13-23.

Mary and Joseph had to leave town quickly. They left during the night and headed to Egypt because a leader named Herod knew that Jesus had been born. He knew Jesus would be a threat to his power, so he tried to kill Jesus. But the angel warned Mary and Joseph, and they kept Jesus safe by taking him away from Herod to Egypt. Finally, when it was safe in Israel again, they returned, but they didn't go back to Bethlehem where Jesus was born. Instead, they went to Nazareth. Long before Jesus was born, people called prophets had said these things would happen. God had told them, and they told the people. And later, after Jesus was born, others would hear these prophecies and know that Jesus was the Messiah—the person they had been waiting for to save them. Because Mary and Joseph listened to God, Jesus was kept safe. He lived, and he grew up, and he would one day save the people from their sins.

Just like God asked the prophets, as well as Mary and Joseph, to listen, God asks us to listen too. Our situations may be different, but God still knows what's best. God knows the right thing to do. When we listen, when we follow God's directions, God can do amazing things. Because the prophets listened to God, the people discovered that Jesus was the Messiah. Because Mary and Joseph listened, Jesus survived. God can use us too. All we have to do is listen and obey. When you feel like God is talking to you, listen!

## Discussion and Prayer

1. Ask your family to talk about ways they feel like God has spoken to them. What has God asked them to do?

2. What is God asking you to do as a family?

3. How can you know what God is asking you to do? Talk about ways that you can hear from God.

4. Pray, thanking God for speaking to us and asking for help to listen and obey.

# January

## Epiphany
### First Week of January
### Matthew 2:1-12—"Star GPS"

### Your Story

Talk about a time when you didn't know where you were going and had to follow someone or something (like your GPS). Did the person (or thing) you were following get you there okay? Did you get lost? What was it like trusting someone or something else to know where you were going?

### My Story and the Bible Story

Most of us take our phones for granted. We trust that Google Maps or Waze or whatever app we use will get us safely to our destination. We enter the address and set off. Sometimes traffic happens or there's a detour, but for the most part our map apps get us where we are going, even when we aren't sure how to get there. One Thanksgiving, I was heading home to Macon. I left on Tuesday night with my cat Lucy. It was a trip I'd made many times before, but I still used Google Maps just in case there was traffic. Sure enough, there was a ton of traffic. I followed Google Maps off the interstate into unfamiliar territory. I drove down dark back roads and had no idea where I was going. I saw eyes in the bushes on the side of the road (I think it was a raccoon). I started to worry about where I was going, but Google Maps continued with its directions—go straight, turn right here—and eventually it took me back to the interstate, allowing me to avoid the traffic. I made it safely to Macon, and I thanked Google Maps for getting me there. It was hard to trust that it knew where it was going when I was on those dark back roads, but it got me where I wanted to go.

Read Matthew 2:1-12.

Thousands of years ago, Magi from the East used what may have been the first GPS: a star. These wise men or kings followed a star to the Christ child. And they didn't just follow that star for an hour or two. They followed that star for a long, long time. It would have been easy for them to change their minds and turn around. After all, they weren't sure where they were going or how long it would take. They didn't know what would happen on the journey. And yet they trusted God. They trusted that the star in the sky was important and that it would lead the way. Finally, they arrived. They saw the Christ child and rejoiced because they had found the Savior. The first GPS didn't let them down; it showed them the way.

It can be hard to trust when we don't know where we are going. We may want to turn back or try to find a different way on our own. It can be hard to trust that God knows where we are going when God asks us to do something that doesn't make much sense. But if we trust God, if we follow where God tells us to go, then like the Magi so long ago, we won't be disappointed. God won't lead us in the wrong direction. God knows where we should go. It won't always be easy, but God will always be with us. We can trust God. Sometimes our map apps let us down. Sometimes they can't find our location or get us stuck in traffic. Sometimes there's a glitch and they stop working. But we can trust that God will never let us down. God will always be there. And if we pay attention, God will show us the way to go.

## Discussion and Prayer

1. Talk about how God has led your family. You can also talk about how God led your parents, grandparents, or another family member, if that is relevant.

2. Talk about times when you had to trust God and accept that God would show you what to do.

3. Ask your children to talk about times when they followed God even when they were not quite sure what God was doing.

4. Pray, asking God to help each member of your family trust God more. Ask for help in knowing what to do and where to go.

# Second Week of January
# Isaiah 42:1-9—"The Lighthouse to the Nations"

## Your Story

Talk about a time when you have needed a light to show you the way.

## My Story and the Bible Story

My mother loves lighthouses. She enjoys collecting statues of them and visiting them. When I was growing up, every time we went to the beach, we tried to find a lighthouse. We would climb its steps all the way to the top and step out into the cool breeze. We could see for miles up there. And at night, the light shone as a beacon, showing ships where the land was, keeping them safe. Without it, they might crash into the land. But with it, they could safely reach their destination.

Isaiah tells us that Jesus is a light to the nations, kind of like a lighthouse.

### Read Isaiah 42:1-9.

Back when Isaiah wrote this, he didn't know about Jesus. But he did know that a Messiah was coming. This person would be God's servant. He would live among the people and be a lighthouse for them. During Advent, we read that "the people walking in darkness have seen a great light; on those living in the land of the shadow of death a light has dawned" (Isa 9:2). When Jesus came into the world, he brought light with him. He is the light, shining to show people the way to God. As our lighthouse, Jesus shows us the right path to take. He shows us the obstacles that are in our way and how to avoid sin. But sometimes we stumble. Sometimes we choose to do the wrong thing and we mess up. Even then, his light still shines, showing us the right way. The next time you see a lighthouse, remember that Jesus is our lighthouse, showing us the way to God.

## Discussion and Prayer

1. Ask your children to talk about a time when they had to use a flashlight to see their way in the dark. Talk about how hard it

is to walk in the dark without a light and how much a flashlight helps.

2. Talk to your children about how Jesus shows us the way to God.

3. Pray, thanking God for sending Jesus to be our lighthouse. Ask God to help us know the way to go.

# Third Week of January
# Psalm 40:1-11—"God Hears Us"

## Your Story

Talk about a time when God answered your prayers.

## My Story and the Bible Story

There was a time when I lived in a place that was far from my family and friends. I felt very alone. I knew that I was where God wanted me to be, but I was also sad and lonely. Passages like this one from Psalm 40 reminded me that God was always with me, even when I was alone. It reminded me to wait patiently for the Lord because God would hear my cry and answer my prayers. And eventually, God did. God "put a new song in my mouth, a hymn of praise." God "gave me a firm place to stand" and reminded me that God is always there.

Read Psalm 40:1-11.

Sometimes we feel left out and alone. It seems like nobody understands us and nobody hears us. But God hears our cry and will lift us up. The psalmist writes that God sets our feet on a rock and gives us a firm place to stand. This means that we belong to God and can trust that God will be there. God has so many plans for each one of us, and if we wait and watch, God will show us the way. God is quick to give us mercy when we make a mistake, and God's love is always with us. We can trust that God will hear us even when nobody else does. God's promises always come true.

## Discussion and Prayer

1. Ask your children to talk about times when God has answered their prayers. What did they pray for? How did God answer them?

2. Ask them if they'd like to share some things they are praying about so that you can pray for them as well.

3. Pray, thanking God for always hearing us. Ask God to open your eyes to see the answers to your prayers.

# Fourth Week of January
# Matthew 4:18-23—"Fishers of Men"

### Your Story

Talk about a time when God asked you to do something unexpected or when you saw God at work in something that changed your life.

### My Story and the Bible Story

Has anyone ever said to you, "Stop what you're doing and follow me"? That's not quite how I became a children's minister, but it's close. From the time I was a young teen, I knew I wanted to be an accountant. I was good with numbers, and people who like numbers tend to be accountants. Then, during my freshman year of college, my campus minister came to me saying he thought I would be a great children's intern at a church in town. Soon I realized that God wanted me to serve in children's ministry. My story isn't as dramatic as the calling of Andrew and Peter, but God still changed my life.

Read Matthew 4:18-23.

Peter, Andrew, James, and John left everything to follow Jesus. They left their nets and their boat, and, in the case of James and John, they even left their father to follow Jesus. These men were fishermen. Every day they went to the lake to catch enough fish to feed their families and to sell for money to live on. These were not rich men, and yet, as soon as Jesus called, they left the only way they had to make money so that they could follow him. They trusted that Jesus was important enough for them to leave everything. They believed in Jesus.

Most of the time, God isn't going to ask us to leave everything behind and follow like that. But even if God doesn't ask us to leave everything, God can still change our lives. Maybe God is nudging you to do something right now. Maybe God is asking you to sit with the person who is alone at lunch. Maybe God is asking you to be kind to someone who isn't kind to others. Maybe God is asking you to give up something or give something to someone who doesn't have much.

Jesus asked Peter, Andrew, James, and John to take a leap of faith. Taking a leap of faith means trusting that Jesus knows the way and that God will give us what we need to follow. Sometimes following Jesus is hard. Sometimes it makes us uncomfortable. Peter, Andrew, James, and John followed Jesus when he asked, and their lives completely changed. They were no longer fishermen. Instead of catching fish, they taught people about Jesus. They showed people how much God loved them, and they "caught" believers. Their whole lives changed when Jesus showed up at the lake. Because they trusted Jesus, the good news of Jesus spread throughout the land and eventually throughout the world. We believe in Jesus because these men trusted Jesus enough to follow him. If you trust God enough to listen to God and do what God says, your life will be changed. But it won't just be your life that changes. If you follow God and do what God says, you may even help to change the lives of the people around you.

## Discussion and Prayer

1. Talk about a time when you said yes to something God asked you to do. What happened?

2. Talk about a time when God showed up unexpectedly (when God surprised you).

3. Pray, thanking God for challenging us to follow. Thank God for the faith of Peter, Andrew, James, and John. Ask for courage to say yes to what God asks us to do.

# February

## First Week of February
## Micah 6:1-8—"What Does God Want from Us?"

### Your Story

Talk about a time when someone told you what to do but you didn't understand what they meant. Did you get clarity? If so, how?

### My Story and the Bible Story

I like to know exactly what is expected of me. If someone asks me to do something, I ask questions to make sure I know what I'm supposed to do. I hate disappointing people just because I wasn't sure what they wanted, so I make sure to ask. Sometimes we worry about disappointing God. We're not always sure what God wants us to do. We're not sure what the right thing is, and we're afraid to act because we don't want to disappoint God. The people in Micah had disappointed God in a big way, and they weren't sure how to make God happy again.

Read Micah 6:1-8.

At this time, the people made sacrifices when they did something wrong. They brought animals to the temple and sacrificed them to God. This sounds strange to us today, but it was a way for these people to show that they knew they were wrong and wanted to do better in the future. But then they really messed up. In this passage, it seems that they got tired of following God and maybe even started following a different god (there were people who worshiped a lot of different gods back then). They made some huge mistakes, and they were trying to get back to God. God wasn't happy with their animal sacrifices and didn't want them. Instead, God wanted them to do what God had asked of them. God wanted them to do what is right, to love mercy, and to walk humbly with God.

Imagine making your parents upset and trying to give them a cookie to calm their feelings. But then you turn around and do the same thing all over again. The people kept turning away from God. They kept ignoring

God and what God wanted them to do, and God was tired of their offerings. Instead, God wanted them to do what is right, to love mercy, and to walk humbly with their God. God wanted them to obey.

Sometimes it's hard for us to know what God wants us to do. While we may not turn away as much as the Israelites did, there are still times when we don't really want to do what God wants us to do. Or maybe we sort of know what God wants us to do, but we're not sure, so we do our own thing instead. The prophet reminds us that we can't just say, "God didn't tell me what to do," and do what we want to do. We know what the Lord requires, what God asks of us. Verse 8 is a great reminder: "the LORD has told you what is good, and this is what he requires of you: to do what is right, to love mercy, and to walk humbly with your God." This means we can't say to God, "I didn't know what you wanted!" We know exactly what God wants. God wants us to do what is right, to love mercy, and to walk humbly with God. If we do those things, we'll be following God and doing what God wants us to do. And then God can use us to do amazing things!

## Discussion and Prayer

1. Ask your children to talk about times when they weren't sure what to do. What happened?

2. Talk about what it means to love mercy (that is, to show compassion). Also talk about what it means to walk humbly with God (that is, to live in ways that show respect and honor to God above ourselves).

3. Discuss ways you can walk with God this week.

4. Pray, thanking God for showing us what to do and asking for courage in doing what God wants.

# Second Week of February
# Matthew 5:13-20—"This Little Light of Mine"

## Your Story

Tell about a time in your life when you felt like you were clearly shining God's light for others to see. Or tell about a time when you witnessed someone else clearly shining God's light.

## My Story and the Bible Story

Read Matthew 5:13-20.

These are the words of Jesus as he preached what we call the Sermon on the Mount.

This passage always reminds me of the song "This Little Light of Mine": "This little light of mine, I'm gonna let it shine . . . Hide it under a bushel, no! I'm gonna let it shine . . . ."

When we accept Jesus, we become a light for God. Our lives change because of Jesus. When we listen to God, we are kinder to others and we show them how much God loves them. In this way, we are a light. It's kind of like we're all walking around with candles. When it's dark, a candle is a beacon of light. When it's dark, a candle shows us what way to go. God is like that. When we aren't sure what to do or what way to turn, God shows us the way. And when we listen to God and follow God's way, we help show the way to others too.

If you have a brand-new toy that you're excited about, do you hide it away? Of course not. You show it to all your friends. In the same way, God wants us to show God's light—or love—to others. Sometimes it's hard to show God's love to others when it feels like you're the only one doing it. But the good news is that you aren't alone. When you go to church, you're in a place that is full of people shining their lights. One candle may not make much of a difference, but hundreds of candles do. You may only have one tiny light, but let your light shine because it shows others God's love. And when your little light joins with everyone else's, it makes a blazing beacon of light, pointing the way to God. Don't hide your light. Don't hide what God has done for you and how much God loves us. Share it with others.

By sharing that light and that love, you can show others how they can be friends with God too.

## Discussion and Prayer

1. Ask your children how they can share God's light with others. How can they let their light shine?

2. Talk about what it means to hide your light. Provide concrete examples (for instance, maybe someone never talks about Jesus and never shows God's love to others).

3. Talk about ways you can shine God's light as a family. Maybe someone in your neighborhood is lonely. Your family could shine God's light by becoming their friends. Or maybe you could shine God's light by sitting with someone at school who is alone or helping an elderly neighbor with yard work.

4. Pray, asking God for courage to share God's love with others.

# Third Week of February
# Matthew 5:21-26—"Anger and Words"

### Your Story

Have you ever said something in anger that you immediately regretted? Has someone ever said something to you that really hurt? Talk about one of those experiences.

### My Story and the Bible Story

"Sticks and stones can break my bones, but words can never hurt me." How many times did we hear that when we were growing up? How many times have you heard that before? When I said this as a kid, it was because someone had said something hurtful and mean to me. I said this to cover up the fact that those words did hurt. Those words made me angry and sad.

And if a good friend said those hurtful words, they hurt much more. Words are important. Our words can help people, or they can hurt people.

Read Matthew 5:21-26.

These are more of Jesus' words from the Sermon on the Mount.

Eugene Peterson's translation in *The Message* makes Jesus' message very clear: "The simple moral fact is that words kill." Jesus understood that simply obeying the commandment "do not murder" wasn't enough. Throughout history, people have used words to hurt others, and at times those words have had deadly consequences. There have been times when teens have hurt themselves or even killed themselves because of how much words hurt. There are times when we have been so hurt by words that we dreaded going to school or didn't ever want to talk to a certain person again. Words can hurt.

Our words are powerful. Our anger is powerful. When we get angry, if we aren't careful, we can lash out at others, wanting them to hurt as much as we do. Anger can make us do things that we didn't think we would ever do. You may be angry with someone, so you make fun of them about something. Pretty soon, everyone at school is making fun of them. Your words can hurt that person deeply.

We all get angry sometimes. When we get angry, let's think about what we say. Let's remember the love of God that lives in us and ask God for help in controlling our anger. God can help us let it go. It's hard not to hurt someone when they hurt us. But words are powerful. People can use words to hurt us, and we can use words to hurt others. We must remember what Jesus said: when we have hurt someone, we should ask for forgiveness. When others hurt us, we should forgive them. God forgives us no matter what we do, and God calls us to forgive others too. So before we say something, let's think about it. Are our words going to help someone, or are they going to hurt someone? Let's try to remember what Jesus said and focus on words that help, not hurt.

## Discussion and Prayer

1. Ask your children to talk about times when they have been hurt by something someone said. Be sensitive to their pain. Make sure to remind them that you love them. Also tell them that God loves them and created them to be who they are (particularly if they have low self-esteem as a result of being bullied).

2. Ask your children to talk about times when they have hurt others with the things they have said. What happened? Did they apologize?

3. Talk about ways they can change their words to be less hurtful or ways that they can learn how to control their anger (if this is an issue).

4. Pray, thanking God for reminding us how important words are. Ask for help in thinking before we speak. Ask for help in forgiving others who have hurt us with their words.

# Transfiguration Sunday
## Fourth Week of February
## Matthew 17:1-9—"Jesus Is Transformed"

### Your Story

Talk about a time when you discovered something new about a friend that you didn't know before. How did you react?

### My Story and the Bible Story

I love stories of transformation. In the story of the ugly duckling, the young bird has a hard time, but eventually he grows into a beautiful swan. In the story of the butterfly, the caterpillar eats and eats and eats, creates a cocoon, and finally emerges, having changed from a fat, wormlike creature into a butterfly with beautiful wings. In the story of Paul, Jesus meets him and transforms his life. Before Paul meets Jesus, he goes around arresting Christians for following Jesus. But after his encounter with Jesus, he is forever changed. He becomes a champion of Christians and travels all over, teaching about Jesus and his sacrifice for all people. Instead of arresting Christians, Paul himself is arrested for being one!

There are many stories of transformation in the Bible. And there are many stories of people who were completely changed when they met

Jesus. In today's story, Jesus himself is transformed. Peter, James, and John discover exactly who Jesus is, in what we call the Transfiguration.

Read Matthew 17:1-9.

When we see someone or something transformed, we want to tell the world! If you've ever seen a caterpillar turn into a butterfly, you want to tell someone what you saw. If your life was changed by Jesus, you want to tell someone. Peter, James, and John were the same way. After all, not only was Jesus transformed in front of their faces, but they also saw Moses and Elijah, important people in the Jewish faith who had died many years before. And they heard the voice of God! If I heard the voice of God, I would want to tell everyone. Peter, James, and John knew what a big deal it was that they saw Jesus speaking with Moses and Elijah. Also, like Moses after he met with God, Jesus' appearance changed so that "his face shone like the sun and his clothes became as white as light" (Matt 17:2). The disciples witnessed Jesus' glory, and they saw something they had never seen before. Then they heard God's voice saying that Jesus was God's Son and that they should listen to him. They knew then that Jesus was exactly who he said he was. Imagine how excited they were to see and hear proof that Jesus was God's Son! And yet Jesus told them not to tell anybody until he had been raised from the dead. Jesus knew that the people wouldn't believe until he had died and come back to life.

There are times in our lives when things seem too good to be true. God's grace and love seem too good to be true since we don't have to earn them. But, as the disciples found out, they are true. We can trust that Jesus is exactly who he said he is and that God gives us love and grace. God can change our lives if we let God work in us. When God changes us, we should tell everyone around us about our own transformation! Sometimes God changes our lives in big ways, and sometimes it's in small ways. But God always changes us. Whether it is helping us be kinder and more loving, or whether it is completely changing our lives, God always changes us. Be on the lookout for the transformation God is working in you and in those around you. When you see it, share it with everyone you meet!

## Discussion and Prayer

1. What are some changes God has made in you?

2. As a family, have each person share a way (or several ways) they think that God has changed them. Help younger children by sharing ways you see that God has changed them.

3. Take a nature walk and be on the lookout for transformations. When you see one, talk about how God transforms us too.

4. Pray, thanking God for changing us in good ways. Ask for help in listening to God.

# Ash Wednesday
## Last Week of February
## Psalm 51:1-17—"The Ashes"

## Your Story

Do the ashes have a particular meaning for you? Talk about your experiences with Ash Wednesday. (If you need more information about this tradition, you can learn about it in a Google search.) Do you ever feel the weight of your sin? You don't necessarily have to share your sins with your family but talk about how it feels when you give them over to God.

## My Story and the Bible Story

I began participating in Ash Wednesday services when I started attending a Catholic middle school. From that first Ash Wednesday service until now, it never ceases to amaze me how much I feel the ashes on my forehead. It's an odd feeling when someone places ashes in the shape of a cross on your skin. For me, the ashes help me feel the weight of my sin. None of us are perfect, and we all do things that are wrong. These ashes remind me of the times when I've been mean or rude or when I've said or done something that I knew was wrong. And should I forget about the ashes on my forehead, I remember as soon as I glance in a mirror. Once again, I feel the weight of my sin. But the ashes have another meaning too. They remind us of our humanity (we came from ashes and will return to ashes when we die) and our sinfulness (because ashes are dirty), but the shape of the ashes—the sign of the cross—reminds us that we are forgiven. God has taken our ashes and forgiven us. God has cleansed us and made us new. So when I wipe away those ashes at the end of Ash Wednesday, I can forget about the weight of my sin and remember that God has made me clean. I am a new creation.

Read Psalm 51:1-17.

David wrote this psalm because he had done something very wrong. He knew that he was guilty and felt the weight of his sin. He even said that "my sin is always before me." He asked the Lord to make him clean. He prayed for God to "create in me a pure heart, O God, and renew a steadfast spirit within me. Do not cast me from your presence or take your Holy Spirit from me. Restore to me the joy of your salvation and grant me a willing spirit, to sustain me." Like David, we feel the weight of our sins. The ashes on Ash Wednesday remind us of our sins. But the cross reminds us that we have been forgiven. God has cleansed us and made us new. When we ask God to forgive us of our sins, God does. God doesn't ignore us or turn away. God create in us a pure heart and renews our spirits. He makes us a new creation. God had mercy on David and He has mercy on us. He saves us. We are forgiven.

## Discussion and Prayer

1. If you have young children, talk about what sin is. Some good definitions for sin are doing something that you know is wrong, hurting other people on purpose, and knowing what is right and not doing it.

2. Talk about how we all do things that are wrong and how, through Jesus, God takes away our sins.

3. If your children have ever participated in an Ash Wednesday service, ask them if they remember what it was like.

4. Have a time of silent prayer in which each person asks God for forgiveness for things they have done that are wrong. At the end of the prayer, say to your family, "God has forgiven your sins. They are gone. God loves you and has made you clean."

# March

## First Week of Lent
### First Week of March
### Psalm 32—"Guilty"

### Your Story

Tell your children about a time when you ignored the rules and felt guilty. What happened? Were you caught?

### My Story and the Bible Story

I sometimes find myself feeling guilty about very small things. Maybe it's a conversation I had, and I feel guilty that I wasn't able to help. Or I feel guilty that I may have sounded rude (most of the time, I'm just imagining it). I feel guilty when I can't get everything done. There are times when we feel guilty about small things. But there are also times when we feel guilty about really big things. The good news is that God is always willing to forgive us for both the small things and for the really big things.

Read Psalm 32.

David talks about feeling guilty and miserable when he refused to tell God about the things he had done wrong. God already knew everything David had done but waited for David to come to God. And then an amazing thing happened: "Finally, I confessed all my sins to you and stopped trying to hide them. I said to myself, 'I will confess my rebellion to the LORD.' And you forgave me! All my guilt is gone!" (Ps 32:5). God forgave David for everything, and God forgives us always. We can never do anything that God won't forgive, but God wants to hear us confess it because it helps us feel better. When David told God everything he had done, he felt much better. He no longer felt guilty. Was David disciplined for the things he did wrong? Of course. There are always consequences to our actions. But God wasn't punishing David. God was teaching him about what was right and what was wrong. Just as our parents discipline us so that we will know the right thing to do, God allows us to live with the consequences of our actions because God loves us and wants us to do what's right. If we listen,

God tells us, "I will guide you along the best pathway for your life. I will advise you and watch over you" (Ps 32:8). God doesn't want us to feel guilty all the time. God wants us to listen to God, hear what the right thing is, and then do it.

## Discussion and Prayer

1. Ask your children to talk about a time when they felt guilty because they did something wrong. You may want to consider telling them that this devotional time is a safe space and they will not be punished if they confess something you didn't already know.

2. Talk about the importance of not holding on to guilt, as well as the importance of forgiveness.

3. Remind your family that we don't always feel like forgiving someone when they have done something hurtful to us, but we should forgive them anyway.

4. Brainstorm ideas to remind each other about forgiveness this week. You might create a poster that says "Forgive" and hang it in the kitchen, or you could take a few minutes every day to talk about how each family member forgave someone or asked for forgiveness that day. What other ideas do you have?

5. Pray, thanking God for always forgiving us. Ask God for help in letting go of any guilt you or another family member feels. Pray that God will guide your family on the best path.

# Second Week of Lent
## Second Week of March
## Psalm 121—"My Hope Is in the Lord"

## Your Story

Talk about a tough time you went through and how you received help from God. Maybe God sent someone at just the right time or something happened to help you recognize that God was at work in your life.

## My Story and the Bible Story

I am a worrier by nature. When things go wrong, I get anxious. Even when things have the possibility of going wrong, I get anxious. So it is comforting to know that the Lord who watches over us doesn't sleep. God doesn't get tired. God doesn't get anxious. My help comes from the Lord, the Maker of heaven and Earth. The Lord can calm me down. The Lord is the one I can always turn to no matter what. The best part is that God already knows what I need, and God knows what you need as well.

God is for us. God wants what is best for us. But we don't always want what's best for us. It's a good thing that our help comes from God, who knows what we need before we ever say the words. Not only does our help come from God, but our hope comes from God as well. During Vacation Bible School, we sang a song called "My Hope Is in the Lord."[2] Here are some of the lyrics:

> I can't help but feel a little down.
> A little worried when I look around.
> That's why my hope is in,
> My hope is in the Lord.
> I fix my eyes upon the God who gives,
> 'Cause all I need is what I have in him.
> That's why my hope is in,
> My hope is in the Lord.
> My hope is in the Lord.
> I belong to him.

---

2. Sanctus Real, "My Hope Is in the Lord," from *Changed*, Framework Records, 2018. See the VBS video here: www.youtube.com/watch?v=tJePCzTaQo4.

He will never let me go-oh-oh-oh.
My hope is in the Lord.
I can count on him.
My hope is in the Lord.

Read Psalm 121.

We can trust that our help comes from the Lord. We can hope in the Lord, who will never let us down. The Lord watches over us and is our help, our hope, and our salvation. When you are having a hard time, remember that God is there. God is not sleeping or playing video games. God is there with you no matter what happens. God loves and cares for you. Our hope is in the Lord!

## Discussion and Prayer

1. Ask your children to talk about times when they have trusted God. What was the situation? What happened?

2. Talk about ways to practice trusting in God during this season of Lent. Maybe for you that means praying every time you feel anxious or worried. Every time you feel scared, you pray. Every time something happens, you pray.

3. Pray, thanking God for never leaving us. Ask for help in remembering that God watches over us. Praise God for being our help and our hope.

# Third Week of Lent
## Third Week of March
## Psalm 95—"Awestruck"

### Your Story

Tell your family about a time when you have been awestruck. Did you praise God in that moment?

## My Story and the Bible Story

Have you ever been awestruck by something, perhaps a sight that took your breath away? For me, those times come most often when I am standing on top of a mountain, gazing out into the distance at the creation God has formed. Depending on the season, creation is either lush and green, alive with various colors, or waiting in the darkness to spring back to life. No matter what time of year, creation is always amazing, always awe-inspiring. Sometimes nature is the best reminder of why we worship—our God is the Creator who created everyone and everything. And our God is very creative!

Read Psalm 95.

Why do we worship? Why do we sing praises to God? Because our God is the best. God created all that we see and yet it will still fit in God's hands. God sculpted the Earth and painted the leaves. We can see how much God loves us and how creative God is simply by looking at nature. God created everything around us not only because it was beautiful and wonderful but also so it could nurture us. Trees give us the air we breathe as well as a shady place to rest. The sun grows our food. Rain gives us water. With God, we have everything we need. When we look at creation, or even when we just think about God, we should worship. We should shout praises to God because God is always with us and created everything we see. God is the best! Let's worship God with singing and thanksgiving!

## Discussion and Prayer

1. Ask your children what they would like to praise God about. Depending on their ages, you may need to guide them a bit (the food we eat, nature, pets, and so on). You might be surprised by their answers.

2. As a family, praise God through song, prayer, a poem, etc. Find a way to offer praise for God's goodness.

3. Pray, giving thanks for all that God has done and for who God is. Ask God to show you more reasons to offer praise.

# Fourth Week of Lent
## Fourth Week of March
## Psalm 23—"My Shepherd"

## Your Story

How has God guided you through your life? How has God given you peace? Talk about your memories of Psalm 23 and what these well-known words have meant in your life.

## My Story and the Bible Story

Most of the time, I associate Psalm 23 with funerals. I don't like to read this psalm because it reminds me of sadness and pain.

### Read Psalm 23.

It is also about being treasured. David says things like, "I shall not be in want" (that is, I will have everything I need), "he leads me," "he restores my soul," and "my cup overflows." David was a shepherd, so he knew what it was like to lead and care for sheep. Without the sheep, there would be no money for the shepherd, so a good shepherd treated sheep like a treasured possession. He cared for the sheep, finding them food and water and places to rest. A good shepherd made sure that even when other animals attacked, the sheep had no reason to be afraid because he was there. He kept the sheep safe and he showed them the way.

It makes sense, then, that David would compare God to a shepherd. God shows us the right way to go. God provides for us, restores our souls, and gives us peace. Even when bad things happen, God is right there beside us. We have no need to fear because the God who created the universe is there with us. Our cups overflow from the love that God gives us.

In this psalm, David doesn't say that God will take us away from the valley of the shadow of death. There will be times when we still must go through hard things. God doesn't always change our situation. But, as David says, we have no need to fear during those hard times because God is right there with us, reminding us of God's love and comforting us. God is our Shepherd, and if we allow it, God will lead us through this life—through the good times and the bad—and our lives will overflow with God's goodness and love.

## Discussion and Prayer

1. Ask your children how God has comforted them when they have been afraid or sad. Guide them to recognize that God can help them through other people, through songs, through Bible stories, and much more.

2. Talk about how God's peace feels when situations are hard. Ask your children if they have ever felt God's peace. Did it help them feel better? Did it change the way they saw a situation?

3. Pray, thanking God for peace and comfort. Ask God to walk beside you, and talk to God about situations you and your family are facing. Give those situations to God.

# Fifth Week of Lent
## Fifth Week of March
## Psalm 130—"Waiting"

### Your Story

Talk about a time when you were waiting for something good to happen. Did time seem to drag on? Did time go by quickly? Talk about what you were waiting for and how things turned out.

### My Story and the Bible Story

Read Psalm 130.

The Israelites were waiting and watching for God. They were waiting for the Messiah—God's promised one—to come, and with the Messiah would come redemption. They waited thousands of years, watching for God to arrive. Then, all of sudden, God was among them in the form of Jesus. Many believed, but some continued to wait. This week, only a few weeks before Easter, is a time of waiting. Lent is a time of waiting. It is also a time to remember the things we have done wrong and to ask God for forgiveness as we prepare for Good Friday, when Jesus died, and Easter morning, when he rose again.

We do a lot of waiting in our lives. We wait thirty minutes after we eat before jumping in the pool. We wait in line for food. We wait for Christmas and birthdays to arrive. We wait for school to be out (and sometimes that feels like an eternity!). We wait for a new game to come out or a new movie to be released. We wait for pizza to be delivered and for siblings to find their shoes. We wait for news. We spend a lot of our lives waiting. Sometimes we wait for silly things. But sometimes we wait for good, important things to happen. We wait for babies to be born. We wait to be able to drive. We wait for college acceptance letters. We wait for summer break. We wait for vacation.

Waiting is hard. It's hard to be patient when you are ready for something to happen. It seems like the hours take twice as long when you are waiting for the bell to ring and school to be out for the day. Christmas seems to take forever to get here. And for the Israelites, it must have seemed as if the Messiah would never come. Thousands of years is a long time to wait for God. And yet they continued to hope and pray and wait, knowing that God would do exactly what God had promised. They knew that they could put their hope in the Lord because the Lord would not let them down.

Maybe you are waiting to hear from God. Maybe you have been praying and praying, asking God for something, and so far you haven't gotten a response. Keep praying. Don't give up. God doesn't always say yes to our prayers, but God is always there and always responds. Like the Israelites, you can put your hope in the Lord. The Lord will never let you down. So keep waiting and keep praying. Don't give up!

## Discussion and Prayer

1. Ask your children to name some things they are waiting for. How long have they been waiting?

2. Talk about different times when you have waited on God. What was God's response to you? What did you do while you waited?

3. Ask your children to talk about times when they have waited on God. What was the outcome?

4. Talk about ways we can use a time of waiting to help others and to grow closer to God.

5. Pray, thanking God for always being there for us and that we can put our hope in the Lord. Ask God for help as we wait for a response.

# April

## Palm Sunday
### First Week of April
### Psalm 118:1-2, 19-29—
### "Celebrate the Lord!"

**Your Story**

Have you ever taken time to celebrate what God has done for you? How did you do that? Alternatively, how might you celebrate what God has done for you?

**My Story and the Bible Story**

I loved to make up songs as a child. Most of my songs were songs of praise to God. They were celebrating what God was doing in my life. Sometimes, it's easy to celebrate what God is doing. But other times, it can be hard to see what God is doing in our lives. The Psalmist reminds us that God uses things and people who are unexpected. God does things in all kinds of ways that we don't think of. And the Psalmist reminds us to give thanks, because God's love endures forever.

Read Psalm 118:1-2, 19-29.

Today is Palm Sunday. It is a day of celebration, when Jesus entered Jerusalem in the midst of a procession. The people waved palm branches and shouted "Hosanna! Blessed is he who comes in the name of the Lord." We, too, give thanks and say, "Blessed is he who comes in the name of the Lord." We give thanks because God answers us. He creates our days and He creates each of us. He has made his light to shine upon us. When we feel as if we are all alone, the Lord is there. God is our Creator, our Redeemer, our Savior, and our Friend. He reminds us of His presence, and He promises to love us no matter what. His love endures forever. When we move, God's love endures. When we change schools or change jobs, God's love endures. When our hearts are breaking, God's love endures. When we are angry, even if we are angry with God, God's love endures. When we think we can't keep going, God's love endures. We give thanks because God is our salvation. He hears us when we call. On Palm Sunday we celebrate Jesus' entry into Jerusalem. But everyday should be a celebration of what the Lord has done for us. So today, find ways to celebrate! Celebrate the day the Lord has created. Celebrate the ways that the Lord has blessed you. Celebrate that God has saved you. Celebrate!

## Discussion and Prayer

1. Talk about things the Lord has done for your family that you can celebrate.

2. As a family, decide how to celebrate these things (i.e. have a party, go get ice cream, write a song to God, send praise and worship music together).

3. Talk about ways to celebrate each week what God is doing.

4. Pray, thanking God for all that He has done for your family and for who He is. Give thanks to the Lord for he is good; his love endures forever!

# Good Friday
## Psalm 31:9-16—"In Times of Pain"

### Your Story

Talk about a painful time in your life. How did your faith see you through?

### My Story and the Bible Story

When I was in college, three people I knew died on January 25. My freshman year of college, a friend from high school died of leukemia on January 25. My sophomore year of college, my great-grandmother died on January 25. My senior year of college, my aunt died on January 25.

After my aunt's death, I struggled to move forward. I was angry and sad. Every January 25, I was filled with fear that something else would happen. Even though I was angry at God because my aunt had died, I still talked to Him. Even though I was in pain, I still said, "I trust in you, O Lord (Psalm 31:14). And slowly, the pain began to lessen. My anger grew smaller. I continued to trust in God and God helped me heal. This experience changed me and helped my faith.

Read Psalm 31:9-16.

Even though Jesus experienced terrible physical pain on the cross, he still trusted God. The words of Psalm 31:9-16 sound like they could be Jesus' words, but they came from the Psalmist. With his strength failing, Jesus was full of grief as almost everyone deserted him. Jesus even felt God had deserted him. But still, he trusted. Still, he called God "Father."

There are times in our lives when we suffer. We all go through times of anguish, times when we feel consumed by grief, times when we feel as if everyone has turned their backs on us. On that seemingly dark Friday, Jesus understood our grief and our anguish. He, too, was deserted by everyone. He, too, was consumed by grief, anguish, and pain. Our Savior can help us in times of need because he, too, has experienced those needs. Jesus' example reminds us that, in the most difficult times, we can still trust in God. And we know that God redeems us, He loves us, and He promises to be with us through it all. He helps us get through. We, too, can say, "You are my God. My times are in your hands." When you go through difficult times, trust that the Lord is right there beside you and will help see you through.

## Discussion and Prayer

1. Talk about difficult times you have faced as a family. Did you rely on God to see you through? If so, how?

2. Ask your children to talk about times when they have been in pain. Help them see how God has helped them through.

3. Pray, thanking God for helping you through difficult times and asking for help for whatever you are currently experiencing.

# Easter
## Second Week of April
## John 20:1-18—"He Is Risen!"

## Your Story

If you went to church on Easter as a child, what were some of your favorite hymns or songs that were sung on that day? Why? If you began going to church as an adult, what are your favorite Easter hymns or songs now? Why have you chosen these?

## My Story and the Bible Story

He is risen! He is risen indeed!

Easter is such a wonderful time. The dark, somber mourning of Good Friday has passed, and in its place is new life, lots of color, and thankful spirits. The best part of our story as Christians is that we are not grave people; we are resurrection people. The grave could not hold Jesus, and the grave cannot hold us. Although we will eventually leave our earthly bodies, that will not be the end of us. We will be forever with God, the created being with the Creator who made and redeems us all.

My favorite Easter hymn as a child was "Christ Arose." It begins low and somber, still in the throes of Good Friday. "Low in the grave He lay, Jesus my Savior, Waiting the coming day, Jesus my Lord." And then suddenly, it bursts forth with new life as it proclaims "Up from the grave He arose! With a mighty triumph o'er his foes, He arose a victor from the dark domain, and He lives forever with His saints to reign. He arose! He arose! Hallelujah, Christ arose!" I loved this hymn precisely because it switched from slow and somber to fast and upbeat. But it also tells us a lot about Easter. It reminds me of the excitement the disciples must have felt when they realized that Jesus was alive. Think about it: here they were trudging along in extreme pain and brokenness, and suddenly, bursting forth with new life and bringing back their hope, there was Jesus! Easter reminds us that we don't have to remain stuck in Good Friday. We don't have to remain in the midst of hopelessness. Instead, we can cling to the hope of Jesus, knowing that he defeated death and that love has won.

Read John 20:1-18.

As resurrection people, we should live as people whose sins have been forgiven, who have been made clean by the Creator of the universe, and who are dearly loved by God. Yet sometimes we allow our sin to pull us down. We allow other voices to crowd out God's, and we begin to believe that we aren't worthy of God's love. We remain in the grave of our sin. But Jesus is there with us, waiting to pull us out of sin and into new life with him. The grave could not hold Jesus. Our sin doesn't have to hold us back. May we live as people who have been forgiven and who are loved no matter what.

## Discussion and Prayer

1. Ask your children about their favorite songs for Easter. What songs do they like to sing to praise God?

2. Give each person in your family a piece of paper and a pen/pencil/marker. Have them write down things they have done wrong. Lead them in a prayer asking for forgiveness. Then tell them that God has forgiven everything they have done wrong and that God loves them. Then burn the pieces of paper or have each person tear theirs into small pieces and throw them away.

3. Praise God for Easter. Thank God for the hope that Jesus brings. Ask God for help in remembering that God's love is more powerful than anything we could ever do wrong.

# Third Week of April
# John 20:19-21—"Don't Be Afraid"

## Your Story

Talk about a time in your life when someone calmed your fears. What were you afraid of? How did that person help? Have you ever calmed someone else's fears?

## My Story and the Bible Story

These days, I find myself needing to hear "Peace be with you" a lot after I listen to the news. When I hear about attacks and shootings, I find myself afraid something will happen to me or to someone I love. Yet God promises to be with us. Jesus tells us "peace be with you." All it takes is someone reminding me of this to help me realize that I cannot live in fear. If I do, I'll never go anywhere. And I'll never do what God wants me to do if I'm constantly afraid.

Read John 20:19-21.

The disciples were afraid. Jesus had been arrested and killed because of who he was. The disciples were afraid that they, too, would be arrested and killed because they followed Jesus. So they hid, locking the doors and hoping people would forget about them. In the verses before verse 19, we read that Mary Magdalene had gone to the tomb and found it empty, so she ran to Simon Peter and John to tell them that someone had taken Jesus' body. The two men ran to the tomb so that they could see for themselves. Then they went back to their homes, but Mary Magdalene stayed by the tomb, crying. And it was there that she saw Jesus again! Jesus told her to tell the disciples that she had seen him. At the point where today's passage starts, the disciples know that Mary has seen Jesus, but they still don't understand what is happening. They haven't seen Jesus and they are afraid of what will happen to them. And then Jesus shows up!

Jesus had calmed their fears before, when they were in the boat on a lake in the midst of a storm. Now Jesus' first words to them after he rises from the dead are "Peace be with you!" He is reminding them that they have no need to fear because not even death has power over him. After they see Jesus, it seems like they are no longer afraid. They finally understand the power Jesus has.

There are times when we are afraid. Sometimes bad things happen, and we are terrified. It seems like there's a lot to be afraid of in our world: hurricanes, tornadoes, earthquakes, terrorist attacks, school shootings, and even bullying. We have a lot of reasons to be afraid. But we also have someone who calms our fears. After Jesus rose from the dead, the disciples' situation didn't change. They still could be arrested and even killed because they followed Jesus. They were no longer afraid because Jesus had given them peace. They suddenly knew that Jesus had power even over death, and there was no reason for them to be afraid. Bad things are going to happen sometimes. There will be times when we are afraid, but Jesus is more powerful than anything else. And Jesus is always there with us, whispering to us,

"Peace be with you." If you let him, he will calm your fears. He will remind you that there's no need to be afraid because he is more powerful than anything else. Nothing can happen that will take you away from God. So when you are afraid, trust in God. He cares for you and will give you peace. Jesus gave the disciples peace when they had a lot of reasons to be afraid. He'll give you peace too. There's no need to be afraid!

## Discussion and Prayer

1. Ask your children to name some things that they are afraid of. Talk about ways they can ask Jesus for peace.

2. Name some things that you have been afraid of in your life (either now or as a child) and how you worked through your fears. Did you give those fears to God? How did you feel after you let go of those things?

3. Talk about some of the things that are frightening in this world (especially terrorist attacks and school shootings). Then talk to your children about how God is always with us, and, although we don't know what's going to happen, we don't have to be afraid because we will never be separated from God.

4. Pray, thanking God for the power God has. Ask God to calm your fears. Ask for peace.

# Fourth Week of April
# Luke 24:13-35—"Recognizing Jesus"

## Your Story

Talk about a time when you saw Jesus in someone unexpected.

## My Story and the Bible Story

Jesus tends to break into our lives in unexpected ways. Maybe for you, it's the bully of the school doing something nice for someone else. Maybe it's the popular kid sitting with the outcast at lunch. However it happens, Jesus usually works through surprising people. We find him when we don't expect to. Through the years, I have found Jesus in very unexpected people, people the world overlooks. When you hear about a homeless person finding someone's life savings and giving it back to them, you see Jesus. When you hear about people running into burning buildings to save others, you see Jesus. Sometimes we see Jesus in the homeless, in a bully, in an outcast, in a prisoner, and even in someone who used to kill Christians (Paul). Church isn't the only place where we can find Jesus. We can see Jesus in the actions of people, and sometimes who Jesus uses surprises us.

Read Luke 24:13-35.

These two followers of Jesus didn't recognize him. They had seen him only a few days before, and yet they didn't recognize him. The story tells us that they were kept from recognizing him, but they weren't expecting to see him there. Sometimes we miss Jesus because we don't expect to see him there either. Jesus is all around us, working in and through the people we meet, but we must be paying attention to see him. We sometimes don't recognize Jesus because we aren't looking for him. These followers were in shock. Jesus had been killed and something strange was happening. The women had told them that they couldn't find Jesus' body. They didn't know what was going on. And while they tried to figure that out, a man came up to them on the road and asked what they were talking about. Surely this man knew what had happened! Where had he been that he didn't know what was going on? They told him all about it, not expecting this man to get angry that they didn't understand. Finally, when Jesus broke the bread, they recognized him and suddenly understood everything Jesus had said to them.

When we look for Jesus, when we expect Jesus to show up and work in our lives and the lives of others, we find him. When someone unexpected is nice to us, when someone does something to help someone else and we didn't think they would, that's Jesus. If we look for him, we will find him. This week, be on the lookout for Jesus. Try to see his face in the people you meet. If you expect to see him in others, you will. But if you aren't paying attention, you'll miss what's going on, just like those two followers almost missed who they were talking to.

## Discussion and Prayer

1. What are some ways that you have seen Jesus in others?

2. What are some ways we can recognize Jesus in the people around us? How can we show Jesus to others?

3. Pray, asking God for help seeing Jesus in others and acting like Jesus to others.

# May

## First Week of May
## John 10:1-10—"The Shepherd"

### Your Story

Talk about a time when you were lost in a group of strangers or simply when you felt very alone. Was it easy to find something familiar?

### My Story and the Bible Story

"Don't talk to strangers." It's what my mother told me when I was growing up, and maybe you say it to your own children. It can be hard to tell if a stranger might do us harm. Getting lost in a crowd of strangers can be scary. We don't know where to turn, and nobody looks familiar. We stand there, frozen and fearful. As adults, for the most part, we can pick out someone who might be safe to ask for help. But for children, being lost in a crowd can be terrifying. Imagine the joy, then, when a parent or someone you know finds you. That person is familiar. That person can be trusted. That's who you follow.

Read John 10:1-10.

In our Scripture today, Jesus basically tells people not to talk to strangers. He says that when the sheep are in their pen, anyone who tries to enter without using the gate is up to no good and may be someone who is trying to steal the sheep. But the one who enters using the gate is the shepherd. The watchman knows who the shepherd is and opens the gate for him. The sheep know who the shepherd is and follow him.

In this Scripture, we are like the sheep, and Jesus says that he is both the gate and the shepherd. We know that we should only follow what Jesus wants us to do, but sometimes we forget. We decide to stop listening to Jesus and start listening to other people, who may want us to do the wrong thing. We do the wrong thing and get hurt, but then we find our way back to Jesus. The amazing thing is that Jesus welcomes us back with open arms! He knows that we sometimes listen to those who want to hurt us, but he promises that when we listen to him and follow what he wants us to do, we will have a full life.

Sometimes it's tempting to talk to people who make promises that sound great. What they offer us may seem better or easier than what Jesus wants us to do, but the only way to have a full life and to please God is by listening to Jesus, our shepherd, and by obeying his voice.

## Discussion and Prayer

1. Talk about how easy it can be to listen to what other people want you to do. Remind your children that God has given them a conscience, a part of their minds that helps them know what is right and what is wrong. Remind them that they can always come to you if they aren't sure whether or not they should do something.

2. Ask them if there's ever been a time when they got lost in a crowd with nothing familiar around them. How did they feel? How did they feel when someone they knew found them?

3. Help your children practice ways to say no when they know something isn't right.

4. Pray, asking God to help you and your family know what is right and what is wrong. Pray for strength for your children so that they will listen to Jesus, their Shepherd.

# Second Week of May
# Psalm 31:1-5, 15-16—
# "God Is Our Fortress"

## Your Story

Talk about how God has been a rock or refuge in your life. Talk about a few times when you have turned to God during difficulty and struggle.

## My Story and the Bible Story

There have been many times in my life when it seemed like a storm was raging around me. Sometimes it was because there were actual storms and even tornadoes. In those times, I prayed for God to protect me and keep me safe, to calm my fears and remind me that God is always there with me. Other times, there weren't actual storms, but it seemed like everything was falling apart. My friends were mad at me or I couldn't do something well or I didn't make the team. Whatever it was, life wasn't great. In those times, just like with the actual storms, I prayed, asking God to be with me, to keep me safe, and to remind me that God is always there. God is our rock and our strength, a refuge and a strong fortress for us.

Read Psalm 31:1-5, 15-16.

Have you ever seen a fortress? They are usually castles, and they are built out of rock. They look imposing, like they would be hard to get into. Sometimes there are moats (deep ditches filled with water) that make it impossible to get to the door unless the drawbridge is let down. There are places where archers could shoot arrows at enemies trying to attack. It's hard to get into a fortress if the person inside doesn't want you there.

When I read Psalm 31, it reminds me of these fortresses. Our God is our fortress, a strong fortress to save us. God protects us with love. In a fortress, we are safe. Things can attack, but the walls will hold. It's the same with God. No matter what happens, no matter who is unkind to us, and no matter what we do, nothing can separate us from God. The walls will remain firm because God is holding us close. Does that mean we'll never get hurt? No, it doesn't. We may break an arm or a leg. We will be heartbroken at some point. And someday, we will die. This is true for all of us. But no matter what, God will always be there for us. God will always hold us. When we are afraid, we can pray and ask God to calm our fears. When bad things happen, we can pray and ask for help. God will lead us in the way we should go, and God will save us.

## Discussion and Prayer

1. Ask your children to talk about times when they have needed God to be their rock or refuge. What happened? How did they feel after they prayed?

2. Show your children pictures of fortresses and talk about how they are designed to protect the people inside them. Talk about how God protects us and how we never face things on our own.

3. Talk about people in your lives who may need to know that God can be their rock, refuge, or fortress. How can you help them see that God can be their safe place?

4. Pray, asking God to help you remember that God is always there. Ask for God's peace.

# Third Week of May
# Acts 17:22-31—"Be"

## Your Story

Talk about a time when you felt fully relaxed in God's presence. How did you feel just being with God?

## My Story and the Bible Story

It is difficult for me to slow down, relax, and just spend time with God. In fact, I usually measure the success of my days based on how productive I was and the amount of work I got done. Sitting and just "being" doesn't seem like a great way to find success. And yet God calls us to do just that.

When I was in seminary, my church history class took a day to visit the Monastery of the Holy Spirit in Conyers, Georgia. (If you are telling this story to your children, explain that a monastery is a place where monks live. Monks are Catholic men who have decided to live their whole lives for God. They don't get married or have a family. Instead, they live together at a place called a monastery, where they spend a lot of their time worshiping God. There are no TVs or electronic devices there.) We began our journey to the monastery at 5:30 a.m. Once we got there, we had a silent breakfast with the monks, as they do not talk until after morning prayers. At 7:00 we went to morning prayers with them, and the day officially began. Although we spent a good bit of our day talking about church history, there was time set aside to be with God. During this time, there were no distractions like TVs or phones. Instead, we were supposed to just "be" with God. I found myself walking along the lake and listening. Eventually I sat on a bench. After a few minutes, I began to relax and listen for God. Of course, that didn't last too long as the geese decided to squawk, and all too soon my busy life began again. But for those moments, I understood what it meant to be with God. I understood the verse in Acts that says, "in him we live and move and have our being" (17:28). These moments where we can simply be with God are precious. They change us. And although we must move back to our busy lives, we are never quite the same.

## Read Acts 17:22-31.

In this Scripture, Paul is teaching the people of Athens, Greece. He is speaking from a place called Mars Hill. The people had been worshiping other gods, but they also had an altar for "an unknown God." Paul was able to tell them who God is and the wonder of God's love. He reminded them that although the other gods that they sacrificed to always needed things from them, God doesn't.

Have you ever thought about that? Unlike us, God doesn't need anything. Acts 17:25 says, "Nor is God served by human hands, as though he needed something, since he is the one who gives life, breath, and everything else." Let that sink in for a second. Our God, the God of the universe, created everything. He doesn't need anything. We often get so caught up in doing God's work (helping others, volunteering, etc.)—even though these are good things—that we start to think God needs us. We think that if we don't do something, nobody else can do it, and God depends on us to get it done. It is true that we are called to be God's hands and feet on this Earth, to help those who need it. But God doesn't need us to do those things. Instead, God wants us first and foremost to simply be with God. God wants to spend time with us and wants us to be connected to the Source that gave us life. Since God created everything around us, it is "in God we live and move and have our being" (Acts 17:28). When you get caught up in and worn down from the busyness of life, remember to stop and just *be.* Relaxing and spending time being with God is one of the best ways to be filled and to feel rejuvenated. Things will get done, but take the time, as much as you can, to stop, slow down, and simply be.

## Discussion and Prayer

1. As a family, talk about intentional ways that you can all can slow down to spend time together and time with God.

2. Are there things you need to say no to?

3. Find ways this week to spend time together without distractions (no TV, no cell phones). Have conversations together. Perhaps have a family dinner a few times per week. Encourage your children to sit for a few minutes and talk to God like they would talk to their best friends.

4. If you have a closet or small room that isn't being used, create a prayer room for the family. Talk about how each of you can go in this room to spend time with God. Make it a comfortable space with few distractions.

5. Pray, asking God to help you slow down. Pray that God will show you if you need to say no to something or remove some of the busyness from your life.

# Ascension
## Fourth Week of May
## Acts 1:1-11—"A New Chapter"

### Your Story

Tell your children about the first time you left them in the church nursery or with a babysitter when they were infants. Talk about ways you tried to make it easier for them and how happy you both were when you returned.

### My Story and the Bible Story

When I went away to college, I only moved to the other side of town. Even though I was in the same town, my mother still had to leave me at Mercer

University. After we finished unpacking my things, there came a time when she had to go and I had to stay. She gave me a big hug and left me. She knew that it would be hard for me, though, so she sent me a letter every few days to encourage me. She knew I would be happy and that this was a new chapter in my life, but she also knew it would be hard in the beginning.

New chapters are exciting but also a bit scary. Moving to college was an important step for me, and it was part of being able to do things on my own. In the book of Acts, the disciples begin to face a new chapter of their own.

Read Acts 1:1-11.

Jesus knew that the disciples needed to start this new chapter: it was time for him to leave. He also knew how hard it would be for his closest friends. Jesus' death was sad and difficult for the disciples, and they were so excited to have him back after he rose from the dead. But now he had to go back to God. As we read in Acts, Jesus didn't leave them alone. He promised that the Holy Spirit would come to them. We know that the Holy Spirit would give them everything they needed to keep going, to start this new chapter, and to spread the good news of Jesus. At the time, though, it was probably scary for the disciples. They knew they would have to keep going without Jesus, and they really didn't want to.

There are times when we have to keep going without the people who feel safe and comforting to us. When your parents drop you off at day care, school, etc., you must go through your day without them. But you trust that eventually they will come back. As you grow older and eventually go to college or get a job, you will start a new chapter where you do things for yourself. Even then, your parents will be there to encourage you and give advice. Jesus sent the Holy Spirit to encourage the disciples and help them know what to do. The Holy Spirit is still with us today, leading and guiding us. New chapters don't have to be scary because we, like the disciples, have the Holy Spirit beside us.

## Discussion and Prayer

1. Ask your children to talk about how it feels to be left at a new place (school, activity, etc.). Then ask them how it feels after they've been there for a few weeks.

2. Talk about how the disciples must have felt when Jesus left them (unsure, scared, excited about a new chapter).

3. Discuss what the Holy Spirit is. Talk about ways the Holy Spirit helps us know the right thing to do, comforts us when we are scared, gives us peace when we are worried, etc.

4. Pray, thanking God for the Holy Spirit and all it does in our lives. Ask God for help in listening for what the Holy Spirit tells us to do.

# Pentecost
# End of May/Beginning of June
## Acts 2:1-21—"Pentecost"

## Your Story

Talk about a time when God did something amazing in your life. How did you feel? What did you do?

## My Story and the Bible Story

For as long as I can remember, I have loved the French language. As soon as I got to high school, I started taking French. Because I went to a private Catholic school, one of the first things I learned in French was the Lord's Prayer. When I was about 17 years old, we went to a wedding in a tiny town in Quebec. I was so excited that I got to use my French! The wedding was in both French and English, and I was thrilled when the congregation began to say the Lord's Prayer in French. I knew what they were saying, and I joined in. It was a wonderful thing to understand their prayer and to be able to recite it with them.

Read Acts 2:1-21.

The Jews in Jerusalem were amazed! They were from every nation and spoke many different languages, but they all heard about God in their own language! They understood what the disciples were saying. It didn't matter what language they spoke; they all heard about God's love. The disciples spoke Aramaic, so anyone who didn't understand Aramaic couldn't hear about God's love until an amazing thing happened—the Holy Spirit came upon the disciples like tongues of fire, and suddenly everyone understood what they were saying! It was a miracle. That day, it was revealed that God's love was for everyone. God showed them that everyone who calls on the name of the Lord will be saved and that the gospel—the good news of Jesus—is for everyone.

Maybe you haven't learned another language yet, and that's okay. There are people who tell others about God in every language. Think about the first time you heard about God's love. Now imagine all the people who spoke all kinds of different languages learning about God's love for the first time! That is what happened at Pentecost. On that day, everything changed for them because they heard about Jesus in their own languages. We can share Jesus with others too, whether or not they speak our language. There are Bibles written in nearly every language, and we can be kind to everyone we meet. Look for ways to share God's love with others this week.

## Discussion and Prayer

1. Is there anyone in your life who speaks a different language than you do? How can you share God's love with them?

2. Has God done something amazing in your life to help you understand something? Talk about that with your family.

3. Pray, giving thanks that God's love is for everyone. Ask God for help in sharing it with others.

# June

## First Week of June
## Matthew 28:16-20—
## "Sharing Jesus with Others"

### Your Story

Talk about a time when you told someone else about Jesus. What were the circumstances? Did you tell a friend or a stranger? How did the person receive it? You could also talk about a time when you shared something amazing that Jesus has done in your life. How did the person receive that story?

### My Story and the Bible Story

As a young teenager, I remember telling one of my best friends about Jesus while we were at a slumber party. She was having a hard time and she was crying. Her parents argued a lot, and she was worried about what was going to happen. Everyone else was already asleep, and I was doing my best to make her feel better. Finally, I told her about Jesus. I told her how Jesus helps me when I'm upset, and I know that even when everyone else leaves, Jesus never will. Hearing and talking about Jesus actually helped her stop crying. It made her feel better to know that Jesus would always be there for her. I don't know if that changed her life. I don't know if she became a Christian because of that conversation. But I did tell her about Jesus and how much he loves her.

Read Matthew 28:16-20.

Through the years, many of us have viewed this passage as instructing us to go to faraway places to tell people about Jesus. But as a child, and even as an adult, it can be hard to get on an airplane and go somewhere far from our homes to tell others about Jesus. Throughout history, there have even been times when we have ignored the people around us to go tell others in faraway places about Jesus. We can read this passage as a call for us to go to faraway places, but we can also read it in a different way. Instead of "go," we can read it "as you are going." *As you are going, make disciples of all nations.*

When we look at it this way, we discover we don't have to go to faraway places to tell people about Jesus. Instead, we can tell people we see every day. As you are going . . . as you are going to school, as you are going to the grocery store, as you are going to soccer or gymnastics or play dates or the pool. Whatever you are doing, you can tell others about Jesus.

And here's the really important thing: yelling at others about Jesus isn't helpful. People don't like it when you yell about things. But if you see someone upset, you can tell them how Jesus helps you when you are upset. If you see someone who is all alone, you can go talk to them and be their friend. Eventually, you may find out that they need to hear about Jesus. Then you can tell them how much Jesus means to you. When you tell others about Jesus in your everyday life, things start to happen. Some people will accept Jesus and discover how much he loves them. Other people won't accept Jesus. That's okay, because you did what you were supposed to do. You told them about Jesus. For the people who listen, you can change their lives by telling them about Jesus. Everyone needs to hear that they aren't alone in this world. Jesus says in Matthew 28:20, "surely I am with you always, to the very end of the age." Jesus is always with us. He will never leave us, no matter what. That is great news to share with everyone!

## Discussion and Prayer

1. Talk about positive ways to share Jesus with those around you.

2. As a family, have each person share ways that Jesus has helped them.

3. Talk about places where you can share Jesus with others.

4. Pray, thanking God for Jesus and asking for opportunities for you and your family to share Jesus with the people around you.

# Second Week of June
## Matthew 9:35-38—"We Are Called"

## Your Story

Talk about a time when you told someone else about Jesus. What happened?

## My Story and the Bible Story

When I was in eighth grade, I had a friend who knew about Jesus, but she didn't have a relationship with him. Even so, she was open to talking about Jesus. Whenever I could, I told her how Jesus was making a difference in my life. I told her about how Jesus helped me through tough times and how Jesus would help her too. When her family was going through a difficult time, she and I talked about how Jesus would always be there for her. I shared Jesus with my friend because she was important to me, and I shared Jesus with her because he's the most important person to me. I wanted her to have him in her life too.

Jesus called the disciples so that they could share God's love with others, and he also tells us to share God's love with others.

### Read Matthew 9:35-38.

Jesus said to the disciples, "The harvest is great, but the workers are few" (Matt 9:37). When Jesus said that, he wasn't looking at fields of wheat or corn. He was looking at a crowd of people. He knew that everyone in the crowd needed God's love. He knows that everyone on Earth needs God's love. We have all been created by God, and we all have a hole in our lives that only God's love can fill. So when Jesus said the harvest is great, he was talking about the number of people. Everyone needs God's love, but not everyone shares God's love. Jesus told the disciples to pray that God would send more people to share love with everyone around them. That's where we come in! You see, like the disciples, we are called to share God's love with others. We are God's workers!

There are lots of ways to share God's love with others. We can do something kind for someone else, like bake cookies when they are sick or help clean their yard after a storm. We can share God's love with others by listening to them when they have a bad day or when they need a friend. We can share God's love with others by giving to help them have enough to eat or warm clothes to wear. We can share God's love with others by telling our friends how God helps us. You could stand on the sidewalk and shout,

"God loves you!" to everyone you see. But when you do things to help others, when you listen to others, and when you tell your friends how God helps you, you are doing more to spread God's love than you ever could by yelling at strangers on the sidewalk.

Just like the disciples, we are called to share God's love with others. How will you share God's love this week?

## Discussion and Prayer

1. Talk about ways to share God's love this week. What are some tangible things you and your family can do to share God's love?

2. Talk about ways others have shared God's love with you.

3. Choose a few ways to share God's love with others, and take action steps to make sure you do these things.

4. Pray, giving thanks for how much God loves us and asking for help in sharing God's love with others.

# Third Week of June
# Psalm 86:1-10, 16-17—
# "Our Bighearted God"

## Your Story

Talk about a time when someone went above and beyond to help you. How did that make you feel? Has there been a time when you have gone above and beyond to help someone? How did you feel after you helped?

## My Story and the Bible Story

When I was in preschool, I had a teacher named Miss June. I loved Miss June. She had a big heart and was very sweet, but the thing I loved most about her was that she kept me company when everyone else was taking a nap. I had to do a breathing treatment for my asthma every day after lunch. While everyone else napped, I had to stay awake and use my nebulizer.

I'm sure there were a lot of other things Miss June could have done while everyone else was asleep, but she kept me company. She talked to me and even shared her cottage cheese with me. It meant a lot that she stayed with me. I didn't feel weird having to do something different from everyone else because Miss June made me feel special.

In Psalm 86, David reminds us of what a big heart God has.

Read Psalm 86:1-10, 16-17.

In *The Message*, Eugene Peterson translates verse 5 as "You're well-known as good and forgiving, bighearted to all who ask for help." Our God is a bighearted God. God listens to us, is there for us, and helps us. God knows what we need before we even ask. And God loves us enough to want what's best for us, even if what's best for us is hard. When we are alone, God is there. When we are surrounded by people but still feel alone, God is there. When we are happy, God is there. When we are sad, God is there. When we are angry, God is there. When we are scared, God is there. We can be confident that God will answer us when we call. You never have to worry about God's phone going to voicemail.

There are many songs that remind us that God is for us and not against us. God loves you! When you fall, when things don't go the way you planned, when people make fun of you, when things are hard, then, as David says, God will "gently and powerfully put [you] back on [your] feet." Even when you don't feel God's presence, God is there. Even when you're angry with God, God is there. Even when you're sad, God is there. God hears your prayers. God bends down and listens to your cries. When you are in trouble, when everything is falling apart, you can cry out to God and know without a doubt that God will always answer you.

## Discussion and Prayer

1. How do you see God's bigheartedness in your own life?

2. Has someone ever helped you when you didn't think anybody would? How did you feel?

3. Have you ever helped someone whom nobody else helped? How did you feel? How did it make them feel when you helped?

4. How can you show others how much God loves them?

5. Pray, thanking God for always being there for you and for listening to your cries for help. Give praise for how bighearted God is!

# Fourth Week of June
# Psalm 89:1-4, 15-18—"The Love of God"

## Your Story

How do you talk about God's love?

## My Story and the Bible Story

We often sang a hymn called "I Love to Tell the Story" when I was growing up. This hymn always reminds me of how much Jesus loves us. It's a story that never gets old, and one that we should never get tired of telling.

> I love to tell the story of unseen things above
> Of Jesus and his glory, of Jesus and his love.
> I love to tell the story, because I know 'tis true;
> It satisfies my longing as nothing else can do.
> I love to tell the story, 'twill be my theme in glory
> To tell the old, old story of Jesus and his love.[3]

### Read Psalm 89:1-4, 15-18.

"Your vibrant beauty has gotten inside us—you've been so good to us!" Have you ever thought about that? Our creative God's vibrant beauty, beauty that is a living, breathing thing, has gotten inside us. Not only has it gotten inside us but it also makes us beautiful. There's a saying that beauty is only skin deep, and to some extent that's true. The way you look on the outside may not necessarily match who you are on the inside. You can be beautiful on the outside and be a grumpy, mean person nobody wants to

---

3. "I Love to Tell the Story," music by William G. Fischer, lyrics by Katherine Hankey.

be around. Inner beauty, the kind that helps others, is compassionate to others, listens to others, and encourages them. This kind of beauty comes from God.

When God's vibrant beauty is inside of us, we can't help being beautiful, and that beauty overflows. As the psalmist says, we can't keep quiet. When we know how much God loves us and how much God loves everyone, we can't stop telling others about the story of God's love. We can't stop telling everyone how faithful God is. God is always faithful. God's love is the foundation for our lives. It's what keeps us grounded in our faith and steady when times are hard.

Your roof is on your house to keep you safe. It keeps things like trees, rain, and storms out of your house. It keeps you safe. God's faithfulness is like that as well. It is the roof over our world, keeping us safe. God is always with us. God holds us and will not let us go. No wonder the psalmist says that he is forever telling everyone about how faithful God is and the story of God's love! There's no other love like God's. Even the people who love you the most (your parents, grandparents, etc.) cannot always be there for you. But God is *always* there. No matter what happens, God is there. That's the story we should tell everyone we meet: the story of God's love and faithfulness.

## Discussion and Prayer

1. What are some ways in which God has been faithful to your family?

2. Ask your children about the ways they share God's love.

3. How can you share God's love and faithfulness this week?

4. Pray, giving thanks for God's love and faithfulness. Ask for help in sharing it with others.

# July

## First Week of July
## Matthew 11:28-30—"Our Burdens"

### Your Story

Talk about a time when you carried something really heavy. Be specific about what it was and how you felt when you were carrying it.

### My Story and the Bible Story

When I was a kid, we went to Mount Vernon, George Washington's home. It was also a farm, and you could carry water, rake, hoe, and do other chores to see a bit of what it was like for the slaves who lived on the farm. I have a picture of me carrying a heavy wooden contraption with buckets on either side of it. This was carried across the shoulders so that a bucket hung on either side of you, helping you to balance enough to carry the water. For me, it wasn't too heavy since there was no water, but I imagine it was heavy and hard to maneuver when the buckets were full. It could easily be a burden for the person carrying it, weighing heavily on their shoulders as they tried to get water back to the house. I tried to imagine carrying it back and forth many times a day. I would have been very tired by nightfall! Even just a little water in the bucket would feel like it weighed a ton. A person's back and shoulders would be tired, and eventually they might start walking stooped over. It would have been a hard burden to bear.

Although people can't see some of the burdens we bear, they can still be pretty heavy. Instead of carrying water, we carry things like guilt. Sometimes we feel guilty because of something we did. Even though we ask for forgiveness, the guilt doesn't go away. It can start to feel heavier and heavier. We carry things like worry. If we worry all the time, it starts to feel too heavy. We carry things like pain. Sometimes, things happen that hurt our feelings. Maybe a friend was mean to you or a bully picked on you. Maybe people in your family fight all the time, or nobody wants to be your friend. When these things happen, they can really hurt us, and that pain can feel very heavy. Whatever burden we bear, it feels heavy. That's part of why Jesus came.

Read Matthew 11:28-30.

A yoke is similar to the piece of wood that went over my shoulders and held the water buckets. It's a heavy wooden harness that fits over the shoulders of an ox to help the animal pull a heavy piece of equipment. We have invisible yokes that hold our guilt, our pain, and our worry, and they can get very heavy. But Jesus tells us to give him our burdens. He wants us to tell him what's wrong. He wants to take away our guilt, our worry, and our pain, and he will give us rest! He will give us his yoke that is much easier to carry. Instead of being heavy, his is light. When Jesus takes away our guilt, our worry, and our pain, does that mean bad things will never happen? Does that mean we will never again feel guilty or worried? It doesn't. There will still be times when we feel guilty. There will be times when we are worried about something. There will be times of pain and hurt. But Jesus reminds us that he is there with us. He's waiting to take our burdens from us. All we have to do is pray and give them to him. When we do, we find peace and rest. It's like we are trying to carry a piano (those are really heavy!) and Jesus swaps it for a newspaper. Our burdens become much lighter and we can find rest. That is great news!

## Discussion and Prayer

1. Ask your children if there are things that worry them. Ask them if they are carrying any pain. Listen intentionally as they share.

2. Write about your pain, your worries, and any guilt you are feeling. Then, as a family, tear up the papers and throw them away or burn them (depending on the age of your children). Explain that God takes our burdens and throws them away. God gets rid of them so we can have peace.

3. Pray, thanking God for giving us rest. Specifically give each of your burdens to God. Ask God for help in letting go of them.

# Second Week of July
# Psalm 65—"Everything that Grows"

## Your Story

Talk about a time when you were awestruck by the beauty of creation.

## My Story and the Bible Story

Spring and fall are my two favorite times of the year. Seeing the wonderful colors of leaves as they change in the fall fills me with delight. Likewise, seeing everything bloom and grow in the spring reminds me that new life comes every year. Winter does not have the last word. Things that seemed dead begin coming back to life as the temperature rises. I love seeing cherry trees bloom. My favorite part of my hometown is all the cherry trees. I love seeing cherry blossoms everywhere I go. When I see them, I imagine that heaven must be filled with those light pink blossoms. When we look around us and see the beauty of creation, it's easy to see God's handiwork. The Bible reminds us that it takes both sunshine and rain to make all of this grow.

Psalm 65 reminds us of God's presence and how God takes care of us as well as creation.

## Read Psalm 65.

Can you almost hear the Earth singing for joy to the Lord? God takes care of creation, sending rain to make the flowers and the fields grow. Everything bears fruit because of the care the Lord gives it. And God doesn't just make creation grow. God makes us grow too! We won't start sprouting plants on our arms or anything like that, but God helps us grow into who we are and who God wants us to be. When we arrive on God's doorstep, when we come to God, we do that because we need help. Our sins are too much for us, and we know that we need saving. So we go to God, and God does something amazing: God takes all that stuff away! God gets rid of our sins and throws them away, then invites us in. We are reminded that God is always with us and loves us no matter what. When we listen to God and follow God, we can bloom with God's fruit, the fruit of the Spirit.[4] Just as God makes the flowers and the trees bloom, the grass and the wheat fields

---

4. Galatians 5:22-23 tells us that the fruit of the Spirit is love, joy, peace, patience, kindness, goodness, faithfulness, gentleness, and self-control.

grow, and on and on, God makes us bloom as well. Imagine a spring day when everything is blooming and the Earth is bursting with possibility. If God does this for creation, imagine how much God can help us grow too! God loves us no matter what and is always ready and willing to help us grow. Listen to God because God cares for you. Follow God, and God promises to help you grow.

## Discussion and Prayer

1. Talk about your favorite parts of creation. How can you see God in those things?

2. Think back over the last few months. How has God helped you grow?

3. As a family, talk about the fruit of the Spirit and how God helps us become more like Jesus.

4. Pray, thanking God for saving us and asking for help to grow in God.

# Third Week of July
# Psalm 139:1-12, 23-24—"God Sees It All"

### Your Story

Talk about a time when you knew someone was watching over you in a helpful way. How did you feel?

### My Story and the Bible Story

When I was seven years old, I had to ride the bus for the first time. I rode the bus to my house, where my mom met me after school. And every day that I rode the bus, my grandmother would follow it. I knew that when I turned around on the bus, Shug's car would be right there, making sure I was safe. And when I got off the bus stop, she would follow me home. She knew that I needed to ride the bus, but she made sure I was safe.

Read Psalm 139:1-12, 23-24.

God knows and sees everything. God knows what we're thinking and what we're going to say before we even say it. No matter where we go, God is there. There's nothing we can do that God doesn't see. Like my grandmother followed my bus to make sure I was safe, God is always with us.

Sometimes you may feel like you're all alone. It may be when you go to a new school and don't know anybody. It may be when you go off to camp and you're homesick. Or it could be the middle of the night when there's a bad storm outside. There are times when we feel as if we are all by ourselves, but the good news is that we're never alone. We are never out of God's sight. Wherever we go, God is there. Whether it is dark outside or the sun is brightly shining, whether we are happy or sad, whether we are saying nice or mean things, God is there. God sees it all and knows it all. No matter what we say or do, God will never stop loving us. God knows every single thing about us, the good and the bad, and God loves us no matter what.

## Discussion and Prayer

1. Ask your children to talk about a time when they knew someone was watching over them. How did they feel?

2. Talk about how knowing that God is always there can help us make better choices.

3. As a family, talk about times when each of you has felt alone. How does it feel knowing that you're never actually alone?

4. Pray, giving thanks that God is always there. Praise God for always loving us, even when we do and say things that aren't very lovable.

# Fourth Week of July
# 1 Kings 3:5-12—"What Do You Want?"

## Your Story

What was your big dream as a child? Did you want to be famous? Did you want to be rich? Did you want to be powerful? Did you want to help people? Tell your family about your dreams as a child. If they changed as you grew up, talk about those as well.

## My Story and the Bible Story

As a child, I wanted to be a singer, an actress, an astronaut, a doctor, and a teacher. I wrote songs for a bit. Then I got a sparkly dress and dressed like a movie star every chance I got. Then, when I got a grade book, I decided I wanted to be a teacher. I graded the papers of my dolls and stuffed animals and kept very detailed notes. As I grew up, my dreams changed. And if you had asked me what I really wanted as a kid, I wouldn't have answered like Solomon did in the passage. I would have said, "more books!"

As a child, Solomon wanted something too. He could have asked for lots of things; after all, he was the king. Instead, Solomon asked God for something surprising.

### Read 1 Kings 3:5-12.

Solomon was a child when he became king. Everything was his, and God told him to ask for anything. Instead of asking for what he might have wanted (riches, long life, etc.), Solomon asked God for what he needed. Solomon knew that he had no idea how to be king, and he wanted to lead the people well. So he asked God for help. He asked for a heart that listened to God so he would know the best thing to do and the right choices to make. He asked God for wisdom in making decisions. Thousands of years later, Solomon is still known as a wise king. God gave Solomon what he asked for, and because Solomon asked for a heart that listened to God, God gave him so much more than he asked for.

Wisdom is priceless. Listening to God and doing what God wants you to do is worth more than all the money in this world. Pleasing your Creator and living your life doing what God says is the best thing you can do. Sometimes it means life is harder. It may mean you don't get to be rich or famous. But it does mean you will see God's blessings in your life. It means you will live your life the way God created you to live it. And when you live your life following God, you are living the best version of your life.

Money, power, and fame can be good things, but the better thing to ask God for is wisdom. If you ask, God will always help you know the right thing to do. Having the God of the universe help you make decisions is priceless.

## Discussion and Prayer

1. What do you need in your life? Talk about ways you can ask God for it.

2. Talk about what wisdom may look like in your child's/children's lives.

3. Pray, thanking God for knowing what is best for us. Ask God for wisdom. If you have a big decision you have to make, ask God for help in knowing what to do.

# August

## First Week of August
## Psalm 145:8-9, 14-21—"Don't Give Up"

### Your Story

Have you ever been ready to quit? Has something ever frustrated you so much that you were ready to give up? Talk about that with your family. Did you give up? Talk about how it felt if you did, or how you kept going if you didn't.

### My Story and the Bible Story

I love learning different languages. I took French for seven years in high school and college and I absolutely loved it. I knew what I was doing and I was good at it. When I got to seminary, I had to take a semester each of Hebrew and Greek. I loved Hebrew and grasped it quickly. It was like a puzzle, because you have to read Hebrew right to left instead of left to right. But when I got to Greek, I had a hard time. I didn't understand why the language worked the way it did, and it was literally "all Greek to me." I was frustrated, and I wanted to give up. But eventually, the more I studied, the more I understood it.

### Read Psalm 145:8-9, 14-21.

Sometimes we are ready to give up. We get frustrated with something and we want to quit. Maybe for you it's a team sport. You made the team but you've been stuck on the bench all season. Everyone else gets to play, but you're still sitting there waiting. You're tired of waiting and ready to quit. Or maybe it's math class. Maybe you just don't understand and you're ready to give up. Maybe you're being bullied at school and no matter what you do, the bully doesn't stop. You are ready to give up. Whatever it is, there are times in our lives when things are hard, when we are discouraged and ready to quit. In those times, we can turn to passages like Psalm 145, where it says that "GOD gives a hand to those down on their luck, gives a fresh start to those ready to quit." God sees everything and knows exactly how we feel. God knows when we are ready to quit, and God is there, ready to help us through. God can give us a hand and help us make a fresh start. All we have to do is pray and ask God for help.

Does that mean that the bully will stop or you will suddenly understand math class? Maybe, but maybe not. What it does mean is that the God who created the universe will help you make it through. God will give you the strength to keep going and will be right there beside you, encouraging you not to give up. As Psalm 145 says, "Everything GOD does is right—the trademark on all his works is love. GOD's there, listening for all who pray, for all who pray and mean it. He does what's best for those who fear him—hears them call out, and saves them. GOD sticks by all who love him." God sticks by you through the good and the bad, when you are happy and when you are sad, when things are great and when you're ready to give up. So don't give up, because God is right there with you, ready to help.

## Discussion and Prayer

1. Ask your children to talk about a time when they wanted to quit or give up. What happened? What did they do?

2. Talk about ways you and your family can encourage one another when someone wants to give up.

3. Talk about ways to encourage others (friends, people at school, etc.) when they want to give up.

4. Pray, thanking God for helping us not give up. Thank God for always being there for us.

# Second Week of August
# Genesis 37:1-4, 12-24—
# "Standing Up for Others"

## Your Story

Talk about a time when you stood up for someone else, or someone else stood up for you. What was the situation? What happened?

## My Story and the Bible Story

I confess that I haven't always stood up for people I didn't like. When I was in middle school, there was a guy in my homeroom who didn't have many friends. His locker was next to mine, and he always wanted to talk. I didn't want to talk to him because he seemed weird. I was polite and answered any questions he asked, but I never went out of my way to stand up for him or to be his friend. Looking back, I might have been more like Reuben than Jesus in that situation.

### Read Genesis 37:1-4, 12-24.

Joseph was the favorite son, and it seems that he liked to tell on his brothers. He was a bit of a tattletale and the favorite, and his brothers hated him for it. They hated him so much that they plotted to kill him. But Reuben knew how much Joseph meant to their father, so he stood up for Joseph . . . kind of. Reuben told his brothers not to kill Joseph but instead to throw him into a cistern. We know that Reuben intended to go back and rescue Joseph, but as we find out later in the story, that didn't happen. Instead, the brothers sold Joseph to traders and he became a slave in Egypt. Reuben kind of stood up for Joseph because he asked for Joseph's life to be spared, but at the same time, he still went along with the brothers, putting Joseph in danger. Imagine that you are in Reuben's shoes. Your little brother the tattletale is trying to tag along again. Your father always believes him when he says things about you, and you know he's your father's favorite. But you also know that it's wrong to hurt him. So you stop your brothers from doing that, but you still take part in scaring him.

Sometimes we have to stand up for people who annoy us. Maybe there's someone at school who doesn't have friends. You know you should talk to them, but they irritate you. Maybe they are the person the bully picks on. It can be hard to stand up for someone, to put yourself in harm's way, especially when they drive you crazy. But Jesus stood up for the people whom others didn't like. He stood up for the people whom others made fun of and viewed as unworthy. Jesus calls us to stand up for these people too. Reuben kind of stood up for Joseph, but he still allowed the others to scare him. It's hard to stand up for someone when everyone else is making fun of them. It's scary. You may worry that the bullies will hurt you too, or maybe they won't want to be your friend anymore. But if you pray and ask God for courage, God will help you stand up for someone else. In doing so, you will show God's love to that person. You may lose a few friends because of it, but you'll be doing what Jesus did and what God wants you to do.

## Discussion and Prayer

1. Talk about a time when you stood up for someone else or when someone else stood up for you. How did that feel?

2. Talk about a time when you felt like God was telling you to stand up for someone. What happened?

3. As a family, talk about ways we can stand up for others.

4. Pray, thanking God for standing up for us when we didn't deserve it. Ask God for courage to stand up for someone else.

# Third Week of August
# Genesis 45:1-15—
# "Look on the Bright Side"

## Your Story

Talk about a time when something good came out of a hard situation. How did you respond?

## My Story and the Bible Story

When I was in the sixth grade, there was a big argument at church. Everybody took sides and people weren't nice to each other. It got so bad that

I didn't have any friends, and I came home from church crying every Sunday. It was a tough time in my life and I was very sad. We started going to another church, a church with warm, welcoming people who always greeted us with smiles. I made new friends in the youth group, and it was there that I learned how important it is to spend time with God each day. Something good came out of a hard time in my life: I made new friends and developed a personal relationship with God.

In the Bible, Joseph was in a tough situation. His brothers hated him and sold him to some traders (after they talked about killing him). He was sent to Egypt, was important in Potiphar's house until Potiphar's wife told lies about him, then was thrown in jail, where he interpreted the dreams of two of Pharaoh's servants. From there, Pharaoh eventually heard about what Joseph had done and sent for him. Joseph became a trusted advisor to Pharaoh and was in charge of a lot in Egypt. Still, his brothers had put him in a hard situation. Joseph could have easily been angry with his brothers. He could have refused to forgive them for what they did to him.

## Read Genesis 45:1-15.

Joseph could have stayed angry with his brothers, refusing to tell them who he was and not sharing any of the food in the Egyptian storehouses. He could have given them what they asked for, nothing more, and sent them on their way. But Joseph forgave them. He could see the bright spot in everything. Because his brothers sold him into slavery, he was sent to Egypt. Because he was in jail in Egypt after Potiphar's wife lied, he was able to hear the dreams of Pharaoh's cupbearer and baker. Because God helped him interpret those dreams, eventually Joseph began to work for Pharaoh. And finally, because Joseph was working for Pharaoh, he was able to save plenty of food for the people to last through the famine, a time when nothing would grow. Eventually, all of that led Joseph right back to his brothers. He could see how God was working in the things that happened in his life. He trusted that God had a plan and that God would be there for him.

Sometimes bad things happen. We find ourselves in hard situations where we are unhappy or even scared. But we can trust that God is always with us and that God can take anything that happens and make something good come out of it. Because Joseph's brothers were mean to him and sold him into slavery, Joseph was sent to Egypt. From there, Joseph saved millions by making sure they stored up enough food before the famine. Whatever happens in your life, God can take something bad and make something good come out of it. Be on the lookout for the bright side: it's always there, even if you sometimes have to look really hard.

## Discussion and Prayer

1. Talk about a time when something tough happened. Did anything good come out of that situation?

2. Talk to your children about times when your family has dealt with a hard situation and something good came out of it.

3. How can we be on the lookout for God in hard situations?

4. Pray, thanking God for always being there for us. Thank God for helping good things come out of hard situations. Ask God for help in seeing good things in hard times.

# Fourth Week of August
# Psalm 138—"God's Love Is Eternal"

## Your Story

Talk about a time in your life when God's love and faithfulness were apparent.

## My Story and the Bible Story

I love the song "One Thing Remains." It's a song of praise to God, but it's also a reminder to us that God's love is eternal. There's only one thing that remains: God's love. God's love never fails, it never gives up, and it never quits on us. As you read these lyrics to the song, think about the power of God's love.

> Higher than the mountains that I face
> Stronger than the power of the grave
> Constant in the trial and the change
> This one thing remains
> This one thing remains

Your love never fails, it never gives up
It never runs out on me
Your love never fails, it never gives up
It never runs out on me
Your love never fails, it never gives up
It never runs out on me
Your love

On and on and on and on it goes
Yes it overwhelms and satisfies my soul
And I never, ever, have to be afraid
'Cause this one thing remains[5]

### Read Psalm 138.

David's psalm is a great reminder that God's love never fails. God never quits on us. God sees and knows everything about us and still loves us. When people hear what God has to say, they will sing about the glory of God. Their response will be full of thanks. When we talk to God, are we always full of thanks? When times are hard and we are sad, are we full of thanks? When things happen that make us mad, are we full of thanks to God? Sometimes we don't feel thankful. In David's life, he had to fight a giant with a slingshot. His best friend's father, Saul, tried to kill him, and David had to run away. David made big mistakes and hurt people. One of his children died at birth. Yet David was full of thanks to God. Did he always feel thankful? Probably not. But he always thanked God because he knew that God's love is eternal. It never fails us. No matter what happens, God always loves us, and God will always be there.

## Discussion and Prayer

1. Talk about ways to express our thankfulness to God.

2. How do you see God's love in your own life? How has God helped you?

3. What are some things we can do to remind us that God's love is eternal?

---

5. Jesus Culture, "One Thing Remains," *Come Away (Live)*, 2010.

4. Pray, giving thanks that God's love never fails and that God never gives up on us. Give praise for who God is.

# End of August/Beginning of September Exodus 3:1-15—"Paying Attention"

## Your Story

Tell about a time in your life when God used something to speak to you. How did you know you were hearing from God?

## My Story and the Bible Story

When she was reading her Bible, a friend of mine felt God calling her to be a kindergarten teacher. She saw the word "kindergarten" in big letters as she was reading that day, and she knew it represented what she was supposed to do. Later, she tried to find the page where it said "kindergarten." She wanted to show everyone how she had found her calling, but she couldn't find the word. It didn't seem to be written anywhere in her Bible. After a few months, she stumbled across the word "kindergarten" in one of the devotions in her Bible. It was in small letters, the same size as all the other words. But because she was paying attention that day, God used a devotion in her Bible to show her what God wanted her to do.

Read Exodus 3:1-15.

Moses could have easily walked by that burning bush. Surely he had seen a small fire like that before. But when Moses looked at the bush, he noticed something. It was burning but it wasn't burning up. So he went over and the Lord spoke to him. Moses was paying attention. He may not have been waiting for God to speak to him, but he paid attention to what was going on around him. He was open to hearing God speak. In this passage, we also see that God was paying attention. God saw what was happening to the people. God knew that they were suffering and wanted to help them. Our God pays attention. God knows every detail of our lives, like when we trip and fall, when we fall off our bicycle, and when we score the winning goal in soccer. God knows when we study as much as we can for a test and get the best grade in the class, and when we study hard but still don't do well. God knows everything about our lives. God pays attention to us.

Because God pays attention, God sees our potential. That means God sees the best person you can be and the best I can be. God knows what we can do. But in order for us to be the best people we can be, we have to pay attention too. Yes, we need to pay attention to people in authority, like parents and teachers and bosses. But it's also important to pay attention to God. It's important to be open to hearing from God and to listen for God. God may not speak out loud, but God will become known to us in some way. Moses was paying attention. He could have walked past that burning bush and God would have found someone else to lead the people. But Moses noticed. He was listening for God and he saw the sign God sent him. We may not get a burning bush like Moses did, but God still speaks to us . . . if we pay attention.

## Discussion and Prayer

1. Has God ever spoken to you? If so, how?

2. Talk about ways God speaks to us (through other people, through the Bible, through music, through prayer, etc.).

3. Talk a walk around your neighborhood and tell everyone in your family to pay close attention to your surroundings. Then talk about things you may not have noticed before.

4. Pray, thanking God for speaking to us. Ask for help in paying attention.

# September

## First Week of September
## Psalm 119:33-40—"Following God"

### Your Story

Talk about a time when someone helped you follow the rules. Maybe it was a friend of yours, or perhaps it was one of your parents or a teacher. How did they help you follow the rules? Were you able to follow them after that?

### My Story and the Bible Story

I loved to talk when I was a kid. I talked all the time. At school, there are times when you're supposed to be quiet, but sometimes I couldn't help myself and I talked to the people around me. Of course, I got in trouble. I got I's (needs Improvement) and sometimes U's (for Unsatisfactory) on my report card for talking. My mom needed to help me learn how to follow that rule, so she told me that if I worked hard to be quiet and got an "S" (Satisfactory) on my report card, then she would pay me. I forget how much she said she'd give me. It was probably only $5, but it motivated me. I learned how to stay quiet, and when my report card came, I was proud to show my mom that I had done it! I had gotten an S. She gave me the money, and then she said that now I knew how to stay quiet, and she expected me to be quiet when I was supposed to be. It worked! I didn't have a problem with talking at school when I was supposed to be quiet. Sometimes we need help following the rules.

Read Psalm 119:33-40.

Sometimes it's hard to follow the rules. It can be hard to remember everything we're supposed to do. Sometimes, the rules don't seem to make sense, and we have a hard time understanding why we should follow them. For instance, why can't I carry an ice cream cone in my back pocket on a Sunday? (That's illegal in Georgia.) Why can't I keep a donkey in my bathtub? (Also illegal in Georgia.)[6] These are silly, but sometimes even the rules we have at home or school don't make sense.

There are times when God's rules don't make much sense either. But instead of saying, "These are stupid, so I'm not going to follow them," the psalmist does something different. He writes, "Teach me, O LORD, to follow your decrees; then I will keep them to the end. Give me understanding, and I will keep your law and obey it with all my heart." The psalmist asks for help in following God's laws. He asks God to teach him to follow and to help him understand why those laws are important. It can seem like God has a lot of rules, and sometimes it seems like those rules don't make sense, or they get in the way of what we want to do. But if, like the psalmist, we ask God for help following these rules, and we ask for help in understanding why the rules are important, it will be easier for us to follow them. Here's the thing about God's rules: there's a reason for them. God's rules help us live better, and they help us show love to others.

When you need help understanding God's rules, all you have to do is ask. And when you need help following them, you can ask for that too. God is always there for you and always ready to help. All you have to do is ask!

## Discussion and Prayer

1. Ask your children to talk about a time when they needed help following the rules. Who helped them?

2. Talk about some of God's rules that are sometimes hard to follow (for instance, loving your neighbor as yourself, not lying about something, etc.).

3. Ask your children if there are rules that you can help them follow.

4. Pray, asking God for helping in following God's laws. Ask God to help you and your family understand these rules.

---

6. Amanda Northern, "These 15 Crazy Laws In Georgia Will Leave You Scratching Your Head In Wonder," *Only in Your State*, 3 July 2015, www.onlyinyourstate.com/georgia/crazy-laws-in-georgia/.

# Second Week of September
## Exodus 14:19-31—
## "God Always Finds a Way"

## Your Story

Talk about a time when what you felt like God was telling you to do seemed impossible. How did God help you through?

## My Story and the Bible Story

Looking back and seeing God's fingerprints in your life is a lot easier than seeing them in the moment. There are times in my life when things seemed impossible. When I was upset and hurting in the sixth grade as our church fell apart due to arguments and division, it seemed impossible that I would ever be happy again. But God made a way at a new church. When I was an accounting major and my campus minister mentioned children's ministry, that kind of career seemed impossible. Who would switch from accounting to children's ministry, and how could I do it well? Yet God made a way, and here I am, loving my job as a children's minister. There are times in our lives when things seem impossible, but nothing is impossible with God.

### Read Exodus 14:19-31.

Moses and the Israelites were in a tough spot. The Egyptian army was behind them, getting closer and closer. In front of them was the Red Sea. They had nowhere else to go, but the angel of God and the pillar of cloud moved behind them. They kept the Egyptians from seeing the people. And then something amazing happened: the Red Sea parted! The people were able to walk across on dry land. When the Egyptians saw what they were doing, they started crossing as well. After the last Israelite crossed, Moses stretched out his hand and the Lord sent the sea flowing back into place. The Lord protected the Israelites when it seemed like all was lost. God did something impossible and saved the Israelites.

In our lives, there are times when things seem impossible. There are times when we struggle to trust God because we think, "There's no way God can do this." Yet God saved the Israelites by parting the Red Sea. God gave Jesus the power to perform miracle after miracle. God raised Jesus from the dead. What is impossible for us isn't impossible for God. When it seems like God wants you to do something and things look impossible, remember that God can do the impossible. Trust that if God wants you to do something, God will make it possible for that to happen. God always finds a way!

## Discussion and Prayer

1. Is there something you feel like God is asking you to do that seems impossible?

2. Has there been a time in your life when things seemed impossible and God came through for you? Talk about that time.

3. As a family, talk about how we can trust God because God is always there for us, never lets us down, and always finds a way.

4. Pray, asking for help in trusting God when things seem impossible. Ask God to help you find a way to do what God wants you to do.

5. For older children: This story shows how God miraculously saved the Israelites in an event that also resulted in the deaths of many Egyptians. Why did that happen? How do you think God felt, knowing that his miracle in saving the Israelites also killed many Egyptians?

# Third Week of September
# Matthew 20:1-16—"That's Not Fair!"

## Your Story

Talk about a time when you deserved punishment but were given grace or about a time when someone was very generous to you. You can also talk about a time when you were very generous to someone else or gave someone grace who perhaps didn't "deserve" it.

## My Story and the Bible Story

"That's not fair!" Growing up with a younger sister meant that I said, "That's not fair" a good bit. There were times when she got to do things much earlier than I had, or she got her way when I really wanted mine. There were times when it seemed as if she got away with doing more than I ever got away with. Things didn't seem fair. If you have siblings, you know what I'm talking about. You've probably said, "That's not fair!" more times than you can count. Or maybe someone at school got something you wanted, something you thought you deserved. We don't get what we earned. We are punished and someone else isn't punished at all. Someone else gets a bigger piece of cake or more ice cream. Whatever it is, there are times in life when things just aren't fair.

Read Matthew 20:1-16.

In this story that Jesus tells, people who worked for an hour received the same amount of money as those who worked the whole day. It doesn't seem fair that those who only did a small amount of work got paid the same as the workers who worked all day long. The manager decides to be generous to those who hadn't worked all day, and he still paid those who worked the whole day a fair wage. He didn't cheat the ones who worked all day to pay those who didn't. He simply decided to be generous with the ones who came late.

Grace is like that. It is sometimes hard for us to accept grace because it's not fair. God gives grace to people we think deserve it and to those we think don't deserve it. There's a song that says, "the beauty of grace is that it makes life not fair."⁷ Grace is a gift. It's not something we earn, and it's not something we deserve. We make mistakes. We do the wrong thing. We look at our sin and think it's not as bad as what someone else did. We may think to ourselves, "I lied but at least I didn't cheat." Or "I cheated but at least I didn't steal." God doesn't see things that way. For God, all sin is wrong, and none of us deserve grace. There's no way we can earn grace because we aren't perfect. There will always be times when we choose the wrong thing.

Life isn't fair, but that's the beauty of it. If life were fair, none of us could have a relationship with God. If we only got what we deserved, we would never have Jesus. We would never know God's love. If life were fair, we would have to follow every single rule 100 percent of the time in the hope that God would think we deserve God's kind of life. Life isn't fair. There are times when people get good things that they didn't earn or don't deserve. There are times when people deserve to be punished and aren't.

---

7. Relient K, "Be My Escape," *MmHmm*, 2004.

But those are times when we can see God's grace too. We see God's grace when someone lets us avoid our deserved punishment. We see God's grace when someone is generous with us, like the manager in today's passage was. The next time you find yourself saying, "That's not fair," think about God's grace and remember that grace isn't fair either.

## Discussion and Prayer

1. Ask your family about times when they deserved to be punished for something but were given grace. Talk about times when someone was generous to them.

2. Ask your family about times when they gave grace to someone else. Has there been a time when they were generous to another person?

3. Talk about ways to show God's grace when things aren't fair. How can we respond when we are punished for something someone else did? How should we respond when someone is given grace?

4. Pray, thanking God for grace. Ask for help in recognizing that none of us deserve it. Ask for help in sharing God's grace with others, particularly when we feel like they don't deserve it.

# Fourth Week in September
# Philippians 2:1-13—"Our Attitude"

**Your Story**

Talk about a time when you accomplished something that you wanted everyone to know about. Who did you tell? Then talk about a time when you put others before yourself. How did that feel?

## My Story and the Bible Story

When I was a kid, I loved everything about school, and I loved good grades. I wanted to be the best. But here's the thing: there was always someone better than me. No matter what I did, no matter how hard I tried, there was always someone ahead of me. There were a few times when I came in first for something, but there was usually someone else who did better than I did. I did really well, but I was never first. Looking back on it, I think there was a reason I was never first (aside from the obvious one that the other person did a better job than I did). I think God knew that being first would go to my head. I would have tried to put myself ahead of everyone else in my quest to stay number one, and that's not how God wants us to live. In a way, I think it was better than I wasn't usually number one. I learned how important it is to respect others and to see that we are all equal. None of us is better than anyone else, because we are all created by God. If Jesus, God's own Son and the only perfect human who ever lived, didn't act like he was better than everyone else, then how can we?

Read Philippians 2:1-13.

Eugene Peterson translates verse 4, "Forget yourselves long enough to lend a helping hand." It's easy to get caught up in being the best. It's easy to think about what we want. It's easy to only think about ourselves. But there are times when everyone needs help. Maybe there's someone at school whom nobody talks to, and you're afraid you won't be popular or people will make fun of you if you talk to that person. Or maybe there's a toy you've been saving up for and you have enough money, but your friend's family doesn't have enough money for food. In order to be a Christian, in order to become more like Christ (which is our goal as Christians), we have to think about others and what they need. Jesus thought about us. Jesus was living with God in heaven, but he came to Earth in human form. He had to deal with cuts and scrapes and hurts just like we do. And he loved us enough that he did what was best for us, giving up what he had in heaven and coming to Earth to die for us. Jesus put us ahead of what he wanted and did what was best for us. He wants us to do the same for others. So when someone needs help, try to help them, even if that means you don't get a new toy right away or people don't understand why you're being nice to someone nobody else talks to. Think about what Jesus did for us, and help others. When you do that, you'll be doing what Christ did, and you'll be following what God wants us to do. You may not get to be number one, but you'll make the Creator of the universe happy. And that's a lot better than any reward!

## Discussion and Prayer

1. Ask your children if they know someone who needs help. If so, brainstorm ways that you as a family can help.

2. Talk about concrete ways to put others first (letting your sister use the bathroom to get ready before you, helping your mom set the table, letting someone else have the last cookie, etc.).

3. Find different organizations that help others, and as a family talk about which one you'd like to volunteer with.

4. Pray, asking God for help in putting others first. Thank God that Jesus was willing to do what was best for us so that we could always be with God.

# October

## First Week of October
## Philippians 3:4b-14—"Being the Best"

### Your Story

Have you ever worked really hard to be the best at something? Did you achieve it? If so, how did you feel once you got there?

### My Story and the Bible Story

One semester in college, I asked my professor what I got on my final exam. He said something like a 94, and I asked what questions I missed. I'll never forget his response: "Why does it matter? You got an A." I was still trying to find out how I could do better, even though I got an A. It sounds silly, but I always wanted to be the best at everything I did. And I almost never was. There was always someone who did just a little better than I did. It reminded me that no matter how hard I try, there would always be someone better. All I can do is my best, and that is good enough. In Philippians, Paul reminds us that we don't have to try to be the best with God. In fact, we can never be good enough for God. But God doesn't want us to be. That's not the way God works.

Read Philippians 3:4b-14.

Paul did all the right things. He was the best of the best in Jewish life. He was from the tribe of Benjamin, he was circumcised, and he was a Pharisee. He strictly obeyed the Law. He even made trouble for the church. He did everything the Law demanded, and it still wasn't enough. He thought he was the best . . . until he met Jesus on that road to Damascus and everything changed. Suddenly, none of his work mattered. All of it was garbage. Paul discovered that everything he thought was important wasn't because none of it could save him. It didn't matter how good he tried to be; he could never be perfect. He could never be good enough for God. But he discovered that God doesn't want perfection or for Paul to earn his way. Instead, Christ died for him so that he could always be friends with God.

We, like Paul, sometimes fall into the "good enough" trap. We try to do all the right things, to be the best of the best, in hopes of earning our way to God. We try to make God proud of us and to be good enough for heaven. But nothing we do is good enough. It doesn't have to be—because of Christ. God offers us a prize because of Christ, not because we earned it. Our prize is that we are called to heaven to spend forever with God. We will never be the best of the best. There will always be someone better than us. And that's okay, because God doesn't expect us to be the best. Instead, God wants us to know and follow Christ. When we do that, we have a far better prize than anything we could ever earn. We have the prize of spending forever with God!

So try your best, but remember that you don't have to earn your way to God. God opens that way for you freely. That is great news!

## Discussion and Prayer

1. Ask your children if they have ever tried to be the best at something. What happened?

2. Talk about how, even when we feel like failures, we still have God. We can't earn God's love because God gives it to us freely.

3. Imagine how our lives might look different if, instead of being focused on being the best, we focused on Christ and God's love for us. What might change?

4. Pray, thanking God for Christ and that we don't have to earn our way into heaven. Ask for help letting go of our desire to be the best of the best.

# Second Week of October
# Philippians 4:1-9—
# "How Should We Live?"

## Your Story

Talk about a time when you felt like you were following God's will. What did that look like?

## My Story and the Bible Story

I am a worrier by nature. I worry about all kinds of things. I worry about my family and my friends. I worry about safety. I worry about whether an event is going to turn out well and if people are going to show up. I even worry about other people's problems! When I worry like this, it threatens to steal my joy. It is hard to be joyful when I am worried all the time. Sometimes my worries overwhelm me. There are times when they become too much for me. When that happens, I always remember that I haven't given my worries to God. And when I finally talk to God about everything I'm worried about, I start to feel better. I realize that God is in control and is far more powerful than I am. I remember that God is always with me. Whenever I am worried and I pray, God always gives me peace.

We are reminded in Philippians about how God wants us to live. In this letter to the church in Philippi, Paul reminds us that God wants us to have peace, to worry less, and to have more joy. And God wants us to work together!

### Read Philippians 4:1-9.

Paul says, "Always be full of joy in the Lord" (v. 4). Paul doesn't say, "Whenever you feel like it, be full of joy" or "When things are going well, be full of joy." He says, "Always be full of joy." We should live by being filled with joy. That doesn't mean we are happy all the time, but it does mean we have joy knowing that God loves us and is always there. Therefore, even in the midst of hard things, we can have joy knowing that God is with us.

Paul also says, "Don't worry about anything; instead pray about everything. Tell God what you need and thank him for all he has done. If you do this, you will experience God's peace" (vv. 6-7a). Another way we should live is with God's peace. God doesn't want us to spend our lives worrying. Doing so overwhelms us and steals our joy. Instead, we are to tell God what's going on, to give God our worries and fears. God promises to give us peace. That doesn't mean God will make every situation better, but it does mean we can have peace knowing that God is with us.

Finally, Paul says, "Fix your thoughts on what is true and honorable and right. Think about things that are pure and lovely and admirable. Think about things that are excellent and worthy of praise" (v. 8). Paul reminds us to think about good things. Instead of being focused on everything that is happening around us, we should think about things that are true and right, things that are excellent and worthy of praise. When we are thinking about the things of God, it is much easier to have God's peace. It's easy to focus on the terrible things that are happening in our world, but when we spend time with God, God reminds us of what we should focus on. God gives us joy and peace and helps us find ways to share those with others. How should we live? By being full of joy, by giving our worries to God, and by allowing the peace of God to settle our souls. When we do that, we can show others a different way of life: God's way!

## Discussion and Prayer

1. Allow each person to share their worries. Then, take time to give each of those worries to God.

2. Ask your family members what they think God wants them to think about. What are some things that are true, right, noble, excellent, and praiseworthy?

3. How can you remember to be joyful?

4. Pray, thanking God for peace and asking God to take away your worries. Pray that you can always be filled with joy.

# Third Week of October
# Exodus 33:12-23—"Who Goes with Us?"

## Your Story

Talk about a time when you felt the presence of the Lord with you.

## My Story and the Bible Story

My grandfather fought in the Korean War. In fact, he almost died in that war. In the few times that he ever talked about it, he told us that after he had been wounded, when he thought he was dying, he saw an angel who told him it wasn't his time yet, that he wasn't going to die that day. Then one of his fellow soldiers picked him up and carried him to safety. My grandfather spent almost a year in the hospital, but he survived. And on that day, he knew God was with him. He knew God was watching over him even in the midst of war. That story always reminds me that no matter what, God is there with us. Sometimes we need to be reminded of God's presence. In Exodus, Moses needed a reminder that God was with him.

Read Exodus 33:12-23.

Moses was asking for the presence of the Lord. He wanted to make sure he and the people were doing the right thing, and he knew that if the Lord's presence were with them, they would succeed. The only way they would be able to make it through the wilderness was with God beside them. Moses also wanted to see God. He wanted to know the One he was talking to. Although Moses was only able to see God's back, his face still glowed from being in the presence of God (Exod 34:29). He was radiant from God's presence.

Although we have never seen the Lord, the Lord's presence still changes us. Like God said to Moses, God has mercy and compassion on us. God gives us grace. When we are in God's presence, God gives us rest. We find peace. We feel loved. And we know that God will never leave us. My grandfather felt the presence of God on that battlefield so long ago. His life was changed because of the presence of God. When God asks us to do things that seem scary or things that we're not sure about, like God asked Moses to do, we can know that the presence of God goes with us. God gives us the strength we need and helps us know what to do. If we listen to and follow God, we know that God goes with us. There's no need to be afraid because God will always be by our side.

Rest in the presence of God because God will never leave you.

## Discussion and Prayer

1. Ask your family if they have ever felt the presence of God with them. Have them talk about those experiences.

2. Talk about how sometimes we feel God's presence in a big way, but at other times, God's presence is in something small that happens.

3. Talk about ways you can know that you are following God.

4. Pray, giving thanks for God's presence that is always with us and asking for help in knowing what God wants us to do.

# Fourth Week of October
# Matthew 22:34-40—
# "What Is the Greatest Commandment?"

## Your Story

Talk about ways you have shown your love for God. Talk about ways you have shown love to your neighbor.

## My Story and the Bible Story

As a rule follower, I also want to know the order of the rules. Which rules are most important? Are there rules that we can actually ignore? Which is the rule we absolutely must follow? The Ten Commandments are important rules. "Don't murder" is really important. But so are "don't steal" and "don't lie about your neighbor." "Don't covet your neighbor's stuff" is important too, because that could lead to stealing your neighbor's stuff. And "only worship God" is very important, and so is "put God first." All of these commandments are important, but which one is most important? Are there ones that we can ignore?

The Pharisees thought they could trap Jesus with these kinds of questions. After all, Moses got the Ten Commandments from the Lord. The people knew they were all important, so they asked Jesus which one was *most* important. No matter which one he said, they could get him in trouble if he left out the rest. If he said that "worship God" was most important, then what about "do not murder"? Could they let people get away with murder? Certainly not! So the Pharisees thought they had Jesus trapped. But in Matthew 22, Jesus takes the Ten Commandments and uses two to show the people what the greatest commandments are.

### Read Matthew 22:34-40.

Love God. Love people. These are the two greatest commandments. In fact, Jesus reminds his listeners that everything else is based on these two commandments. "Don't murder" falls under "love your neighbor as yourself." "Don't covet," "don't steal," and "don't lie to your neighbor" also fall under "love your neighbor." "Put God first" and "only worship God" fall under "love God with everything you have." All of the Ten Commandments, and everything else the prophets told the people to do, fall under these two commandments.

When we prioritize the rules, we do so in order to try to get out of following all of them. We try to see which rules are okay to break and which ones are important. But Jesus reminds us of what we are supposed to do: we are to love God with everything we have and to love our neighbors as ourselves. Our neighbors are the people around us, people we like and people we don't like, people who live next door and people who live around the world. Our neighbors are everyone God has created—and God has created everyone on Earth.

A lot of times, we are guilty of trying to fit God into our lives, of spending five minutes with God when we have a free moment and then ignoring God for the rest of the day. But when we love God with everything we have, that means we put God first. We put God before our friends and before video games. We put God before homework and before dinner. We live our lives putting God first instead of putting God last. We live our lives in prayer, telling God about what's going on, giving thanks for what God has done, and asking God for help. And we remember that God is in charge, not us.

What is the greatest commandment? There are two of them: "love the Lord your God with everything you have," and "love your neighbor as yourself." When you do these things, you will be following God.

## Discussion and Prayer

1. Have you put God first this week? Talk about ways to put God first in your lives.

2. How have you shown love to your neighbor this week? How can you show love to those around you?

3. Pick a specific way to show love to the people around you in the coming week.

4. Pray, giving thanks that God tells us how to live. Ask for help to put God first and to show love to our neighbor.

# November

## All Saints' Day
## First Week of November
## Matthew 5:1-12—"Blessed Are You"

### Your Story

Tell your family about someone you know who lives out the Beatitudes.

### My Story and the Bible Story

Every time I read the Beatitudes, I think about Mother Teresa. Mother Teresa spent her life caring for the poor and forgotten. She showed mercy to those who seemed unlovable, and she did her best to bring about peace. Through it all, she was kind to everyone she met, even when they made fun of and insulted her. She embodied the Beatitudes. Many times I struggle to live out the Beatitudes. It is hard to be meek when someone insults you. It is hard to be a peacemaker in a world that glorifies getting your own way. It can be hard to live out the Beatitudes, yet this is the way Jesus calls us to live.

*Read Matthew 5:1-12.*

These words that Jesus spoke to the crowd that day are called the Beatitudes. They start with "Blessed are . . . ." They show us that God's Kingdom is different from our world. Our world says that if you are successful, good-looking, famous, or wealthy, then you are blessed. In God's Kingdom, things are different. In God's Kingdom, we are blessed when we mourn because we will be comforted. We are blessed when we are hungry, not for power, but for righteousness. We are blessed when we show others mercy. We are blessed when we work toward peace. We are blessed when we are insulted and made fun of because of our belief in God.

In 2016, Pope Francis offered an updated version of the Beatitudes:

Blessed are those who remain faithful while enduring evils inflicted on them by others and forgive them from their heart. Blessed are those who look into the eyes of the abandoned and marginalized and show them their closeness. Blessed are those who see God in every person and strive to make others also discover him. Blessed are those who protect and care for our common home. Blessed are those who renounce their own comfort in order to help others. Blessed are those who pray and work for full communion between Christians.

This week we celebrate All Saints' Day. We remember those who have given their lives for Jesus. We remember those who have remained faithful in the face of persecution. We remember those who have spent their lives helping others. We remember those who are well known saints and we remember those who are the saints in our own lives. We remember the people who have gone before us and have taught us about God. We remember the people in our own lives who showed us what it means to be a Christian. And as we think about their lives, may we take these Beatitudes to heart. May we live them out ourselves. May we remember that God is with us, that He gives us courage to remain faithful when others persecute us. May we remember that God wants us to see those in need and to help them. May we see God in every person we meet and show God's love to them. May we remember the legacies of these Christians and live them out in our own lives.

## Discussion and Prayer

1. As a family, talk about people the world may not consider blessed, but God would. Talk about people you know who fit with some (or all) of the Beatitudes.

2. Talk about ways you can live out the updated Beatitudes. Help your kids think of ways that they can see God in every person. Remind them that God created each of us and help them find something good or kind in each person they think of.

3. Talk about what it means to give up your own comfort in order to help others. What is one way your family can do this in the coming week?

4. Pray, thanking God that Jesus showed us how we should live. Ask for help in living out the Beatitudes.

# Second Week of November
# Psalm 78:1-7—"Tell Me the Story"

## Your Story

Who told you the story of Jesus? Talk about the people in your life who told you about Jesus and about how much God loves us.

## My Story and the Bible Story

I grew up in church. For as far back as I can remember, I had Sunday school teachers telling me about Jesus and how much he loves us. My preacher knew who I was, and he told me about Jesus too. My mom told me about Jesus, and my grandparents told me about Jesus. I knew that I was surrounded by God's love. We tell the story of Jesus because it's the most important one we know. We tell the story of Jesus because it shows others the way to God. The story of Jesus points us to God's love. Telling stories isn't new. In fact, it's the way the people of the Bible handed down important teachings. It's even how the Bible got started: the people would tell the stories of God. They told their children the stories of things that God had done, and their children told their children, and so on, until eventually the stories were written down.

## Read Psalm 78:1-7.

The writer of this psalm knew how important the stories of God were. We know that we can trust in God when we hear story after story of how God can be trusted. When we read that God rescued the Israelites from the Egyptians, that God used Moses to save the people, that God took Abraham and his family on a journey and protected them, that God was with David, that God gave Esther courage to stand up for her people, that God was with Joseph and used him to do amazing things, and that God sent Jesus at just the right time to die for us, we learn that we can trust God. We see that God used ordinary people to do extraordinary things, and we know that God can use us too. When we read these stories, we learn what God is like. We learn that we can trust God, that God is always with us, that God will always love us, and that God will show us what to do. When we know the stories of the Bible, we learn who God is. But the stories of the

Bible aren't the only stories that tell us who God is. We have our own stories of how God has helped us, of how we trusted God and God came through for us, of how we have felt God's love. When we share these stories, we help make God more real to others. We show them that God can be trusted and that God loves us no matter what.

The psalmist reminds us that we should share our stories. Parents should share the stories of God with their children. They should share the things that God has done in their own lives. Children can also share their stories with their parents and with their friends. Our grandparents share their stories of God with us too. Other adults in your life can share stories of what God has done. When we tell our stories, we add to the kingdom of God. We add our own stories to the big God story, and we show people how God works in our lives and in the world.

When God does something in your life, when you hear from God, when God shows you what to do or what not to do, share it with others. Tell the stories of God to others. Share God's love with them. When we share such stories, we help others see who God is.

## Discussion and Prayer

1. Talk about ways you have seen God in your life. Do you have any stories to share about God's love or about how you have heard from God?

2. How can you share your stories with your friends? With others who don't know God?

3. As a family, write down important stories of things God has done in your lives. Start a family tradition of writing the stories of God's work in your lives. Collect other family stories of how God has worked in your grandparents' lives and in the lives of other relatives. Start a journal or scrapbook that you can hand down to future generations.

4. Pray, thanking God for always working in our lives. Ask for courage to share your stories of God's love.

# Third Week of November
# Matthew 25:14-30—
# "Using What God Gives You"

## Your Story

Talk about the gifts and abilities God has given you. How are you using them?

## My Story and the Bible Story

I'm a good organizer and I like to plan events, but I didn't realize how these gifts would help me in ministry. I had planned on being an accountant, but God had other plans for me. Now, as a minister to children and families, I can see how God gave me the right gifts to use for what God wanted me to do. God equipped me for my job, and I am using the abilities God has given me.

I could have ignored God's call on my life. I could have decided that I wasn't going to listen and that I would be an accountant instead. I could have thrown away the gifts God has given me by not using them. Jesus told a parable about that in Matthew 25.

### Read Matthew 25:14-30.

The money that the master gave is like the gifts and abilities God has given us. God gives each of us talents—things that we are good at doing. We are given gifts and abilities to use to do what God has called us to do. God gives us what we need to be able to do these things. The first servant doubled the money he was given. He used what was given to him, and he doubled what he had. The second also used what was given to him and also doubled what he had. But the third didn't use what he was given. In fact, he buried it.

When we don't use the gifts and abilities God gives us, it's like we are burying money. We can't do what God wants us to do when we don't use the gifts and abilities God gives us. When we bury these gifts, we ignore God. And when we ignore God, we can't play our part in God's kingdom. When the servant buried his money, the master was furious and threw him out.

Sometimes you might be afraid to do what God has called you to do, but remember that God has given you gifts and abilities. When you use them, when you do what God asks, God can use you to do amazing things for the kingdom. But when you ignore God and don't use your gifts, then God can't use you to do great things for the kingdom. God doesn't make us do anything, but when we ignore God, we miss out on a lot. Sometimes our gifts go away when we don't use them. Think about the gifts and abilities God has given you, and listen to see how God wants you to use them!

## Discussion and Prayer

1. As a family, talk about the gifts and abilities God has given each of you. Help your children (if needed) by pointing out some of the gifts and abilities you see in them.

2. Ask if there are things your family feels like God is telling them to do. How can you help them follow God's leading?

3. Talk about how God gives us many chances to use our gifts and abilities. Assure your children that making a mistake doesn't mean God can't use us.

4. Pray, giving thanks for the gifts God has given you and asking for help in knowing how to use them.

# Fourth Week of November
# Matthew 25:31-46—
# "For the Least of These"

### Your Story

Talk about a time when you helped someone who was less fortunate than yourself. How did you help them?

### My Story and the Bible Story

My youth group went to serve lunch at a homeless shelter when I was a teenager. I wasn't sure what to expect, but I wanted to help. We began by helping prepare the food and by making sandwiches for the people to take with them when they left. I was happy being in the kitchen preparing things, but I felt uncomfortable being around the homeless. Then, I was asked to go into the dining room and refill glasses of tea. I was nervous, but I went. And as I went around refilling glasses, I saw people who were grateful for a meal. I saw that I didn't need to be afraid, because they were people just like me. I came to one man, and when I asked him if he'd like a refill, he said yes, and he handed me a Christmas card. These were cards that he sold to earn money, and he was giving me what he had to say thank you. All these years later, I still remember that Christmas card. Even though I was the one helping him, this man taught me an important lesson about the homeless. He helped me see past my fear so that I could help.

Read Matthew 25:31-46.

Sometimes we are afraid to help others. Sometimes we just don't want to help. But Jesus reminds us of how important it is to God that we help others. In this passage, Jesus tells us that everyone is created by God and that when we help people who are hungry, thirsty, homeless, shivering, sick, and in prison, it is like we are helping God. Can you imagine that? It's like we're helping God when we care for other people. We please God by caring for others. God cares about us and what happens to us. God cares about each person God created. As a result, God cares about what happens to them. So when we feed the hungry, give water to the thirsty, give clothes to those who need them, give a place to stay to those who have none, help someone who is sick, and care for someone in jail, we are doing it all for God.

God gives us gifts and abilities to do God's work and also gives us resources so that we can help others. We can keep everything we have for ourselves, or we can use it to help others. We can ignore the needs around us and, in doing so, ignore God. Or we can help the people around us and, in doing so, help God. The choice is ours. When we love God and love our neighbors, we are doing what God commands us to do. Part of that is caring for the needs of the people around us. It's almost Thanksgiving, a time when we remember all the things for which we are thankful. Look for someone you can help. This is one way you can thank God for all the blessings God has given you.

## Discussion and Prayer

1. Ask your children about ways that they have helped others in the last few weeks.

2. What are some things you are thankful for? How can you use them to help others?

3. Talk about specific ways that your family can help people around you. Choose one way to help others this week.

4. Pray, giving thanks for the many blessings God has given you and asking God to open your eyes to the needs around you.

# Year B

# December

## First Week of Advent
### First Week of December
### Isaiah 64:1-9—"Hope"

### Your Story

Has it ever seemed like you were hoping for something that would never happen? How did you keep your hope alive when all seemed lost? Did what you were hoping for come true? Share your story with your family.

### My Story and the Bible Story

I saw the Star Wars movies much later than many others. I was in my early twenties before I watched any of them, but when I did, I found a familiar story: of hope. For so long the darkness had ruled, but a small band of rebels thought the light could defeat the darkness. They worked and they dreamed, hoping that one day the light would win, that the light side of the Force would be strong enough to defeat the dark side. If you've ever seen the Star Wars films, you know what happens. It seems as if the dark side will win. At one point, hope is nearly lost. But just when it seems as if the dark side will be triumphant, something surprising happens: the one representing the dark side starts to change. He starts to remember the hope he once had, and the rebels win! Hope and light defeat the dark side. This is a familiar story this Advent season, not only because we see it over and over in the movies but also because it is lived out in the Bible.

### Read Isaiah 64:1-9.

The people were crying out to God for salvation. They desperately needed to hear from God. They had chosen to do the wrong thing for so long that it seemed as if God had abandoned them. The prophet Isaiah asks, "Is there any hope for us? Can we be saved?" Even though it seems as if God abandoned them, they remember that God is still their Father. God is still the One who made them. In spite of what seems like a hopeless situation, they are able to maintain hope that God will remember them and save them.

Today begins the Advent season, a time of waiting for the Savior. It is a time when we remember that for thousands of years, the people hoped and prayed and worked for the Messiah's coming. There were times when they were filled with hope and times when they were filled with despair. But through it all, they had hope that God would come through. Maybe you and your family need to remember hope today. As we light the candle of Hope, we remember the hope that God brings into our world. There are times when it seems as if the darkness will win. There are times when hope is dim and it seems as if God has abandoned us, but we know that God did not abandon the Israelites. Instead, at just the right time, God sent the Messiah. There may be times when we hope for things that never happen, but we can always hope in the Lord and know that God will come through for us. God promises to never abandon us, and God will do the things God has promised. The Lord is our Creator and Savior who will hear our cry. So take heart and have hope, for the Lord who created the universe is still working. God is still our potter, and we are still the clay. We are God's people, and God will never leave us.

## Discussion and Prayer

1. Talk to your children about what it means to have hope. Explain the difference between the hope that we will pass a test or get a certain toy for Christmas and the hope we have in God.

2. Ask your children to name some things for which they have hoped. Talk about whether or not those things happened.

3. Find ways this week to share God's hope with others.

4. Pray, giving thanks that we can always have hope in God. Ask for strength and courage to always believe in that hope.

# Second Week of Advent
## Second Week of December
## Isaiah 40:1-11—"Peace"

## Your Story

Have you ever been comforted by someone after a difficult time? If so, talk about the experience.

## My Story and the Bible Story

We did an experiment a few years ago in Vacation Bible School with dry ice, dish detergent, water, and food coloring. We started with clear water, and then we began to talk about all the hard things that can happen in life: someone bullies you, you get in trouble at school, you get a bad grade, you lose a pet, you have to move away from your friends, your parents fight a lot, a loved one dies, your parents get a divorce, and the list goes on. As we listed each of these things, we put food coloring into our water. The water that started off so clear was suddenly dark and murky. It was filled with all of these hard things. After adding a little dish detergent, we put in a few chunks of dry ice to represent God, who comes in the midst of the hard things of life to comfort us. God is there with us and helps us through. All of a sudden, bubbles started to rise. Our container was filled and over-flowing with bubbles. The water was still dark, but the bubbles were light and fluffy. It was a picture of how God comforts us. God is there with us, helping us get through. The situation may still be there. Things don't magi-cally change. But God comforts us and gives us peace. God did the same thing thousands and thousands of years ago for the Israelites.

### Read Isaiah 40:1-11.

The Lord comforts us. Everything else may fade around us, but God's word stands firm and forever. We can trust that God will care for us, comforting us in the midst of hard times. As we light the candle of peace this week, we remember the peace that God brings us. Jesus brought hope with him when he came to Earth, reminding everyone that the Lord had not forgotten them. He also brought peace; it doesn't change our circumstances, but it helps us get through them. God is always with us and will give us peace.

## Discussion and Prayer

1. Talk about some difficult things you have faced as a family and the ways you saw God's presence.

2. Ask your children to talk about some hard things they have faced. Help them see how God has been there for them.

3. Read Philippians 4:4-7: "Rejoice in the Lord always. I will say it again: Rejoice! Let your gentleness be evident to all. The Lord is near. Do not be anxious about anything, but in everything, by prayer and petition, with thanksgiving, present your requests to God. And the peace of God, which transcends all understanding, will guard your hearts and your minds in Christ Jesus" (NIV). Help your children get into the habit of asking God for peace.

4. Pray, telling God about any hard situations you are facing and asking God for peace.

# Third Week of Advent
## Third Week of December
## Isaiah 61:1-4, 8-11—"Joy"

### Your Story

Talk about a time when you felt joyful. Perhaps it was after the birth of a child, and you were filled with a joy that was much deeper than happiness. Or perhaps it was when you were facing a difficult time but you felt the presence of the Lord.

### My Story and the Bible Story

I have a friend named Joy (she's one of the 8-year-olds at church), and her name suits her personality. She always has a smile on her face and a radiant attitude. Is she always happy? She's not. There are times when she doesn't get what she wants or things don't go her way. There are times when she fights with her sisters and times when she has a hard day at school. But through it all, she radiates joy. You can look at her and tell that her smile is much more than happiness. It is the deep contentment of knowing that God loves her and is always with her. It is knowing her Savior and knowing that no matter what happens, God is there. It is happiness that depends not on good things happening in life but on the steady faithfulness of God. We read about joy in today's passage from Isaiah.

Read Isaiah 61:1-4, 8-11.

Can you hear the joy in this passage? God sent Isaiah to preach good news, to heal the heartbroken, and to announce freedom! If you've ever been stuck in a car on a road trip for hours on end, you know a small taste of what freedom feels like once you finally reach your destination. The people's cities had been destroyed and many of them were held captive, but Isaiah had come to remind them all of the good news of the Lord. The cities would be brand new, the people would be free, and the world would know that the people were God's people and they were blessed.

There are times when hard things happen. There are times when we are sad, hurt, upset, and frustrated. There are even times when we are angry. If we are depending on happiness, we will be disappointed. Happiness goes away. But joy stays. God's joy is deep within us. It reminds us that God is there and will take what is happening and make something good out of it. God will make all things new. We can be filled with joy because we know that God loves us no matter what and that our God is faithful. He'll never leave. May you, like my friend Joy, radiate God's joy. And as we light the candle of Joy, may you think about all the ways God has blessed you and your family.

## Discussion and Prayer

1. Ask your children about times when they have felt joyful.

2. Talk about choosing to be joyful no matter what, and how we can learn to be joyful in the hard times when we remember the ways God has blessed us in the past.

3. Talk about ways to share God's joy with others.

4. Pray, thanking God for always being there. Thank God for freeing us, for rescuing us, and for giving us joy.

# Fourth Week of Advent
## Fourth Week of December
## Luke 1:26-38—"Love"

## Your Story

Talk about a time when you have felt God's love.

## My Story and the Bible Story

I can't remember a time when I didn't feel loved by God. I grew up in the church, and I remember standing on top of the pew and sharing the hymnal with my mother. I knew without a doubt that God loved me. In fact, when I was a kid, I wrote these words in a Christmas card I made: "Don't forget about Jesus!" I have known that God loves me for as long as I can remember, and the reason I know God loves me is something that happened over 2,000 years ago.

### Read Luke 1:26-38.

God loved us enough to send Jesus as a baby to rescue us. God became human and came down to rescue us. God showed great love for us by being human, by feeling our joys and our hurts, by seeing and feeling pain, and finally by dying on the cross. When we told God no, God told us yes. Romans 5:8 reminds us that we were still sinners when Christ died for us. We were still stuck in bad behaviors and harmful thoughts, but when Christ died for us, God showed us that no matter what we do, God still loves us. Jesus was God's great rescue plan.

Mary showed how much she loved God by trusting God. God was asking her to raise the Savior, and Mary showed her love by trusting that God knew what God was doing. When Jesus was born, Mary loved and cared for him. As we light the Advent candle of Love, we remember the great love God has for us and the love that Mary had for God and for Jesus. We celebrate God's amazing love that came to us at Christmas. What better gift could we receive?

## Discussion and Prayer

1. Ask your children about ways that they feel God's love.

2. Talk about how you can share God's love with others.

3. Pray, giving thanks for God's amazing love. Ask for help in sharing it with others.

# Christmas
## Luke 2:1-20—"Jesus is Here"

### Your Story

Talk about a time when God took something ordinary in your life and made it extraordinary.

### My Story and the Bible Story

I confess that I have a favorite Christmas story. I love Luke's story of Christmas. This is the Christmas story that my family read every Christmas Eve. It's the one that I can almost recite by heart. I love Luke's story because he focuses on the ordinary. It's an ordinary day that becomes extraordinary. These are ordinary lives transformed into extraordinary lives by the birth of a child.

Read Luke 2:1-20.

Mary and Joseph must go to Bethlehem to register for the census. They ride into the town on a donkey, but then there's no room for them. There's no such thing as hotel reservations and there's no more room. They go out to the stable to rest, and there a miracle happens. The best thing to happen to the world comes into it quietly and is placed in a manger, a trough from which animals eat their hay. Then, who finds out about Jesus' birth first? Not a king or a ruler but lowly shepherds, tending their flocks. The angels appear before these shepherds, scaring them out of their ordinary night. After the angels leave, the shepherds run to find Jesus. They believed the angels, and they dropped everything to see this miracle.

Jesus breaks into the ordinary and turns it into something extraordinary. How often does God do that for us? We live our lives in the ordinary. We go to school, we go to work. We eat breakfast, lunch, and dinner. We spend a lot of our day in the car, going from activity to activity. But sometimes something amazing happens. God breaks into the ordinary of our lives to do something extraordinary. We meet someone who changes our lives. Our children are born. We find a place to belong. Whatever it is, God has a knack for taking the ordinary and making something extraordinary. How might God be taking an ordinary day in your life and making it extraordinary?

## Discussion and Prayer

1. Ask your family to talk about ordinary things in their lives that God has made extraordinary.

2. Ask your family to talk about people/events in their lives who/ that God has used to change them.

3. How might God be turning something ordinary into something extraordinary in your life?

4. Pray, thanking God for taking an ordinary day and using it to change the course of history. Ask for help in seeing how God is working.

# The Last Week of December
# Luke 2:22-40—"The Waiting Is Over!"

## Your Story

Talk to your children about when they joined your family. Tell them how you felt as you first met them, when the wait was finally over.

## My Story and the Bible Story

One Christmas as a child, I really wanted a toy called "GoGo My Walkin' Pup." She walked and barked, and I desperately wanted her. So did every other child that year. My mom tried her best, but the toys were sold out everywhere she went. She had to order GoGo, and the toy didn't come in until after Christmas. Mom had to tell me (as a 4-year-old) that I would have to wait a little longer for the Christmas present I really wanted. It was coming, but I had to wait. Finally, after what seemed like forever, my present finally came! I loved that toy. She was worth the wait!

Luke tells us the story of Simeon, a man who had waited a long time to meet the Messiah. As he waited, he trusted God. He believed it when God said that he would live to see the Messiah. But as the days and months and years went by, I am sure there were times when Simeon wondered when the Messiah would come. Then everything changed one day at the temple.

Read Luke 2:22-40.

The waiting was over! The Messiah was finally here! Simeon and Anna praised God that they were able to meet the Messiah, the promised one—Jesus. The one whom they had prayed for and hoped for and trusted in was finally with them. It took a long time for the promised Messiah to come, and there were probably times when the people struggled to understand why they had to wait.

Sometimes it feels as if we are always waiting. It can feel like we have to wait a long time for God as well. There are times when we pray and wait for an answer, and it seems as if we wait and wait and wait for God. The Israelites felt the same way. It took a long time for the Messiah to come, but Jesus came at just the right time. God's timing is perfect. God always comes through. God always answers us and always listens to us. God knows exactly what we need and when we need it. At just the right time, God gives it to us. The people waited a long time for the Messiah, but now the waiting is over! The Messiah is here!

## Discussion and Prayer

1. Ask your children to name some things for which they are waiting. Talk about good things they can do during that time of waiting.

2. As a family, share ways that you are waiting on God. Are there things you have prayed for and are now waiting for?

3. Talk about some of the people in the Bible who had to wait a long time for God's promises. Talk about how God always fulfills promises.

4. Pray, being thankful that God knows what we need. Ask for help in waiting on God. Offer praise that the Messiah has come!

# January

## Epiphany
### First Week of January
### Isaiah 60:1-6—"The Light Has Come"

**Your Story**

Talk about a time when you felt the light shining in the darkness. Perhaps it was at the end of a long journey and you were finally almost home. Perhaps you were going through a difficult time and you were finally moving out of it.

**My Story and the Bible Story**

"There's a light at the end of the tunnel." "You're almost there!" "Blue skies are coming." We use a lot of phrases to talk about how the light is coming. When we are going through hard times, we talk about the light at the end of the tunnel. We talk about blue skies around the corner. There's even a song that says, "Gray skies are gonna clear up. Put on a happy face." These sayings give us hope that soon things will be better. The light is coming. We will make it through. The Israelites had been through a time of great darkness. They were waiting for the Messiah to come. And as we read during Advent from Isaiah, "the people walking in darkness have seen a great light. On those living in the land of the shadow of death a light has dawned" (Isaiah 9:2). And that light was the Messiah, the Savior. Isaiah goes on to tell the people to be filled with joy, for their light has come. In Isaiah 60:1-6, Isaiah reminds the people of the hope they have in the Lord.

Read Isaiah 60:1-6.

As we celebrate Epiphany, we remember that the light has come. When darkness covered the Earth, a star shone. The magi followed the star to find the Savior. They knew that this light was special, and so they followed it to find the light of the world. They came from nations far away to find the light of the world, and these kings bowed down to the Savior. The people who had been in darkness could finally lift up their heads. The light had come!

There are times when we feel as if we are in darkness. Maybe you worry about the actual darkness and find yourself afraid when you turn off the light. Or maybe you find yourself in a tough situation and feel as if you are in darkness. Or maybe you have been suffering for a long time and feel like things will never get better. Maybe you are being bullied at school and can't see a way that things will improve. The good news from Isaiah is that the glory of the Lord is with us. The light has come! You can lift your eyes and look about you, for the Savior of the Lord has come. When you are facing difficult times, remember that God is with you. God will help you through. The Light of the World is there with you, shining His light on your life. When you feel like things won't get better, ask God for help. Ask God to remind you that He sent His light into our world, and that He makes the darkness bright. Rest in knowing that there is a light at the end of the tunnel, and that light is the Lord.

## Discussion and Prayer

1. Ask your children to talk about ways they feel like they are in the dark (i.e. if they are going through something tough at school, if they are afraid of the dark, etc.).

2. Talk about how we can remind ourselves that the Light (Jesus) has come (perhaps by shining a flashlight in the darkness or writing a reminder in your school planner or memorizing verses, etc.).

3. Talk about ways to share the Light (Jesus) with others?

4. Pray, thanking God for sending the Light into our world. Ask God for help in remembering that He is always there, and that He shines brighter than anything else.

# Second Week of January
# Genesis 1:1-5— "Being Creative"

## Your Story

As a family, take turns talking about something each of you has created that you are proud of. If you are like me, it is a song. Or maybe you've written a story or painted a picture. Talk about how it felt to create that thing and how you felt when you finished it.

## My Story and the Bible Story

As a child, I loved making up songs. I'd make up the tune as well as the words and sing these songs to myself as I played. Occasionally I even wrote down the words. These songs were about anything and everything: sometimes they were songs about God, and other times they were songs about what I was doing at the moment. I recently came across one of these songs that I had written down. I no longer remembered the tune, but it was fun to see something I created all those years ago.

### Read Genesis 1:1-5.

Take a few moments and ask everyone to close their eyes. Imagine when the world was dark and nothing was here. There was inky blackness as far as you could see. Then imagine God's voice speaking, creating everything— light, sky, land, plants, the sun, the moon, fish, birds, reptiles, bugs, wild animals, and, finally, humans. Imagine what it must have been like to see all of God's creation coming to life. God, the Creator of the Universe, took time to speak each thing into life, from the sun and the moon, all the way to the tiny ants and bugs that walk on the ground.

We like to create things. We build things out of Legos and draw pictures. We make new recipes and we write new songs. We dream up new ideas and we create new things. We like to create. And we create because our Creator does the same. God is still creating. He created you and me and everything we see. What a wonderful Creator we have!

## Discussion and Prayer

1. Ask each member of your family what their favorite animal is. Then talk about each person's favorite part of creation. Is it the

mountains or the ocean? A lion or a whale? A lightning bug or lightning? A rose or a salamander?

2. Talk about the creative gifts you have in your family. Is someone musical? Does someone like to write? Draw? Paint? Build with blocks?

3. Talk about how you can use your creative gifts to help others.

4. Find a way this week to celebrate God's creation.

5. Pray, giving thanks for all that God has created and for giving you the ability to create as well. Ask God to show you ways to use your creative gifts to help others.

# Third Week of January
# Psalm 139:1-6, 13-18—
# "Wonderfully Made"

## Your Story

Talk about a time when you realized that God loves every piece of you. This may be a time when you doubted yourself and didn't feel worthy, and then you realized that God formed you and knows you inside and out and loves you.

Or talk about how you know your children inside and out; you know their hearts, the random freckles on their feet, how they react to things, what they love.

## My Story and the Bible Story

As a teenager, I didn't always feel pretty or worthwhile. There were many times when I doubted myself, particularly as a middle schooler. I had braces and I had to get glasses in middle school, and it was an awkward time. I will never forget when I first learned these verses in Psalm 139. We first talked about being "fearfully and wonderfully made" in my youth girls' Bible study. We clung to verse 14 when we had a hard time accepting ourselves.

I love this verse because it reminds me that God made me and loves me the way I am made.

Read Psalm 139:1-6, 13-18.

If you ever doubt yourself, think you aren't pretty or handsome enough, or think you aren't cool enough, remember that the God of the Universe created you. The God of the Universe shaped you inside and out, making you bit by bit as you grew. And the God who made you thinks that you are a marvelous creation. God not only made you but also knows everything about you. God knows what you are thinking, sees you at every moment, and knows what you're going to say even before you say it.

Sometimes what we say or do isn't very nice, and God sees and hears it all. But no matter what we say or do, God knows exactly who we are and loves us. God created us to be who we are. Think about that for a minute: who we are is who God created us to be! When you don't feel good enough or smart enough or cool enough, remember that God created you to be you. Be who you are, because that's who God made you to be. God didn't make you to be someone else; God made you to be you and loves you for who you are.

## Discussion and Prayer

1. If you didn't in the beginning, talk about the different ways you know your children and how you've watched them grow. Then talk about how much more God knows us.

2. Ask your children how it feels to know that God knows everything about them. Talk about how that might seem scary, but it's actually comforting to know that God knows everything, the good and the bad, and still loves us.

3. Talk about ways to show others that God made them to be who they are and that God loves them.

4. Pray, thanking God that we are fearfully and wonderfully made. Praise God for the amazing things God does. Ask for help in remembering that God created us to be who we are.

# Fourth Week of January
# Psalm 62:5-12—"God Is Our Refuge"

## Your Story

Tell your family about a time when God was your refuge. Perhaps, like me, you were afraid of storms and God comforted you. Or maybe God was there for you during another trying time of your life. Talk about how it feels to know that God is with us.

## My Story and the Bible Story

I was terrified of thunderstorms as a child. The thunder would get so loud that I just knew something bad would happen to me. I would run to my mom, crying, when the thunder boomed and scared me. I couldn't wait for those storms to be over. As I got older, my mom taught me to pray in the midst of storms. As the thunder boomed, I'd pray that God would keep me safe and that the storm would soon be over. Passages like Psalm 62 would comfort me and remind me that I could trust God and that God was my refuge in the storm. I would pray for peace, and although the storm wasn't over, I would feel God's comfort, reminding me that God was there. The storms would eventually end and I would feel safe again. It was during these storms, though, that I learned that God is always with us.

Read Psalm 62:5-12.

Our hope comes from God. God is our refuge and we can trust God, both through actual storms and through the storms of life. Our God has created us, loves us, and is always there for us. Bad things will still happen and there are times when we will be hurt, but we can trust that God will always be there and will be our refuge. Because we live in this world, we will still have pain, but we can always run to God no matter what. We can trust that God will take our pain and turn it into something good and that, in the end, God's love will conquer all.

## Discussion and Prayer

1. As a family, talk about ways that each of you needs to trust God. Perhaps it is trusting God in the storm like me. Or maybe

your child needs to trust God to help with a bully. Talk about how God can be our refuge.

2. Remind each other this week that God is our refuge and that we can trust God.

3. If you have a neighbor, family member, or friend who is going through a hard time, share this passage with them as well as a story from your own life about how God has been your refuge.

4. Pray, thanking God for always being there for us. Ask for help in trusting God through everything that happens.

# Fifth Week of January
# Psalm 111—"What God Creates"

## Your Story

Talk about a time when it was difficult for you to figure out the truth. How did you determine what it was? Was it your word against someone else's? Who was believed?

## My Story and the Bible Story

Ask your parents for pictures of clothing styles that were popular when they were kids. You may think some of those pictures are pretty funny. Clothing styles go through trends. Once, it was popular for women to wear corsets and petticoats under their dresses. In fact, there was a time when giant hoops that went under dresses were popular and women had a hard time fitting through doors! In the 1960s and 1970s, bell bottom jeans were popular. In the 1980s, big hair was popular. In the 1990s, plaid shirts and hair scrunchies were popular. And in the early 2000s, glitter was popular. The clothes we wear right now may be popular, but they won't always be. There will be new trends and styles. Kids will outgrow their clothes and eventually get rid of them. Even if we keep our clothes for twenty years, they won't last. They will fade and get holes. We will have to throw them away at some point. We will move on to different shirts and pants and different styles.

The things we have—toys, clothes, bedding, etc.—are all things that we will outgrow in some way. They will break, we'll stop playing with them, or we won't wear them anymore. But the things of God are guaranteed to last.

Read Psalm 111.

God "manufactures truth and justice." That means God creates them. The works of God are honest and true. We can trust in truth and justice because God created them, and they are 100 percent guaranteed! Unlike our stuff, truth and justice never go out of date and never become obsolete. We always need them. God is our compass. Without God, we would lose our way. Without God, right might seem wrong and wrong might seem right. Without God's guidance, we wouldn't know what the truth is. Sometimes it's hard to know the truth, and it can seem that the truth, just like clothing from the 1970s, has gone out of style. It can seem like truth is relative, and it can feel like the truth is different depending on who you talk to. When that happens—when it's hard to know what's true and what's real—look to God. God is the creator of truth who will help us know what's true. We can trust God to be steadfast and know that the truth, God's truth, will never be out of date or obsolete. Sometimes the truth isn't popular, but if we follow God, we'll be doing what is true.

# Discussion and Prayer

1. As a family, talk about peer pressure. Ask your kids about peer pressure they have faced. How did they handle it?

2. Talk about the pressure to lie, whether to help someone else or to keep yourself from getting in trouble. Then talk about God creating the truth and why we should be honest and true.

3. Talk about ways to encourage each other to tell the truth.

4. Pray, asking God for help in knowing what the truth is. Ask for courage to always tell the truth.

# February

## First Week of February
## Psalm 147:1-11, 20c—"Praise the Lord!"

### Your Story

Talk to your family about a time when God healed your broken heart and bound your wounds. Were you able to still praise God during this time? Were you angry with God?

Talk to your children about how it's okay to be angry with God sometimes. Explain that God understands our feelings. Talk about how sometimes we don't understand why things happen, but we know that God can use bad things to do something good.

### My Story and the Bible Story

My aunt died suddenly of a heart attack when I was a senior in college. The shock, combined with the grief, made it a very difficult time. We were heartbroken that she was no longer with us. I struggled with my grief and with anger that she died after she had finally gotten her life together.

Read Psalm 147:1-11, 20c.

You may wonder why I tell this sad story when this psalm is about praising the Lord. I tell it because in Psalm 147:3 we read, "He heals the broken-hearted and binds up their wounds." God heals the brokenhearted. Because we live in a world filled with disease, pain, and death, we will all be broken-hearted at some point. But we can take heart and praise the Lord; God not only "determines the number of the stars and calls them each by name" (v. 4) but also heals our broken hearts and binds our wounds. When your heart is broken, you feel wounded. Perhaps no one can see your wounds on the outside, but on the inside it feels as if you are breaking. Even so, the Lord doesn't leave you alone in your pain. God sees your pain and comforts you, binds your wounds, and walks beside you. Eventually, you don't feel as broken. You never forget, but your wounds do heal. That is why we can praise the Lord even in the midst of the pain.

## Discussion and Prayer

1. If your child has experienced loss (whether a person or a pet), ask them how they felt when it happened. Talk about how God comforts us. Ask them how they feel now.

2. If your child hasn't experienced loss yet, talk about how they might feel if someone they love dies.

3. As a family, discuss how you can find the good things that God is doing even when you're sad.

4. Has someone you know recently lost a loved one? Find ways to help them this week: take them a meal, bake cookies for them, take their children to school, listen to stories about their loved one, etc.

5. Pray, thanking God for comforting our hearts and for helping us heal after a loss. Offer praise that God knows all the stars and yet cares for us and is always there. If you are grieving, ask God to heal your broken heart.

### *Note*

Make sure to tell your children that God doesn't take anyone away from us—death happens because we live in a sinful world. Our bodies aren't made to last forever. But when someone we know dies, Jesus welcomes them with open arms. (If your child is old enough, you can talk to them about how that person needs to believe in Jesus, but the point of this conversation is that God doesn't take a loved one away.)

# Transfiguration Sunday
## Second Week of February
## Mark 9:2-9—"Jesus Is Transformed"

## Your Story

Talk about a way that God has changed you. How has God made you better than you were before you followed God?

## My Story and the Bible Story

God has changed my life in a lot of ways. For starters, I've never felt totally alone because I know that God is always with me. God has helped me get through some difficult times. God has helped me become kinder and gentler with others. God's love changes us. It's called "sanctification," which means that we become more like Christ. When we follow God, God changes us to be more like Jesus. God helps us become more of who He created us to be. God has a way of changing us. God has a way of showing us things we never dreamed.

### Read Mark 9:2-9.

Jesus transformed before the disciples' eyes! He changed, and all of a sudden Peter, James, and John could see who he was. They could see his holiness. Instead of simply seeing the man, they saw Jesus: the Son of God. God transformed him right in front of them. Like many people who saw angels in dazzling white, these men were frightened. Jesus changed, and they weren't sure what to do. But Peter knew that something amazing had happened. Jesus had changed, and Elijah and Moses, who had both been dead for a very long time, were in front of them. Peter wanted to stay on that mountain with a transformed Jesus and Elijah and Moses. They heard a voice say, "This is my Son, whom I love. Listen to him!" Jesus was transformed that day, but so were Peter, James, and John. They had seen the Lord, and they wanted to tell everyone. But Jesus told them to wait until it was time. When the time came, we know that Peter, James, and John told everyone about Jesus and all they had seen.

If we are willing, God transforms us and changes our lives. For some of us, that means God changes the things we do. For some of us, it means God changes the way we act. But whatever it is, God changes us. God transforms us. If we are willing, God will shape our lives so that everyone can see God's love. God transforms us but doesn't leave us. God tells us to go back down that mountain and tell others what He has done. Don't be afraid to share with others how God has transformed and changed you.

## Discussion and Prayer

1. Ask your children about ways that God has changed them. Talk about changes you have seen in your kids that appear to be God's work in them.

2. Talk about how your family can share with others what God has done for each of you.

3. Pray, thanking God for changing you. Ask God for help in sharing with others how you have been changed.

# Ash Wednesday
## Second Week of February
## Isaiah 58:1-8—
## "What We Do Matters to God"

### Your Story

Talk about a time when you helped someone else.

### My Story and the Bible Story

I tend to give up soda every year for Lent. Part of it is because there's a ton of sugar in soda and it's not good to drink it every day. But part of it is also because soda is my crutch. When I'm stressed, I drink a Coke. When I'm upset, I drink a Coke. Instead of giving my worries and my fears to God, instead of talking to God about it, I try to solve things on my own. I drink a Coke and try to work things out. Giving up soda for Lent so that I turn to God when I'm stressed, worried, or upset, is good. It's good for me to rely on God in those times instead of trying to do things on my own. But when I read passages like this one in Isaiah, I think that instead of giving up something for Lent, I should decide to do more. Instead of fasting from soda (or TV or Facebook or whatever it is you lean on), we should focus more on working to help those around us.

Read Isaiah 58:1-8.

The people were seeking the Lord. They wanted to know His ways. They even fasted to be closer to God. But they weren't loving their neighbor. They were arguing with each other and hurting others. And in Isaiah, God reminded them that He didn't care how much they fasted. What He cared about was how they were loving their neighbor. The way to be closer to God is by loving your neighbor, by sharing your food with the hungry, by giving clothes to those who need them, by providing shelter to those who need it, and by caring for others. Then, when we do that, when we show our love for our neighbors, then, "your light will break forth like the dawn, and your healing will quickly appear; then your righteousness will go before you, and the glory of the Lord will be your rear guard." God wants us to seek Him. But He also reminds us in Isaiah of how important loving our neighbor is. Giving up things doesn't mean anything if we aren't showing God's love to our neighbors. It doesn't matter how much we give up at Lent if we are ignoring the poor and hurting. As we begin Lent this year, find ways that you can show love to your neighbor. By doing so, you will be seeking after the Lord. And the glory of the Lord will go with you.

## Discussion and Prayer

1. Talk about concrete ways to love your neighbor this Lenten season.

2. Use this list to create a schedule of ways to love your neighbor each week during Lent. Or, use this list to create a grab bag in a bowl at your home so that each week, each person draws a way that they can show love to their neighbor that week.

3. Talk about what fasting means and its purpose.

4. Pray, thanking God for reminders to love our neighbor. Ask for help in finding ways to share God's love with others.

# First Week of Lent
## Third Week of February
## Genesis 9:8-17—
## "Why Are There Rainbows?"

## Your Story

What promises has God made to you? What promises have you made to God?

## My Story and the Bible Story

As a child, I always loved rainbows. I loved drawing them, and I really loved seeing them in the sky. Something about all the different colors coming together after the rain made me smile. As an adult, I still like rainbows. Seeing one unexpectedly still makes me smile, and it also reminds me of God's promises. When someone asks, "Why are there rainbows?" we can talk about how a beam of sunlight hits a raindrop at a certain angle and produces the colors we see. A beam of sunlight is actually made up of a bunch of different colors, but we can only see the spectrum when the light hits water and bounces off at certain angles. There's another reason for rainbows, though. Genesis 9 explains what the rainbow means to God.

### Read Genesis 9:8-17.

The rainbow is a reflection of sunlight through a raindrop, but it's also a reminder of God's promises. After the flood, God promised Noah that there would never again be a flood that destroyed the Earth. And God has kept that promise. Every time we see a rainbow, we can remember God's promise for Noah and God's promise to us: a flood will never again destroy the Earth. We can remember God's other promises as well. God promises never to leave us.

The next time you see a rainbow, remember that God loves you and will never leave you. We can be thankful for rainbows because they help us remember all the promises God has made, and we can trust God to keep these promises.

## Discussion and Prayer

1. As a family, talk about some of the promises God has made in the Bible. What are some of your favorite promises God has made?

2. Talk about the promises you and your family have made to God. Talk about how important it is to follow through with those promises. Also talk about God's grace and how even when we fail, God loves us no matter what.

3. What are some things that can help you remember God's promises?

4. Pray, giving thanks for all of God's promises. Ask for help in remembering that God is always there for us.

# Second Week of Lent
## Fourth Week of February
## Romans 4:13-25—
## "Why Are We Called Children of Abraham?"

### Your Story

Talk about a person who helped you believe in God and Jesus.

### My Story and the Bible Story

When I was a kid, we used to sing a song called "Father Abraham." It went like this: "Father Abraham had many sons. Many sons had Father Abraham. I am one of them, and so are you. So let's all praise the Lord." I always wondered why we sang that Father Abraham had many sons. If you read in Genesis, Abraham had two sons: Isaac and Ishmael. That's not many; that's just two. Yet God promised Abraham that he would be the father of many nations. That doesn't mean we are all descendants of Abraham. Abraham isn't necessarily our great-great-great-great . . . grandfather. It means that Abraham believed in God. He trusted God and followed God. Because he trusted and followed God, God used him to do big things. God used someone nobody knew to hand down the faith to future generations. Abraham trusted God, did what God wanted him to do, and shared his faith with others. Then his children and grandchildren and great-grandchildren trusted God, all the way down to Jesus. As Paul reminds us in Romans, Abraham is our faith father.

Read Romans 4:13-25.

When everything was hopeless, Abraham believed. He believed in God's promises and had faith in what God was doing, so God made him the father of a multitude of people. Abraham showed us how to trust in God during the good times and the bad and to trust even when things seemed impossible. Abraham is our faith father because he showed us how to follow God. Sometimes Abraham made mistakes. There were even a few times when he tried to tell everyone that Sarah (then called Sarai) was his sister and not his wife. But even though he made mistakes, he followed God. He trusted in God's promises when things seemed impossible.

Sometimes things seem impossible in our own lives, but we can trust that when God promises something, God will follow through. What God says will happen *does* eventually happen. And when God shows us what to do and we do it, God can use us to do great things.

## Discussion and Prayer

1. Are there things that God is asking you to trust God about? Talk about them with your family.

2. Are there things in your life that seem impossible? How might God be working?

3. What are some ways that God can use us?

4. Pray, giving thanks that nothing is impossible with God. Ask for help in knowing what you should do. Ask for help in trusting that God will always follow through with God's promises.

# March

## Third Week of Lent
### First Week of March
### Exodus 20:1-17—
### "Why Do We Have Rules?"

**Your Story**

Talk about a time when you didn't follow the rules and got in trouble or got hurt. Talk about why that rule was established.

**My Story and the Bible Story**

When I was in first grade, we had a fire drill. Our teacher told us we needed to be quiet as we walked outside, but I had a hard time being quiet. I talked all the time, so I wasn't quiet during the fire drill. My teacher knew it. She called my mom and told her about it, and I got in trouble. Looking back on it, I know now that my teacher wanted us to be quiet so we could hear directions. It might be okay if one person is talking, but if everyone is talking, it will be hard to hear. In fact, if that fire drill hadn't been a drill—if there was an actual fire—we could have gotten hurt if we couldn't hear directions. The rule was there not to get us in trouble or to ruin our fun but to keep us safe.

God does the same thing for the Israelites.

### Read Exodus 20:1-17.

God gave the Israelites these rules to keep them safe, to help them know how to worship God, and to show them how to live. Taking a day of rest was important because it helped them be ready for the next week. It also reminded them that they were not God and they did not have to try to be in control of everything. God wanted to make sure they treated their neighbors well. God wanted to make sure they knew that they were God's people. In a time when everyone around them was worshiping many different gods (because in those days people believed there were gods for lots of different things), the Israelites needed to know that their God was the one true God.

Why do you have to follow rules? You follow rules for the same reason the Israelites did: rules keep you safe. "Don't play in the road." "Look both ways before you cross the street." "Don't talk to strangers." "Don't talk during the fire drill." "Don't touch the stove." Rules like these, and more, keep you safe. They help you know what is dangerous. You also follow rules to keep other people around you safe. "Don't hit." "Don't take what doesn't belong to you." Rules like these help us be nice to each other.

We follow rules for all kinds of reasons. Rules keep us and the people around us safe, and God's rules show us how we should live. The next time you have to follow a rule, think about why you follow it. Does it keep you safe? Does it keep the people around you safe? Does it help you live a great life? Rules can be frustrating, but they also help us.

## Discussion and Prayer

1. What rules are the hardest for you to follow? Why?

2. Think about some of the rules you have as a family. Talk about the reasons behind those rules.

3. As a family, decide what will happen if someone breaks one of those rules. Talk about why that will happen.

4. Pray, thanking God for giving us rules so that we can live our best lives. Ask for help in following the rules.

# Fourth Week of Lent
## Second Week of March
## John 3:14-21—"Why Did Jesus Come?"

### Your Story

Talk about the time when you accepted Jesus as your Savior. How did you feel? Did you feel as if God was judging you, or did you feel God's grace?

## My Story and the Bible Story

There have been times in my life when I have done the wrong thing, and most of the time, I have gotten in trouble for that. But sometimes, even though I really deserved to get in trouble, I didn't. There were times when my mom or my teacher gave me grace instead of judgment, and instead of being punished I was simply forgiven.

Read John 3:14-21.

"God so loved the world . . . ." You can probably say the rest of this familiar verse. Many of us learn it in church at an early age and remember how much God loves us. Why did Jesus come? Jesus came because God loved the world too much to sit by and watch us move farther and farther away. God loved the world enough to send Jesus to us so that whoever believes in him would have eternal life. We all do things that are wrong. We sin. We make the wrong choices. We are sometimes mean to others. We sometimes say nasty things. We hurt each other, and sometimes we hurt ourselves. Jesus is perfect. It would have made sense for Jesus to come and judge the world. After all, there's nothing we could do to ever be perfect. There's no way we can be perfect simply by trying hard enough. But John says that Jesus didn't come to judge the world: "God did not send his Son into the world to condemn the world, but to save the world through him." Jesus came to save us, not to condemn us. Jesus sees what we have done and forgives us.

We deserve to get in trouble with God. We sometimes do the wrong thing. But instead of punishing us, God sent Jesus to save us. When someone asks you why Jesus came, you can say he came because God loves us enough to want to be our friend forever. God loves us enough to forgive all the things we do wrong. Jesus came not to judge us but to save us. Jesus came so that we could always be with God. That is great news!

## Discussion and Prayer

1. Has there been a time when you did something wrong, but instead of getting in trouble you were simply forgiven? How did that make you feel?

2. Have you ever forgiven someone who hurt you when they thought you would be angry with them? How did it feel to forgive someone who didn't really deserve it?

3. Think about the ways God has forgiven you. Write them down. Thank God for forgiving you, then throw your piece of paper away.

4. Pray, thanking God for always forgiving us. Thank God for sending Jesus not to condemn the world but to save it. Ask for help in looking at the world through God's eyes.

# Fifth Week of Lent
## Third Week of March
## Psalm 119:9-16—"How Should We Live?"

### Your Story

Did you grow up in church? If so, talk about your experiences there as a child and youth. Did you enjoy going? Did your parents teach you how to follow God? What were some ways that you learned God's word that helped you remember it? If you did not grow up in church, talk to your family about how you started going to church. How did you discover God? How do you "hide [God's] word in your heart" now?

### My Story and the Bible Story

I loved going to church as a child. I loved Sunday school, Vacation Bible School, choir, worship, and everything else I went to. I wanted to be at church every time the doors were open. In fact, there was one Sunday morning when I woke up late and ran into the living room to ask my mom why she hadn't gotten me up for church. There had been a blizzard during the night, and everything was covered in snow! My mom did a great job of instilling in me a love for God and for church. Learning about God didn't just end with church, though. My mom took time to read Bible stories to me, and later on we did devotions together. She taught me how to seek God. She helped me learn how to hide God's word in my heart, as Psalm 119 says.

Read Psalm 119:9-16.

How should we live as God wants us to? How can the children in our care grow up following God? By reading the Bible. Through the Bible, the Holy Spirit can speak to us and show us how to live. The Bible is full of stories of people trying to follow God, waiting for God to speak, and doing what they believe God has told them to do. Many times they succeed, but sometimes they fail. If we read the Bible and listen for God, God will teach us how to live in God's way. In order for children to grow up following God, they must know and fall in love with God. They must know that God is their Creator and their Redeemer and that God loves them enough to give them the beautiful gift of grace.

## Discussion and Prayer

1. Ask your children to share their favorite thing about church. It might be worship, seeing friends, or eating donuts!

2. Share with your family your favorite thing about church.

3. Discuss ways that you and your family can hide God's word in your hearts (memorize Scripture, write it on mirrors with dry-erase markers, write Bible verses on index cards and keep them in the car, etc.).

4. Find ways this week to read more Scripture as a family. If you have young children, focus on Psalms or the Gospels.

5. Pray, thanking God for the Bible. Ask God to teach you and your family God's ways, as the psalmist does in Psalm 119. Ask for help in teaching your children about God.

# Palm Sunday
## Fourth Week of March (2021)
## Mark 11:1-11—"Celebration and Real Life"

## Your Story

Do you like celebrations? Tell a story about one of your favorite memories of a celebration. How did you feel during that celebration? Were you able to forget about your worries and your fears, or were they still present but you chose to set them aside for a time?

## My Story and the Bible Story

I love celebrations. In particular, I love birthdays. I love finding the perfect present and celebrating who the special person is. I enjoy my birthday as well, but it's always a little odd to me. I look forward to it, yet I always feel slightly let down. It's not because people forget my birthday; the people who are close to me remember. And it's not that I don't have fun; I do. But I always expect to feel different on my birthday, older and wiser, perhaps. And yet when the sun sets and the day is done, I feel the same. I love the anticipation of celebrating, but I also know what comes after my birthday: real life. And that real life is not always easy.

Read Mark 11:1-11.

I wonder if Jesus felt that odd mixture of anticipation and disappointment when he entered Jerusalem. He enters the city triumphantly, riding on a donkey, with people spreading their cloaks on the road and others waving branches in the air, shouting, "Hosanna! Blessed is he who comes in the name of the Lord!" The people, and the disciples themselves, are celebrating. They think this is the best thing that could happen. And yet Jesus knows what is coming after the celebration: real life and death. He knows that those same people who are shouting, "Hosanna!" will soon be shouting, "Crucify him!" But he enters Jerusalem anyway. He knows what is waiting for him and still he goes.

I hope that this time of celebration gave him a reprieve from the heavy burden of knowing that death was coming. That's what celebrations sometimes are for us: a reprieve from our heavy burdens. They are moments in time when we come together and celebrate, either someone or something, and put aside our burdens, our pain, and our worry, if only for a moment.

As we begin Holy Week, may you take time to put aside your worries and your burdens and remember the hope that Jesus brings.

## Discussion and Prayer

1. What are some things, large or small, that you and your family can celebrate this week?

2. Talk about how you think the disciples felt when they heard the crowd shouting, "Hosanna! Blessed is he who comes in the name of the Lord!"

3. Pray, thanking God for celebrations, when we can put everything aside to remember someone close to us. Ask God for help in celebrating God's love and grace even when things are difficult.

# Good Friday
## Fourth Week of March (2021)
## Mark 14:43–15:47—"A World in Ruins"

### Your Story

Talk about a time when your week started well but ended with you feeling disappointed and discouraged. What happened? How did you handle it?

### My Story and the Bible Story

Sometimes things happen all at once, and we aren't sure how we're going to make it another hour, let alone another day. We've all had bad weeks, and some of us have had a week so terrible we couldn't go another step. The disciples had the worst week of their lives that first Holy Week. At the beginning of the week, things were amazing. They were walking with their teacher into Jerusalem, entering that great city victoriously. The people were laying their coats down, waving branches, and shouting, "Hosanna!" It seemed everyone recognized who Jesus was, and finally things would be great. And yet by the end of the week, Jesus had been arrested, Peter had denied even knowing Jesus, the disciples had scattered, and Jesus was dying on a cross.

Read Mark 14:43–15:47.

What do you do when your world has been shattered? What do you do when it seems that the person in whom you placed all of your hopes and dreams was wrong, when it seems as though Jesus wasn't the Messiah at all? Almost all the disciples hid, terrified that they, too, would be arrested and possibly crucified with Jesus. Praise God that we know the story doesn't end on the cross but moves instead to the empty tomb. But on this day, this Good Friday, the disciples had no idea. Jesus was dead, and their world had come crashing down around them. Which way do you turn when your world is in ruins?

## Discussion and Prayer

1. Talk about how you think the disciples felt when Jesus was arrested. If you had been there, do you think you would have tried to fight the people arresting Jesus? Would you have run away?

2. How would you feel if you saw Jesus being crucified?

3. We know that Easter is coming and that Jesus rose from the dead, defeating death so that we could always be with God. But today we remember Jesus' death. We remember how hard it must have been for the disciples. Today we mourn for Jesus so that we can celebrate his resurrection on Easter Sunday. As a family, talk about what you can do to remember Jesus' death today.

4. Pray, thanking God for sending Jesus to die on a cross for us. Confess your sins to God and ask God to forgive them.

# April

## Easter
### First Week of April
### Mark 16:1-8—"What Just Happened?"

## Your Story

Have you ever experienced something confusing? What did you do?

## My Story and the Bible Story

I cannot tell you the number of times that I have said, "Wait. What just happened?" Whether someone said something that didn't make sense or I witnessed something that didn't make sense, I was confused and didn't know what to do. So I asked, "what just happened?" Sometimes I got answers. But sometimes others were just as confused as I was. As hard as we try, sometimes we can't make situations make sense. There are times when we see amazing things, but we don't realize it until later. For the women at the tomb in Mark's Gospel, their experience was confusing. They were afraid and bewildered.

### Read Mark 16:1-8.

I don't know about you, but if I saw an angel sitting in the tomb where Jesus was supposed to me, I would probably be alarmed too. I can imagine that, after listening to the angel, Mary, Mary, and Salome looked at each other thinking "what just happened?" They were so afraid that they ran from the tomb. And Mark tells us that they told no one. I would love to think that if I were in their shoes, I would have shouted from the rooftops that Jesus is alive. But how often do I shout that from the rooftops now? How often to I tell everyone I know that Jesus is alive? It is not as often as I should. And so perhaps, before we judge them for keeping this great news to themselves, we should also remember that we don't always tell everyone that Jesus is alive either. Why did they keep this good news to themselves? Perhaps it was because they were confused and unsure of what was happening. But Jesus had already told them what would happen.

Here in front of them was the proof that Jesus was real, that everything He said was true, and that He was the Son of God. It's possible that in that moment, they panicked, knowing that now they needed to practice what Jesus had taught. It's important to note that at some point, the wonderful news of the Resurrection was told. At some point, they got over their fear and bewilderment to tell everyone about the good news of Jesus. There are times when we, too, may be confused and bewildered by God. God may be doing something that seems strange to us, or He may ask us to do something that doesn't make much sense. In times of confusion, remember that God will make things clear. If you continue to talk to God, He will show you what to do. You might not understand, but God does promise to talk to us. So when you are confused about what God is doing, talk to Him about it. Ask Him to calm your fears and show you what to do. He always will. The good news of Easter was bewildering on that first Easter morning. And it doesn't always make sense to us either. But even though we don't always understand grace, God still gives it to us freely. And that is great news!

## Discussion and Prayer

1. Has there been a time when you didn't understand how God was working in your life? As a family, talk about times when what God was asking you to do didn't quite make sense.

2. Talk about things about God that seem confusing.

3. If you are confused about what God wants you to do, how can you get clarity? Talk about the different ways you can better understand what's going on (i.e. read your Bible, pray, talk to a trusted adult who follows God, etc.).

4. Pray, asking God for clarity in knowing what He wants us to do and for courage to do it.

# Second Week of April
## John 20:19-31—"I Doubt It"

## Your Story

Has there been a time in your life when something seemed too crazy to be real and yet it was? Talk about this with your family. Or you can share my story or talk about a time when you doubted something and it indeed turned out to be false.

## My Story and the Bible Story

When I was a child, we played a game called "I doubt it" when we went on vacation. It was a card game, and the point was to get rid of all of your cards first. The trick was that you had to get rid of them in order. For instance, the first person starts by putting aces facedown in a pile. You can put down one to four cards at a time (more than four and people know you aren't telling the truth). Maybe you say you are putting down three aces, but you only have one. You don't have to have three aces to say that you are putting them down. But any player may say, "I doubt it!" whenever someone puts down cards. Those cards are then turned over; if the player was telling the truth, the doubter has to take the whole stack of cards. If, however, the player didn't actually put down three aces, then he or she has to take the whole stack of cards. This continues until one player is out of cards. This game teaches about number sequencing, but it also teaches how to read people and not always take things at face value. Like in the game, there are times in life when things seem too crazy or ridiculous to be real. It's at those times when we find ourselves saying, "I doubt it!"

### Read John 20:19-31.

Thomas gets a bad rap. He's the only one of the disciples who didn't see Jesus when he first rose from the dead. When the other disciples told Thomas about Jesus, he could only scoff and say that he wouldn't believe unless he saw Jesus and his wounds for himself. For Thomas, and for most of us if we're honest, the idea of resurrection is a crazy one. This had never happened to anyone before, and Thomas probably felt like the other disciples had simply seen someone who looked similar to Jesus. But Jesus understood and appeared before him. He allowed Thomas to see that his wounds were real and that it really was him.

There are times when it seems as if God is too good to be true. There are times when it seems as though our prayers just bounce off the ceiling, yet God is always there for us, waiting patiently and reminding us that God is, in fact, real. How patient God must be as we run ourselves ragged trying to figure things out. In verse 29, Jesus says, "blessed are those who have not seen and yet have believed." Thomas had proof that Jesus was real and this Jesus rose from the dead. He felt the scars and he saw Jesus right in front of him. Living 2,000 years later, we don't have the chance to see Jesus in that way. But Jesus calls us blessed. We are blessed because we continue to have faith and believe in the things we cannot see. We are blessed because when the doubts creep in, God's saving love reminds us of grace and acceptance.

Perhaps God is calling you to take a leap of faith. Trust that God is with you. When the doubts creep in, give them over to God. Allow God's peace to wash over you, and believe that God is always honest and always faithful.

## Discussion and Prayer

1. Ask your kids about things that have seemed too good to be true to them. Were they indeed too good to be true? What happened? Did your kids believe anyway?

2. If God is calling you to take a leap of faith, accept it this week. Take that leap. If not, take time to give God all of your doubts this week. Work on believing that God will come through with all that God has promised, even if it looks different than you thought it would.

3. Pray, asking God to help you believe in things you cannot see. Pray for God's guidance in situations where you need to take a leap of faith. Ask God to help you trust more.

# Third Week of April
# 1 John 3:1-7—"A Blank Slate"

## Your Story

When have you been given a new start? Did you take it? How did things turn out? Share this story with your family.

## My Story and the Bible Story

I loved school as a child. One of my favorite parts about going back to school was buying school supplies. Even if I had pens and pencils at home, I wanted new ones for school. New notebooks were also a must. When I opened the cover of a fresh notebook for the first time, I knew it could hold anything. All of the pages were blank. I could turn it into anything I wanted. If I wanted to draw pictures, the notebook could become a sketch-book. If I wanted to write a book, it could be that too. If I needed to take notes for a class, it became my science or history notebook. Each new note-book was a fresh start, a blank slate.

Our lives can be blank slates as well. There are times when we need a new start. Thankfully, there are times throughout the year when we are given a new start. If you go to school, that new start is the first day of a new school year or the first day of a new semester. At work, it might be the first day of a new job or in a new office. In your life, that new start can begin on your birthday or on January 1 of a new year. There are built-in times for us to have a blank slate and a new start.

### Read 1 John 3:1-7.

The Scripture writer says that "what we will be has not yet been made known" (v. 2). God gives us many blank slates—chances to start over—throughout our lives. As children, we can be whoever we want to be. We can pretend to be astronauts, doctors, teachers, singers, actors, etc. The possibilities for who we can be are endless. Bit by bit, we begin to discover what brings us joy and who we are. God gives us a blank slate when we accept Jesus as our Savior. We get a blank slate/fresh start at the beginning of each new year. And finally, we will all get a blank slate when we are with God forever. However your life looks, remember that what we will be has not yet been made fully known. But we can know for sure that what we are and will always be are children of God.

## Discussion and Prayer

1. Ask your children who and what they want to be when they grow up.

2. If your children have done something wrong this week, give them a fresh start. Talk to them about God's grace and who they are as a child of God. Tell them that God gives us a fresh start when we say we're sorry for the things we've done wrong and mean it. Let them out of their punishment early if possible.

3. Talk about ways that your family can have a fresh start. Perhaps you need to spend more time together. Find ways to set aside time each week to spend as a family.

4. Pray, thanking God for fresh starts. Praise God for always forgiving us and giving us a blank slate when we mess up. Ask God for forgiveness for anything that's weighing on your heart this week.

# Fourth Week of April
# 1 John 3:16-24—"Compassion"

### Your Story

How do you show compassion for others? Did you help others when you were a child, or is it something you have started recently? Talk to your children about ways you have helped or ways you want to help others.

### My Story and the Bible Story

When I was a child, I was sick. In fact, I had to have allergy shots every single day for a time when I was little. My mother cannot stand needles. She would make a wonderful nurse except for the fact that she faints when she sees a needle. But I had to have these shots in order to stay well. It was too much for us to go to the doctor every day, so my mother practiced giving me the shots. The first time she gave me my shot was in the doctor's office. She gave me the shot, calmly put down the needle, and passed out. Eventually she stopped passing out, but even though she was afraid of needles, she loved me and knew I needed these shots, so she gave them to me. She didn't just tell me she loved me; she showed me.

Read 1 John 3:16-24.

"Dear children, let us not love with words or tongue but with actions and in truth" (1 John 3:18). God calls us to love others, but that love must be more than words.

God calls us to show others God's love, but this love doesn't leave people where they are—broken, starving, or hurting. This love calls us to come alongside others, to listen to their hurts and carry their crosses. It requires us to be compassionate and help others when we see their need.

## Discussion and Prayer

1. Ask your children about ways that they have helped others.

2. As a family, discuss ways that you can show compassion or help others this week. Perhaps that means taking dinner to a grieving friend or someone who has been sick. Maybe it means baking cookies for the lonely senior adult across the street. Maybe it means serving food together in a homeless shelter. Find ways to be creative.

3. Thank God for loving us enough to send Jesus to us. Ask God to help you be more compassionate. Ask God to show you the needs of others.

# May

## First Week of May
## John 15:1-8—"Staying Connected"

### Your Story

Think of things that must stay connected to its source in order for it to work. Talk to your kids about the electronics and appliances in your house that must be plugged in for them to work.

### My Story and the Bible Story

I have always loved wisteria. I know that it's a parasite, but it has always been beautiful to me. One of my favorite parts of driving to my grandparents' house as a kid was passing the beautiful wisteria growing in a patch of trees. I loved it so much that one day Pop (my granddad) pulled over on the side of the road to cut me a piece of wisteria. As soon as he cut it off the vine, it wilted. Unlike a flower, wisteria can't survive without being connected to its source.

### Read John 15:1-8.

Like the wisteria, we thrive when we are connected to our source: God. When we are apart from God, when we refuse God and run away, we wilt. The storms of life knock us down and things feel hopeless. Without God, we have no hope. If we remain connected to God, though, the storms may still knock us down, but God will lift us back up. With God, nothing is impossible. We are able to get through anything because the Creator of the Universe loves us and walks beside us. God is always with us. As long as we stay connected to God, we can rest in the fact that God will carry us through the storms. When we stay connected to God, other people can see God's love in us. That is the fruit we bear, the fruit of the spirit: love, joy, peace, patience, kindness, goodness, faithfulness, gentleness, and self-control (Gal 5:22-23).

## Discussion and Prayer

1. What are some ways that you can stay connected to God, both as individuals and as a family? What are things you need to do to remain connected to God?

2. How do you feel when you ignore God for a while, when you "disconnect"? How about when you listen to God and remain connected?

3. Pray, giving thanks that we can be connected to God through Jesus. Ask God for help in whatever ways you want to use to remain connected. Give thanks for God's love and peace.

# Second Week of May
## John 15:9-17—"Friends"

### Your Story

How have you helped or supported your friends? How have your friends been there for you?

### My Story and the Bible Story

We do things for our friends. When I was in seminary, my great-great-aunt passed away. She was the last of my great-grandmother's siblings, and although she was in her nineties, she had been pretty healthy. But then she got in a car wreck and her health deteriorated quickly. I was at school when I got the call that she was gone, and a friend of mine found me crying in the hallway. He comforted me and then we went our separate ways. But that night, he and a few of my other friends brought dinner and ate with me. They listened to stories about my family and reminded me that I didn't have to grieve alone. One of the best things about friends is their care and concern and willingness to be there for us. As friends, we do things like bring food, give rides when cars are being fixed, and help people move. We help each other and confide in each other.

Read John 15:9-17.

Jesus called his disciples friends because he confided in them, helped them (and in turn there were times when they helped him), and cared about them. He chose them and he loved them. We are called to love others the same way that Jesus loved his disciples and loves us. Jesus gave us everything he had when he died on the cross for us. Jesus commands us to love each other not just by saying that we love them but also by showing we love them. That means being present for others, listening when they are in pain, joining them in grieving, celebrating their happiness, and caring about them. Jesus chose to be friends with us. If it were up to us, we would have stayed in our sin, lost and broken without really knowing it. But Jesus knew and he cared, so he chose to be our friend. He chose to meet us where we are so that we could always be friends with God. We are called to show others the same caring and compassion, pointing the way to the One who wants to be their friend forever.

## Discussion and Prayer

1. Ask your children about ways they have helped their friends or their friends have helped them.

2. Explain to them that God wants us to treat everyone like they are our friends. We are called to show God's love to everyone, to be there for them, and to help them when they need it.

3. Talk about ways to be a good friend this week. Choose at least one to put into action.

4. Pray, thanking God that Jesus chose to be our friend. Ask God for helping in showing others' God's love.

# Ascension
## Third Week of May
## Luke 24:44-53—"Being a Witness"

## Your Story

Talk about a time when you witnessed something important. Did it change you?

## My Story and the Bible Story

My grandmother calls herself a "scrap baby." She was born in 1928, on the cusp of the Great Depression. Because she was the baby of her family, she always received the scraps—the leftovers or hand-me-downs. Although she was young during the Great Depression, it forever changed her. She learned how to make things last. She learned the value of money and the importance of not spending more than you have. As an adult, she has a lot more than she did as a child, but she is still careful with her money. I'm fortunate that she passed many of those lessons on to me. Over her ninety years of life, the world has changed dramatically. But no matter how much changes, for the better or for the worse, she has always trusted that God is with her. She hasn't allowed any of the things she has witnessed to take away her faith.

## Read Luke 24:44-53.

The disciples had witnessed Jesus' crucifixion. They knew that Jesus was dead. And Jesus' death changed them forever. But so did the Resurrection. And then, when they witnessed Jesus' ascension to heaven, they knew that everything had changed. And they praised God for what He had done. But that's not the end of the story. Afterwards, they got to work, sharing with everyone they saw about Jesus. They told others what they had witnessed, and they told them about God's amazing love. When we witness something, we don't keep it to ourselves. We tell others about it. My grandmother told me stories about her childhood so that I would understand. She taught me (and continues to teach me) the lessons she learned so that I can be better. The disciples taught everyone what they had witnessed, and their witness changed the world. They shared God's love with others, and those who accepted were changed. It is because the disciples shared what they witnessed that we, 2000 years later, believe in Jesus. When you witness something God does, share it with others! You may just help change their lives.

## Discussion

1. Talk about something God has done in your life. Have your children share what God has done in their lives.

2. How can you share with others what God has done for you?

3. Choose someone this week to tell what God has done for you.

4. Pray, thanking God for the disciples who shared the story of Jesus with everyone they met. Ask for courage in sharing what we have witnessed with others.

# Pentecost
## Fourth Week of May
## John 15:26-27; 16:4b-15—"The Spirit"

### Your Story

Tell your family about a time you relied on the Holy Spirit to help you know the truth. Talk about the situation and how you felt relying on the Holy Spirit.

### My Story and the Bible Story

When I write my children's sermons, I have a process. Usually, I read the Scripture, think about it for a few minutes, and then go do something else. I don't start writing until I find inspiration. I wait for the Holy Spirit to speak to me. It is only when the Spirit speaks to me that I begin to write. I have learned, by trial and error, to wait. If I try to rush the Holy Spirit, I usually end up rewriting. The Holy Spirit inspires us and helps us know what to do and where to turn. And it even helps us know the right words to say.

Before Jesus left, he told the disciples about the Spirit of Truth. He told them that the Spirit of Truth would be coming from the Father and would help them.

Read John 15:26-27 and John 16:4b-15.

In this passage, Jesus reminds the disciples that if he left them, then the Spirit of Truth would come. With Jesus there, the disciples could ask him what they should do, but after Jesus left, they all would receive the Spirit of Truth. We also call this the Holy Spirit. God gives us the Holy Spirit to help us. When we're not sure what to do, the Holy Spirit guides us.

On Pentecost, we remember the day the Holy Spirit came down to the disciples. Acts tells us that the Holy Spirit came upon them like tongues of fire. While we can't see the Holy Spirit the way the disciples did, we know that the Spirit is with us, helping us and leading us. When you're not sure what decision to make or which way to turn, ask God to help you. God will use the Holy Spirit to help you know what to do. Sometimes this kind of help comes through family or friends, sometimes through people at church, and sometimes in a thought you have that you know is right.

## Discussion and Prayer

1. Ask your kids about times when they felt like God was guiding them and showing them what to do. Talk about how that was the Holy Spirit guiding them.

2. Make sure your kids understand that the Holy Spirit comes from God, and that it is part of God. Talk about the Trinity (the Father, the Son, and the Holy Spirit) and how they all work together.

3. Talk about ways you can listen for the Holy Spirit.

4. Pray, thanking God for sending the Holy Spirit to help us. Ask God for help in listening to the Holy Spirit.

# End of May/Beginning of June
# Isaiah 6:1-8—"Holy, Holy, Holy"

## Your Story

When are you most reminded of God's holiness? Is it when the world is quiet and you are walking through nature? Is it when you watch your children sleep? Talk to your family about the times when you think about God's holiness the most.

## My Story and the Bible Story

One of my favorite hymns is "Holy, Holy, Holy."

> Holy, holy, holy! Lord God Almighty!
> Early in the morning our song shall rise to Thee;
> Holy, holy, holy, merciful and mighty!
> God in three Persons, blessed Trinity!
>
> Holy, holy, holy! All the saints adore Thee,
> Casting down their golden crowns around the glassy sea;
> Cherubim and seraphim falling down before Thee,
> Who was, and is, and evermore shall be.
>
> Holy, holy, holy! Though the darkness hide Thee,
> Though the eye of sinful man Thy glory may not see;
> Only Thou art holy; there is none beside Thee,
> Perfect in power, in love, and purity.
>
> Holy, holy, holy! Lord God Almighty!
> All Thy works shall praise Thy Name, in earth, and sky, and sea;
> Holy, holy, holy; merciful and mighty!
> God in three Persons, blessed Trinity![8]

I love this hymn because it reminds us that God is holy, set apart from everything else.

---

8. "Holy, Holy, Holy," words by Reginald Heber, 1826.

Read Isaiah 6:1-8.

God is different from anything else in our universe. He is the Creator, the only One who is holy. I am most reminded of God's holiness during Communion and during Holy Week, the week leading up to Easter. When we remember Jesus' death and celebrate his resurrection, I think most about God's holiness. God is the only One who was willing to die for us. Most of us cannot imagine dying for someone else, unless that someone is your child. But we are all God's children, and God showed love by dying for each of us. What a holy thing to do!

## Discussion and Prayer

1. Talk about how Isaiah must have felt to be in the presence of God. Why did he say that he was doomed?

2. Talk about how Isaiah's sins were forgiven. Talk about how our sins are forgiven so that we can be in the presence of God.

3. What does it mean that God is holy? Ask your children about times when they have been amazed by or in awe of God.

4. Isaiah doesn't stay where he is. After God forgives him for his sins, Isaiah is willing to be God's messenger. In the same way, God doesn't want us to stay where we are. What is God calling you to do this week?

5. Give praise to God, who is perfect. Offer praise for all of God's amazing creations. Thank God for loving us no matter what. Praise God for being holy.

# June

## First Week of June
## 1 Samuel 2:1-10—"God Knows"

**Your Story**

Talk about a time in your life when you felt invisible, like no one else knew your pain and it seemed that you were on your own. Did you turn to God? If you did, talk about how you felt after turning to God (relieved, peaceful, etc.). If not, talk about how it felt trying to handle things on your own.

**My Story and the Bible Story**

There are times when we put a smile on our faces, but inside we are hurting. We may be sad because we lost someone we love. Or we may be sad because we moved and had to leave all our friends or because we're unhappy at school. Many things can make us sad, and sometimes we have to pretend like everything's okay. When that happens, it's easy to feel alone, like nobody knows how we feel and that we are all by ourselves with our pain. That's certainly how Hannah felt in 1 Samuel when she couldn't have a child. But God knew her pain and answered her prayer. God doesn't always answer our prayers with a yes, but God always knows our pain.

Read 1 Samuel 2:1-10.

Hannah reminds us in 1 Samuel that God knows what's going on. God sees everything. We cannot make it in this life on our own. It is only with God's help that we can make it. God sees when we are weak and cares for us. No matter how you feel right now, even if no one else knows it, God does. You can take comfort in the fact that God is walking beside you, ready and willing to give you peace and comfort.

## Discussion and Prayer

1. Ask your family if there is anything they are sad/upset about right now. If so, talk about it as a family.

2. Talk about ways we can know that God is there (the changing of the leaves, the wind blowing, a phone call or visit from someone, a feeling, etc.). Ask your kids to talk about times when they know God is with them.

3. Pray, asking God to take whatever you are feeling and give you peace.

# Second Week of June
# 2 Corinthians 4:13–5:1—
# "Don't Lose Heart!"

## Your Story

Talk about a time when something bad happened in your life and you wanted to give up. Who encouraged you to keep going? Did you look to God for strength?

## My Story and the Bible Story

We all have bad days sometimes. Maybe we forget to do something important like studying for a test or doing homework, we drop things, we step in giant puddles, we are late for an important event, and on and on. But there are also times when bad days become something more. We get a bad grade on a test and feel like a failure. A parent gets fired from a job. Your pet dies. You have to move far away from your friends.

When I was a kid, I had a bad year. I didn't have any friends at school. My church was going through a tough time, and I didn't have any friends there either. My mom and my stepdad were getting a divorce. That was a tough year, and I wanted to give up. But I was reminded of a popular saying that went by the acronym FROG: Fully Rely on God. Relying on God is what helped me through that tough time. It's what Paul tells his readers to do in his letter to the Corinthians.

Read 2 Corinthians 4:13–5:1.

Paul reminded the Corinthians that, even though times were tough, they were struggling, and it seemed like things were falling part, God was with them. Paul reminded them that God continued to work on them every single day and that God was making something new. God's grace was with them no matter what. When things are tough, God's grace is there. When things are good, God's grace is there. We may face troubles, but that doesn't mean God isn't with us. It doesn't matter what is happening in our lives, God is with us.

When we think about eternity with God, our troubles can seem smaller. When we think about last week when life felt so hard, it doesn't seem quite as bad now. God helps us get through tough times and reminds us about all the good times we will have in heaven. Whenever you struggle and whenever bad things happen, don't lose heart! Remember that God is with you. God will help you get through. And someday, all your troubles will be gone. There is a wonderful celebration waiting for us in eternity!

## Discussion and Prayer

1. Ask your kids to talk about hard things they are going through right now.

2. Encourage your family. Remind them that God is always with them.

3. Talk about ways we can remember God is there and recognize how God helps us.

4. Pray, thanking God for helping us through tough times and asking for strength to face today's difficulties.

# Third Week of June
# Mark 4:30-34—
# "The Parable of the Mustard Seed"

## Your Story

Have you ever planted something and watched it grow? Did it grow larger than you expected?

## My Story and the Bible Story

If you have ever planted a flower, you know that it starts from a tiny seed. That seed doesn't look like much; in fact, you might lose it if you drop it. But when you put the seed in soil, cover it, and water it, something amazing starts to happen. Pretty soon, you start to see green sprouts. If you give it sunlight and water, the flower starts to grow big and strong. Think about all the flowers you have seen. Every single one of them started with a tiny seed. Think about the trees you see all around you. Those started from seeds as well. Their seeds may look different (for instance, the seeds for oak trees live in acorns), but they all started with seeds. It took water and sunlight for them to grow, but grow they did. The kingdom of God is like that.

### Read Mark 4:30-34.

A mustard seed is tiny, yet Jesus compares it to the kingdom of God. The kingdom of God started with one small seed: Jesus. Then it spread as the disciples went out and told everyone. As the disciples told people about Jesus, more and more people believed. As they believed, the kingdom of God grew until it had touched billions of people. And still it continued to grow. Thousands and thousands of years later, the kingdom of God is still growing. Like the tiny mustard seed that can grow to be eight feet tall, the kingdom of God continues to grow big and strong. It started as something small, but it grew into something amazing.

You are small too, but you are growing. You are part of the kingdom of God. As you grow, you can do many things for God's kingdom. You can tell others about God's love. You can be kind to others. You can help others when they need it. You can help at church. You can help your parents and your brothers or sisters. You can do many things for the kingdom of God. Every time you tell someone about God, every time you share God's love with others, you are helping the kingdom of God grow. It started out like a tiny seed, but it grew into something big and amazing. You may not feel like you can do big things for the kingdom of God, but know that every small thing you do, every time you are kind to someone or show God's love, you are making the kingdom of God a bit bigger.

## Discussion and Prayer

1. What can you do to help the kingdom of God?

2. Take a walk outside. Stop when you see an interesting flower or tree and talk about how it grows. Remind your family that each plant came from a seed. Talk about some flowers or even vegetables that you may want to plant and watch grow.

3. Ask your children to share what else the kingdom of God might be like. Can they think of other comparisons?

4. Pray, thanking God for the kingdom. Praise God for people who are willing to share God's love with others. Ask for help in sharing God's love with those around us.

# End of June/Beginning of July
# Mark 4:35-41—"The Storms of Life"

### Your Story

Tell your children about a storm in your life when you doubted that God would get you through. It can be about an actual storm or a metaphorical storm. What happened? How did God get you through it?

### My Story and the Bible Story

I've mentioned my fear of storms as a child. The thunder scared me the most, and my mom could never convince me that the thunder couldn't hurt me. One day we were at the beach, swimming in the ocean, when a storm came up. I panicked. I started swimming as fast as I could to shore, determined to get out of the ocean before the storm could hurt me. At first I waited for the grownups, my mom and my friend's mom and dad. But they were moving too slowly for me, so I left them behind and swam as fast as I could. We were all fine, of course. Eventually the storm moved on and we continued with our vacation. But I never forgot how afraid I was of that storm. In that moment, I wouldn't have believed anyone trying to assure me that God would protect us.

Read Mark 4:35-41.

As someone who has never liked bad weather, I love that Jesus can calm even this great big storm. No matter how big the storm, it still has to obey God. God has the power to calm the storms in our lives. And yet the disciples doubted. They had been following Jesus, listening to him teach, and absorbing who he was. Even so, in the midst of the storm they doubted. This passage reminds us that it is okay to doubt, that even those close to Jesus doubted. But it also doesn't leave us in our doubt for long.

Jesus didn't wait for the disciples to get over their doubt before he calmed the storm. The disciples were terrified, so Jesus calmed the storm first and then dealt with their doubt. He didn't make fun of them for doubting, though. Instead, he asked, "Why are you frightened? Don't you have faith yet?" Jesus was basically asking them if they still didn't realize who he was.

Jesus speaks to our fear in this passage too. This story is a reminder to us that there's no need to be afraid. Storms will come and scary things will happen, but our faith will sustain us. No matter what happens, we will spend eternity with God. So when a storm comes along, remember Jesus' words: "Why are you frightened? Don't you have faith yet?"

## Discussion and Prayer

1. Ask your children about their storms in life. What has frightened them?

2. Talk about ways we can remember that God is with us in the midst of these storms.

3. How can we practice our faith during the storms of life?

4. Pray, thanking God for always being there during the storms. Ask for help in trusting God more when the storms come.

# July

## First Week of July
## 2 Corinthians 8:7-15—"Giving"

### Your Story

Share with your children about a time when you gave generously, either your money or your time, to help the church or someone else. Or share about a time when someone gave generously to help you. How did you feel?

### My Story and the Bible Story

One of my favorite stories of giving comes from one of the children at church. At six years old, she received a dollar from the tooth fairy for losing a tooth, but she didn't use that money to buy something for herself. Instead, she put the whole dollar into the offering plate at church one Sunday morning, and she was thrilled to do it. She was so excited about giving her offering that she ran up to me after church to tell me all about it. Giving generously is what we are called to do, whether it is a dollar, ten thousand dollars, or our time.

Read 2 Corinthians 8:7-15.

In a culture where it seems as if we are always pushed to give more, do more, be more, and buy more than we could possibly afford, Paul's words remind us to take a step back and remember why we give. We give because of Jesus' generosity, his sacrifice for us. Jesus became poor, dying on the cross, so that we could be rich by being forever friends with God. Because Jesus was generous, we are called to be generous. Paul tells us that the point of our generosity isn't so we will be hard pressed or "sweat it out," as *The Message* says, while others are relieved or "taking it easy." Instead, we are called to work shoulder to shoulder with other Christians who are working for the kingdom of God. We are each called to be generous and to give generously what we can. For some, giving what they can may not seem like much. For others, it may be a great deal more. It's not the amount that truly matters, for if we each give what we can, it all works out in the end. What truly matters is our heart. We have to desire to give our time, our money, and ourselves. We have to want to be generous. As Paul says, "the heart regulates the hands." We are called to give what we can and work with others who are giving what they can too. If we all give as we are able, then we will continue to help the kingdom of God.

## Discussion and Prayer

1. How can you and your family give generously this week? Talk to your children about what it means to be generous.

2. Have you seen your child do something generous? Praise your child for their generosity and talk about how they can continue that this week.

3. Thank our Savior for being generous with his life by dying on the cross so that we could always be friends with God. Ask God to give you and your family a generous heart.

# Second Week of July
# Psalm 48—"Our Guide"

### Your Story

Have you been a guide before? If so, tell a brief story about what it was like helping others find the way. Was it easy to communicate where they were going? Did they find the way quickly, or did they need extra help? Did you feel like you were successful being a guide? If you haven't been a guide, talk about a time when you have followed a guide, be it a person, a map, or a guidebook. Was it easy to follow the directions? Were you able to trust that your guide knew the way?

### My Story and the Bible Story

For Vacation Bible School one year, our theme was Everest. As the leader of Base Camp Sing and Play as well as Summit Celebration, I was known as a Sherpa. A Sherpa is an expert Nepalese guide on Mount Everest whose job is to guide climbers safely up and back down the mountain. As the Everest VBS Sherpa, it was my job to guide everyone through each part of our assembly time: the skits each day, the singing, the collecting of the offering, and the transition to the first station. Each day the kids had a blast and got where they needed to go, so I'm going to say that my time as a Sherpa was a success!

Perhaps you have been a guide before and were in charge of helping others find the way. Or perhaps you have followed a guide, be it a person, a map, or even a book. Throughout our lives, we find ourselves needing guides in certain places to help us get where we want or need to go. Psalm 48 reminds us of our most valuable guide, our Lord.

*Read Psalm 48.*

Reread the last verse: "our God forever, who guides us till the end of time" (v. 14). God is not only our God forever but is also our guide forever. God didn't create us and then leave us here, not knowing what to do. Instead, God is like a parent, showing us the right way to go and the right thing to do. We can choose to ignore God's guidance, of course, just like you can choose to ignore what your parents say to do. We miss out on so much when we don't do what God wants us to do. Just like you get in trouble when you ignore your parents, we face consequences when we ignore God's guidance. We may not get in trouble, but things may happen that aren't as good as what God wanted for us. Or we may begin to choose the wrong thing if we ignore God's guidance, and we might hurt ourselves or someone else. If we listen, though, God can do amazing things through us. God can guide us through doing things that we could never do on our own.

God's guidance isn't limited to God speaking to us, though. Sometimes it seems as if God is silent when we need God to be our guide. But God hasn't left us alone. We also have a guidebook, the Bible. The Bible is filled with stories of how people heard from and followed God as well as people who ignored what God said to do. In its pages we can find truths about who God is and how much God loves people. While we will not always discover answers to everything in the Bible, the Bible does help us know who God is and how God wants us to live.

## Discussion and Prayer

1. Ask your children how God has guided them in their lives. Was there a certain time when they felt like God was telling them to do something? Did they listen to God? Why or why not? What happened afterwards?

2. Talk about ways that God is our guide through life. Talk about ways to listen to God more as our guide.

3. Pray, giving thanks that God is always there and always willing to guide us. Ask God for guidance in a situation specific to your family.

# Third Week of July
# Psalm 24—"King of Glory"

## Your Story

Do something different today: go to a park or simply walk around your neighborhood with your family. Each time you see part of creation (trees, flowers, rivers, clouds, the sun, people, animals, etc.), have your kids call out "That is God's" or "They are God's!" You can also use this time to talk about your favorite parts of creation.

## My Story and the Bible Story

Third Day has always been one of my favorite Christian bands. One of their songs, "King of Glory," fits this week's passage of Scripture well. Here are the lyrics to verse 2 and the chorus:

> Who is this King of Glory with strength and majesty
> And wisdom beyond measure, the gracious King of kings
> The Lord of Earth and Heaven, the Creator of all things
> He is the King of Glory, He's everything to me
>
> His name is Jesus,
> Precious Jesus,
> The Lord Almighty,
> The King of my heart,
> The King of glory"

---

9. Third Day, "King of Glory," *Offerings: A Worship Album*, 2000. Full lyrics found here: www.thirdday.com/music/songs/king-glory.

Read Psalm 24.

The Lord Almighty is the King of glory. The Earth is the Lord's and every-thing in it. Praise the Lord! Sometimes we forget that everything is God's and that God created everyone. But the more we believe that God is the King of glory and the more we ask God to be the King of our hearts as it says in the song, the more we will see others through God's eyes. When someone is mean to us, it's hard to remember that God made them. Or if someone looks different than we do, it can be hard to remember that God made them too. But as Psalm 24 reminds us, the Earth is the Lord's and everything in it. God didn't ask us to choose who or what God made. Instead, God made everything. As children of God, we are to look to see God in everyone we meet, even if they seem different from us.

## Discussion and Prayer

1. Talk to your children about what it means to see God in each person (to see qualities of God: moments of kindness, gener-osity, love, truthfulness, strength, courage, etc.).

2. Ask your children if anyone at school is bullying them, being mean to others, or seems left out. Work with your child to help them see good qualities in each person. Tell them that it's okay to not want to be a person's friend if they are mean or bullying, but they need to understand that there is a glimmer of God in each of us, even when we are mean.

3. Discuss how we should treat people since each person has a glimmer of God in them.

4. Pray, asking God for help in seeing God's glory in others. Ask for help remembering that God created everyone, so there are glimmers of God in each person. Pray for help in showing to others the glimmer of God that is in you.

# Fourth Week of July
# Ephesians 2:11-22—
# "Jesus Came for Everyone"

## Your Story

Talk about a time when you or someone you know was made fun of for being different. Alternatively, talk about a time when you discovered some similarities with someone who at first seemed very different from you. What did you discover? How did it change your perception of that person?

## My Story and the Bible Story

When I was a teenager, my family sometimes hosted French exchange students in our home. There were times when students from a school in France would come to the United States and stop in Georgia. They would stay for a few days and then move on to another place. I was learning to speak French, but it was still difficult to talk to our guests. We had to work hard to understand each other and to be understood. We seemed very different from each other. But as we slowly started talking, we discovered ways we were similar. We liked spending time with our families. We liked to read. We found out that we weren't as different as we seemed.

It's easy to look for the ways others are different from us. Maybe someone dresses differently, talks differently, or acts differently than we do. Maybe someone has different opinions than we do. Maybe they have a different hair color or skin tone or eye color. Whatever it is, it's easy to look for the ways we are different. The Jews and Gentiles in the Bible were the same way. Before Jesus came, the Jews believed that God was their God and they were God's people, and they thought no one else had access. But Jesus made it possible for the Gentiles to come to God too.

Read Ephesians 2:11-22.

To the Jews, the Gentiles must have seemed very different. They dressed differently, spoke differently, and believed different things. There were centuries of disagreements between the Jews and the Gentiles. But Jesus came so that everyone could have access to God. In Ephesians, Paul reminds everyone that Jesus came for all, for Jew and for Gentile, and that God uses the Gentiles just like God uses the Jews. When it seems as if someone is so different from us that there's no way God can love them, we should read this passage again. It tells us that God created each of us and loves us all. God got rid of what separated the Jews and the Gentiles, once and for all. Let's remember that Jesus came for everyone.

## Discussion and Prayer

1. Have your children talk about someone who seems very different from them. Ask what things they might have in common with this person.

2. Talk about ways we can look for similarities instead of differences.

3. How should we treat others whom God created? Let's remember that God created **everyone.**

4. Pray, asking God for help in finding similarities with people we feel are different from us. Ask for help in showing others God's love.

# August

## First Week of August
## Ephesians 3:14-21— "Roots"

### Your Story

Today's Scripture is about our roots growing in God's love. How do you feel about your life's roots? Have they grown deep in God's love? Share with your family things that you feel have deepened your relationship with God and made you stronger. If you are working to make your roots deeper, share what you are doing to help them grow.

### My Story and the Bible Story

I love picturing our lives as trees with roots growing in God's love. I often think about the giant oak trees in places like Savannah, Georgia, and St. Augustine, Florida. Those trees have lived through hundreds of years and their roots are huge. They have survived things like tornadoes, hurricanes, and other storms. But they didn't survive simply because they clung to life. They survived because their roots were deep enough that they could not be uprooted. The only way for us to survive life's storms (heartbreak, illness, job loss, death, etc.) is for us to be rooted in something. That way, when the terrible times come and threaten to blow us away, our roots will hold.

Read Ephesians 3:14-21.

This is one of my favorite passages of Scripture. Ephesians reminds us of where our roots should be. Instead of being rooted in anything from this world, we should be rooted in God's love. God's love keeps us strong. That love, which is "too great to understand fully," will keep us rooted when everything around us is falling apart.

How can we grow the roots of our lives deep into God's love? The writer of Ephesians has an answer to that as well: Christ will make his home in our hearts as we trust in him. As you give more things over to God, recognizing that God is so much bigger and more powerful than we could ever be, your roots start to grow deeper in God's love. Praying in the good times and in the bad also helps our roots grow deeper because we are talking to God and trusting God with our lives, with our problems, and with our joys. Worshiping God also helps our roots grow deep. Singing praises for who God is deepens our roots. Reading the Bible and learning more about God also helps our roots grow. Hearing from others what God has done in their lives helps our roots grow too.

The thing about roots is that they don't grow overnight; it takes time for roots to cling to the soil and grow big enough to hold a plant in place. It takes years for roots to grow deep enough so that no matter what storm comes, the tree is safe. It's the same with us. Our lives won't be immediately rooted deep in God's love through one prayer. It takes time. But as we trust God, pray, worship, and learn more about God, our roots will begin to grow into God's love. Our loving God will protect us from the storms. Bad things in life will still happen, but God will help us make it through.

## Discussion and Prayer

1. Find a large tree and show your children how big the roots are. If you are gifted in growing plants (or if you'd like to try), buy a small tree or other plant or flower. As a family, plant it in your yard and take turns caring for it. As it grows, talk about how our roots grow deeper as we follow God.

2. Ask your children how they can learn more about God.

3. Make a plan for the rest of the year of ways you and your family can grow your roots in God's love.

4. Pray, thanking God for helping each of you get through the storms of life. Ask God to continue to grow your roots deep in God's love. Give praise that God is able to do so much more in us and through us than we could ever imagine!

# Second Week of August
# Ephesians 4:7-13—"The Body of Christ"

## Your Story

Tell your family about a time when you had to work together with others as a team to be able to get something done. Would you have been able to do that thing alone? How did it feel working together as a team? How did you feel after it was accomplished?

## My Story and the Bible Story

When I was a teenager, we often performed a skit in my youth group called "The Body of Christ." We would all say, "We are the body of Christ, the body of Christ, the body of Christ. We are the body of Christ; the body needs all its parts to work." Then we would say "except for . . ." followed by a body part (hands, feet, ears, eyes, etc.). We would then have to try to do things without those parts. What followed was a funny but eye-opening reminder that, just as it's much easier for us to move with all of our parts, it is much easier for the body of Christ to show people our Savior when everyone is doing what God has called them to do.

### Read Ephesians 4:7-13.

God has given each of us different gifts. Some are called to preach, others to teach, others to make snacks for Vacation Bible School, still others to fix the air conditioner when it breaks, others to build homes, etc. We are all important to the body of Christ. Every one of us has a role, whether we are six years old, sixty years old, or one hundred. When we work together as the body of Christ, we become efficient and graceful, united in our faith in God. Jesus says our faith can move mountains. When we are all united in our faith, impossible things no longer seem quite so daunting, and those mountains start to move.

## Discussion and Prayer

1. Talk to your children about the roles they play in the body of Christ. Ask them which body part they think they are: an elbow, a hand, an ear, etc. Also ask them how they can use the

talents God has given them to share God's love with others
(you may need to help them list their talents).

2. Talk about what role you play in the body of Christ. How can
   you use your talents to further the kingdom of God?

3. Talk about big things your church has done when they have
   been united.

4. What are some ways that you and your family can be the body
   of Christ this week?

4. Pray, thanking God for giving each of us different gifts. Ask
   God to help the people of your church and other Christians
   work together to show love to others.

# Third Week of August
# Ephesians 4:25–5:2–
# "Watch What God Does"

## Your Story

Have you ever been in a place where you learned what to do by watching
others? Perhaps it was in church as a child, or maybe it was in a another
country. Tell your family about that time.

## My Story and the Bible Story

Have you ever been in an unfamiliar place where you didn't know what to
do or how to act? Most of the time, when we are in places like these, we
watch others to see what they do and how they act. Then we do what they
do. I visited a Greek Orthodox Church when I was in seminary. It was part
of an assignment, and several of us went. The church was gorgeous. We
came in, sat down, and opened the worship guide (the Greek Orthodox
church uses books that look like hymnals). One side was in English and
the other side was in Greek. It seemed like it would be easy to follow along,

but the bishop leading the service that morning was Greek with a very thick Greek accent. As a result, it was hard to follow what he was saying in English. I found myself glancing around at others, mimicking what they did so that I wouldn't stand when we were supposed to be sitting and would know when to start singing. Imitation, particularly in unfamiliar situations, is how we learn what to do.

Read Ephesians 4:25–5:2, emphasizing 5:1–2.

"Watch what God does, and then you do it." The author of Ephesians tells us what to do and how to live. We are to watch what God does and then do it. The writer doesn't end there, though. It's almost as if he has heard our question, "But what does God do?" He responds by saying that mostly what God does is love us and everyone around us. God doesn't call us to love others only if they love us. He calls us to love extravagantly, to forgive others when they wrong us, to let go of our anger when others do something wrong, to be gentle with others, and to recognize the gift God has given us. As the writer of Ephesians says, we have a great gift within us: the gift of the Holy Spirit. Part of God is living in us, shaping us so that we can be more like God. God loves us when we are mean, rude, and angry. And God calls us to love others even when nobody else loves them. We are to watch God and see how much God loves others. And then we are to love them too.

## Discussion and Prayer

1. Ask your family to talk about times when they didn't know what to do so they watched someone else and did what they did.

2. Talk about how that your children learn to worship in church by watching you.

3. Pray, thanking God for how much God loves us. Ask God to help you and your family to see others the way that God sees them.

# Fourth Week of August
# 1 Kings 2:10-12; 3:3-14—
# "What Should I Ask For?"

## Your Story

Have you ever asked for something and gotten so much more than you asked for? Perhaps you prayed for a child and ended up with twins. Or perhaps you asked God to help you find a job and you found one you absolutely love. Or perhaps you asked for a friend and ended up with a group of them. Talk about something you asked for and then received that and so much more.

## My Story and the Bible Story

As a child of the 1990s, I cannot tell you how many times I watched *Aladdin*. It was one of my favorite movies. In *Aladdin*, the title character finds a curious lamp, and in the lamp there lives a genie. The genie gives Aladdin three wishes and tells him the rules for those wishes (for instance, he cannot wish for more wishes). At first, Aladdin is dazzled by these wishes. But in the end, he makes the wisest and best wish of all: that the genie would be freed. Aladdin learns what is most important—friendship, justice, and freedom—and sets the genie free rather than wishing for something that would help himself.

God isn't a genie and doesn't really grant wishes. But in our text for this week, God grants a wish to Solomon.

### Read 1 Kings 2:10-12; 3:3-14.

Solomon asked God to make him wise. Because he asked God to help him have good judgment, instead of money or a logn life, he received much more. Solomon's request made God happy. What should we ask God for? Like Solomon, God wants us to ask for wisdom. God wants us to make good choices and knows we need help with that. If we ask God for help in making good choices, we will receive much more than we asked for. If we make those good choices, then good things will follow. For instance, if you choose to study for a test (a good choice), chances are high that you will get a better grade than if you choose not to study. If you choose to help someone who needs help, they will feel better because they got help and you'll feel good about helping them. God won't always give us wealth and fame like God did for Solomon. But God will bless us when we ask for help in making good choices.

## Discussion and Prayer

1. Ask your children to talk about times when they have made good choices. What happened?

2. Has anybody in your family ever prayed for wisdom? If yes, ask about outcomes.

3. Talk about ways to make good choices this week.

4. Pray, asking God for wisdom to make good choices.

# End of August/Beginning of September
# Ephesians 6:10-20—"The Armor of God"

## Your Story

What are some things you have worn to protect you (a raincoat, a helmet, a seat belt)? Was there ever a time when you or someone you know got hurt because you didn't wear protective gear, or didn't get hurt in an accident because you did wear it? If so, share that story.

## My Story and the Bible Story

Have you ever seen some of the equipment necessary for playing sports? Football players put on helmets, chin guards, mouth guards, cleats, and shoulder pads in order to protect themselves when they play. Soccer players wear shin guards and cleats. Hockey players wear helmets with face masks and shoulder pads. It's important to protect yourself when playing sports. In Ephesians, Paul talks about how important it is to protect ourselves with the armor of God. In this world, things will happen that may knock us off course with God. We will be tempted to do wrong, bad things will happen, and we may try to run away from God. That's why the armor of God is so important; it keeps us following God.

Read Ephesians 6:10-20.

The armor of God is "the belt of truth and the body armor of God's righteousness." The truth is always better than lies, because the truth reminds us of who we are and that we belong to God. We know that we will always do something wrong, no matter how great we try to be. God is the only One who is righteous—the only One who always does the right thing—because God is perfect. Thanks to Jesus, God's righteousness (perfection) covers us. The armor of God also includes the shoes of peace, the shield of faith, the helmet of salvation, and the sword of the spirit. As followers of God, we are to bring peace with us wherever we go. The shield of faith keeps us going even when we don't understand what's happening. We have faith that God is there and God knows what is best for us. Salvation is our helmet. And we have the sword of the Spirit, which is the Bible, the word of God. The Bible reveals things to us and shows us how to live. It helps shape us into people of God. God gave us all of these things to help us along the rough journey of life. By using our faith in God, our belief in truth, God's righteousness, God's peace, our salvation, and the Bible, we can follow God no matter what happens.

## Discussion and Prayer

1. As a family, talk about how each of you has used the armor of God.

2. Put on a race, adults versus kids, to see who can put on the armor of God the fastest (a belt for the belt of truth, a vest or button-up shirt for God's righteousness, shoes for the shoes of peace, a piece of cardboard for the shield of faith, a hat for the helmet of salvation, and finally a Bible for the sword of the Spirit).

3. Pray, giving thanks for all that God has given us to help us always follow God. Ask God for strength and courage to tell others about God's love.

# September

## First Week of September
## James 1:22-27—"Do Something"

### Your Story

Have you ever watched a YouTube video about how to fix something? Were you able to fix it after you watched the video? Talk about a time when someone told you how to do something and you followed through. How did you feel after you accomplished it?

### My Story and the Bible Story

Theory and practice are two very different things. I may believe I can do something, but until I do it, who knows whether I can. When I was a kid, I had to learn how to ride a bike with handlebar brakes. I knew how to ride a regular bike, and my dad explained how to use the handlebar brakes, but until I tried the newer bike for myself, I couldn't say I knew how to ride it. After running into a flower pot and falling off a few times, I got the hang of it. I didn't just listen to how to ride that bike; I put the instructions into practice so that I learned how.

Read James 1:22-27.

It's not enough for us to just listen to God's word. We have to actually do something with it. The Bible tells us to love our neighbor. We can't just read that and ignore it. Instead, God wants us to help others, feed the hungry, take care of the homeless, and be friends with people who don't have a friend. As Christians, we can't just sit back and do nothing. James says that if we read the Bible and don't do anything, it's like looking in a mirror, walking away, and having no idea what we look like! Do an experiment with your family. Have everyone look at themselves in the mirror. Then ask them basic questions: What color hair do you have? What color are your eyes? Do you have freckles? Is your hair curly or straight?

After this experiment, talk about how you all remembered what you looked like! As Christians, we're supposed to look like Jesus. That doesn't mean that your hair, skin, or eye color will change or that you'll turn into a boy if you're a girl. But it does mean that God wants us to do what Jesus did.

Jesus made friends with people whom nobody else liked. Jesus fed people who were hungry. Jesus cared about other people, even when nobody else thought they mattered. We're supposed to hear God's word and then follow it because that's what Jesus did. The word "Christian" means "like Christ" or "little Christ." Since we are supposed to be like Christ, we should do the things Jesus did. Then we will be doers of the word of God instead of just hearers.

## Discussion and Prayer

1. Ask your children about learning things that other people have told them how to do (riding a bike, tying their shoelaces, adding and subtracting, reading).

2. Talk about how Jesus shows us how to live in this world. How can your family be like Jesus this week?

3. Pray, asking God for helping with putting what God says into action.

# Second Week of September
# Psalm 125—"Mountains"

## Your Story

Talk about a time when you felt protected by God.

## My Story and the Bible Story

Have you ever tried to move a mountain? That sounds silly, right? I love the mountains. There's something about them that seems peaceful. I think part of it is that I know the mountains aren't going anywhere. They are constant and steady. I like to hike in the mountains when it's cool and the leaves are changing. It's a time of peace and quiet and enjoying nature. But in order to hike a mountain, you have to trust that it's going to stay there. That mountain isn't going to move; if you thought it might move, you wouldn't walk up it. No matter what happens, we can trust that the mountain will be there and will not move.

Read Psalm 125.

Those who trust in God are like a mountain. Our world can seem unsteady at times: storms come and knock down trees, hurricanes come and destroy homes, and other things happen that make us afraid. But if we trust in God, we are like a mountain, constant and steady. No matter what else happens, we know that God is always there. Because we know that, we can face everything that happens. We can cling to God through the bad, scary things, and we can trust that God will help us through.

Psalm 125 takes it a step further, though. Not only are we like a mountain when we trust in God, but God is also like a ring of mountains circling around us. When mountains surround a city, they protect it from storms and from people who wish to do it harm. Those mountains keep the city safe. God is like that with us. God protects us and keeps us safe. Sometimes frightening things will still happen in our lives, but God always surrounds us, walking with us and eventually bringing us home to be with God forever.

## Discussion and Prayer

1. As a family, talk about ways that God has protected your family.

2. Ask your children how they know that God is always with them.

3. Pray, asking for help in always trusting God. Pray for God's protection around your family.

# Third Week of September
# Psalm 19—"Which Way Should I Go?"

## Your Story

Talk about a time when you have been lost—for example, while you were driving, riding, or hiking. How did you find your way?

## My Story and the Bible Story

Have you ever been lost? Have you ever been at a crossroads where everything looked the same? A few years ago, I took a trip to Texas. We knew where we were going (mostly), but then we reached a crossroads where everything looked the same no matter what direction we looked. It would have been hard to figure out which way was right if we hadn't already known. Sometimes life is like that too. It can be hard to know the right way to go unless you already know.

But how can we already know? We can know if we follow God. A still, small voice tells us which way to go.

Read Psalm 19.

As Psalm 19 says, the signposts of God are clear. God places things along our way: people, events, etc., that help us know the right road to travel, the right way to go in our lives. These things are usually not as obvious as road signs, but if we pay attention, God will point out the right way for us to go. And when we choose the wrong way and we repent of our sin, God cleans the slate for us. Each day is a new day for us to choose the way God wants us to go. We can trust that God's way is the best way. As this psalm says (in *The Message*), God's reputation is "twenty-four-carat gold, with a lifetime guarantee." God is the only piece of this world that has a lifetime guarantee. God will never forget you, never grow tired of you, never stop loving you, never break, and never stop pointing you in the right direction. Sometimes we ignore what God wants us to do. There are times when it seems hard to know what the right way is, but if we pay attention and listen to God, we can trust that eventually God will show us the right way. And God's way will be the best way. God is better than a road sign: God is never wrong!

# Discussion and Prayer

1. Talk about times when God has helped you find the right direction in your life.

2. Ask your children to talk about times when God showed them the right thing to do. How did they know what was right?

3. Remind your family that sometimes we have to be patient and wait for God to show us the right way. Sometimes it takes a while, but God always shows us the right way.

4. Pray, asking God to show you and your family the right way in whatever situations you are currently facing. Offer thanks that God gives us a brand-new day each morning with no mistakes!

# Fourth Week of September
# Mark 9:30-37—"Children"

## Your Story

When you were a child, did someone ever make you feel less important than an adult? What happened? Tell that story to your children.

## My Story and the Bible Story

"Children should be seen and not heard." "Go sit at the child's table." Did you hear something like this when you were a child? Maybe you were taught that you should sit quietly and not interrupt the grownups who were talking. Or maybe you were sent to an entirely different table at extended family mealtimes. Maybe someone made fun of you for asking a question because you didn't know the answer. Nowadays, childhood tends to be celebrated. We try to let kids be kids as long as they can. We do our best to love their unexpected answers and to nurture who they are, not as tiny adults but as children.

But it wasn't always this way. Throughout history, children have been seen as less than adults. They have at times been treated as unworthy of important things and as a waste of time for important people. We know that isn't true. We know that children are worthy, that they can say important things, and that they deserve love and respect. Jesus felt the same.

### Read Mark 9:30-37.

In Jesus' time, children weren't viewed as important. They were seen as nuisances, and the disciples probably ignored them. But Jesus didn't. Jesus saw the people whom others ignored and reminded them that they were important too. The disciples were arguing about being first, but Jesus reminded them that it was far more important to help others, to see everyone as a child of God, than it was to be the greatest. Jesus didn't want people who thought they were the greatest. He wanted followers who treated everyone as a child of God: important and loved because of who created them. Jesus changed the way the disciples looked at children. He reminded them that they are important.

It doesn't matter who someone is: child, parent, senior adult, rich, or homeless. What matters is that we are all important to God—every single one of us. God wants us to treat others, even those whom our world says aren't worthy, as important and as people we should love. We don't always have to like someone, but God calls us to recognize that each person is created by God and deserves love and forgiveness.

## Discussion and Prayer

1. Ask your children if there has ever been a time when they felt like they aren't as important because they aren't adults. Talk about how that made them feel.

2. Talk about ways to remember that everyone is important.

3. How can you show others that they are important to God this week?

4. Pray, giving thanks that we are all important to God. Apologize that we don't always treat others like they are important to God.

# October

## First Week of October
## James 5:13-20—"The Answer Is Prayer"

### Your Story

Talk to your family about times when prayer has helped you.

### My Story and the Bible Story

I'm a worrier. It's who I am. I worry about test results, about family members and close friends, about the future, etc. Sometimes my worry feels overwhelming, so I pray about it. Every time I worry, I pray. I pray for friends who are traveling and for family members who are sick. I pray for my future. I pray for whatever I'm worried about. Although my prayers are not always answered with "yes," they are answered with peace. Prayer is powerful because it reminds us that we are not in control but God is, and God is bigger than any of the things we worry about.

Read James 5:13-20.

However you feel, God wants you to pray. If you're sad, God wants you to talk to God about it. If you're happy, God wants to hear about that too. God already knows what's happening in your life but wants to hear about it from you. When you tell God about the scary things in your life, they don't seem quite so scary. When you tell God about the great things, they seem even better. And when you tell God about your worries, God gives you peace. We pray for things that we don't always receive. But God always promises to listen, to give us peace, and to walk beside us through the hard and the good times. Whenever we don't know what to do, we should pray, asking God to help us know what the right thing is. And God will show us the way.

Prayer is powerful. It has the power to change our lives and the lives of those around us. So even when it seems like your prayers aren't being answered, don't give up. Keep on praying! Who knows? Your prayers, like Elijah's in our Bible passage, might be answered in an amazing way!

## Discussion and Prayer

1. Ask your children about times when they feel like God answered their prayers.

2. As a family, talk about favorite places to pray: it could be outside by a lake, snuggled in bed, or even while holding the family pet.

3. Talk about specific things to pray for this week, and commit to praying for them each day.

4. Pray, thanking God for always wanting to hear from us. Ask God to help you not give up when you feel like God doesn't answer your prayers.

# Second Week of October
# Psalm 8—"Small"

## Your Story

Has nature ever wowed you? Have you ever felt small when looking at the ocean or the stars? Talk about a time when you felt awed by something in nature.

## My Story and the Bible Story

Have you ever seen the super moon? What a sight to see! During the last super moon, it was too cloudy for me to see it where I was, but the pictures of the super moon were astounding. The sheer size of the moon in relation to everything else was breathtaking! When I see a moon like that or look up at the number of stars in the sky, I feel very small. And when I think about everything that God has created, I am astounded that God, the Creator of the Universe, wants to have a relationship with me. The God who set the planets spinning, who creates the clouds in the sky and the fish in the sea, who created everything around us, wants to talk to us. When I think about the vast number of things that God has created, I feel small and humbled that God wants to spend time with us.

Read Psalm 8.

David is right. When we look at all the things God has made, we realize that we are a small part of God's creation. We realize that there's no reason God should care about us and yet God does. God loves us not because we have done something amazing but because God made us. We are created in God's image, and God wants to be our friend forever. We may feel small when we look at all of creation, but in God's eyes we are worthy because God has created us.

## Discussion and Prayer

1. Ask your children about things in creation that have made them say, "Wow!"

2. Take time this week to look at the night sky or take a nature walk. Talk about all the things that God has made.

3. Pray, giving thanks for all that God has created. Give thanks that even though we are only a small part of creation, God cares about us.

# Third Week of October
# Psalm 22:1-15—"Where Is God?"

### Your Story

Talk to your family about a time when God felt far from you. What was the situation? What happened? Did you pray anyway? Did God respond?

### My Story and the Bible Story

There have been times in my life when God felt far away. When my church was falling apart when I was a junior in high school, God felt far away. When most of our ministers left and we had to start over at a new church, God felt far away. I couldn't understand all of the factors that caused my church to fall apart, but still, I prayed. I prayed even when it didn't feel like God was listening. Slowly, things got better. I made friends at my new church. I started to feel God's presence again. Of course, God hadn't left. God had always been there.

This can happen to all of us. There are times when we feel abandoned by God. Even David, whom the Bible says was the "man after God's own heart," felt that way sometimes.

Read Psalm 22:1-15.

In the psalm, David feels completely abandoned by God. Others are making fun of him and destroying him while God does nothing. Sometimes we feel that way too. Maybe someone is bullying you and you feel like God should rescue you but nothing happens. Or maybe someone has cancer and you pray for that person but they don't seem to get any better. Sometimes God feels very far away, and it seems like God doesn't care what happens to us. But God does care and is never far from us. Later on in this same psalm, David prays that God will come quickly to help him, and he reminds the people that God doesn't ignore them. God hasn't turned away from them; God listens to their cries. Thousands of years after David wrote this, the same is true for us. God doesn't turn away from us. God listens to our cries. God doesn't ignore us. If God feels far away, it is because we aren't looking hard enough. God is there. God always hears us and never ignores us. Sometimes God's answer to our prayers is "no" or "not yet," but God always answers our cries. When you feel far from God, rest assured that God is not far from you. Praise God for always being there!

## Discussion and Prayer

1. Ask your children if there have been times when it seemed like God wasn't close to them. How did they feel? What happened?

2. Find the popular poem "Footprints in the Sand" and read it together. What does it mean? The first stanza is below:

> One night I dreamed a dream.
> As I was walking along the beach with my Lord,
> Across the dark sky flashed scenes from my life.
> For each scene, I noticed two sets of footprints in the sand,
> One belonging to me and one to my Lord.[10]

---

10. "Footprints," often attributed to Mary Stevenson.

3. Pray, giving thanks that God is always with us. Ask for reminders of that when God feels far away.

# Fourth Week of October
# Psalm 91:9-16—"God Is Our Refuge"

## Your Story

How has God protected you in your life? Talk about some ways that God has answered your prayers.

## My Story and the Bible Story

Sometimes it seems like God isn't there, as we talked about in last week's devotion. This week, our psalm is a reminder that God is always there and that God is our refuge. When I was a sixth grader, I felt lonely and isolated. My mom and stepdad were getting a divorce, my church was splitting, and I had no friends at school. I felt like I had nobody to turn to. So I turned to God. I prayed and prayed that God would help me and that God would remind me that I wasn't alone. God was my refuge during that time. God was the One I turned to when I didn't have anything else, and God rescued me from my loneliness. God sent me a friend. A new girl transferred to my school and we became great friends. Her name was Jessica as well, and we did everything together. I never saw her after that year, but I know that God answered my prayers and rescued me from loneliness.

Read Psalm 91:9-16.

God is our refuge who cares for us. We can trust God to help us. The psalmist even says that we will walk unharmed among lions and snakes. While I don't recommend trying to walk next to a lion or a bunch of snakes, the point is that God is with us. Bad things happen sometimes, but God is always there and we can trust God to take care of us. We are God's children, and no matter what happens, we will always be with God. And God can take whatever happens and make something good in our lives. We can always run to God, and God will not only listen to us but will answer us as well.

## Discussion and Prayer

1. Ask your children to talk about times when God has helped them.

2. Talk about how you and your family can share with others the stories of how God has helped each of you.

3. Thank God for helping you. Ask God to remind you that God is your refuge.

# End of October/Beginning of November
# Mark 10:46-52—"Don't Stop Believing"

### Your Story

Has God ever told you to do something, but everybody tried to talk you out of it? What happened?

### My Story and the Bible Story

When my mom was a teenager, she really wanted to be a youth minister. She felt God's call and knew that she should be a youth minister. But in that time, women weren't usually ministers. People discouraged her, saying that surely God wasn't calling her to ministry. She listened to them and chose something else. Now, looking back, she wishes she had listened to God. She wishes she had ignored everyone and followed God into youth ministry. Although she wasn't a youth minister, she still did ministry. She taught us all about God. She taught us to follow God. And she taught us to believe in our dreams and to listen to God's call. When I felt God telling me to be a children's minister, my mom supported me and pushed me to do what God wanted me to do.

Read Mark 10:46-52.

Bartimaeus knew that Jesus could heal him. He believed Jesus could help him see again. So when he heard Jesus was coming, he shouted for Jesus to have mercy on him. But the people tried to silence him. They assumed that

Jesus didn't have time to listen to a poor beggar, so they tried to get him to be quiet. But Bartimaeus ignored them, knowing Jesus could heal him. Then, Jesus stopped, called Bartimaeus to him, and healed him. Bartimaeus's faith was the reason he was healed. He didn't stop believing that Jesus could heal him, even when everyone else tried to silence him.

Most of the time, unlike Bartimaeus, we aren't trying to get God's attention. But God is trying to get ours. There are times when God tries to speak to us but we miss it because we aren't paying attention. There are also times when we hear God speaking to us, but we let other people silence us. There are times when God tells us to do something, but when we tell someone else about it, we hear, "You can't do that. You're too young. You're too small. There's no way you would be able to do that." When we hear those words, we start to doubt what God told us to do. Sometimes we let other people drown out God's voice. We miss out on doing what God wants us to do. Bartimaeus didn't let the others drown him out. He knew how important it was to talk to Jesus, and he refused to let everyone silence him. Don't let others silence God when God shows you what to do. Don't let them drown out God's voice. Listen to what God says and follow it. It may be hard, but you'll never regret it. Don't stop believing that God knows what's best for you.

## Discussion and Prayer

1. Ask your family to talk about a time when they felt like God was telling them one thing, but everyone else was saying something different. What did they do?

2. Talk about how we can know that God is speaking to us. Share ways that God has spoken to you in your own life.

3. Talk about ways your family can support each other when God asks one of you to do something. How can you be encouraging?

4. Pray, thanking God for showing us what to do. Ask God for help in listening to God in spite of what other people may say.

# November

## All Saint's Day
### First Week of November
### Isaiah 25:6-9—
### "When We All Get to Heaven"

### Your Story

Talk about special loved ones who have died. Tell your children about their importance in your life. Focus especially on those who trusted in God.

### My Story and the Bible Story

I love singing the hymn "When We all Get to Heaven." It reminds me that even though some of my loved ones have died, I will see them again. Here are the words:

> Sing the wondrous love of Jesus,
> Sing his mercy and his grace;
> In the mansions bright and blessed
> He'll prepare for us a place.
>
> When we all get to heaven,
> What a day of rejoicing that will be!
> When we all see Jesus,
> We'll sing and shout the victory!
> While we walk the pilgrim pathway,
> Clouds will overspread the sky;
> But when trav'ling days are over
> Not a shadow, not a sigh.[11]

"While we walk the pilgrim pathway, clouds will overspread the sky." When we are walking through life, we will face hard times. There will be

---

11. Words by Eliza Hewitt, 1898.

bad things that happen and there will be hard days. Though there will be good days as well, those clouds will still be there. But, when the traveling days are over, when we leave this Earth, those shadows will be gone. We can rejoice because we will see Jesus!

Read Isaiah 25:6-9.

Isaiah reminds us that the Lord will prepare a feast for us, that God will swallow up death forever and wipe away our tears. And we will be able to say that we trusted in God and he saved us. Death is part of our lives, and we grieve in many ways when someone we love dies. Isaiah tells us that eventually, God will get rid of death forever. And he promises that if we trust in God, He will save us. Today we celebrate All Saint's Day. We remember important Christians who have gone before us and taught people about Jesus. We remember people in our own lives who helped us believe, and we remember our loved ones who have died. We remember those who trusted in God, and we believe that they are with God. Isaiah gives us a beautiful promise of heaven, that God will prepare a feast and that we will all be together. He promises that God will wipe away our tears. We can remember our loved ones with smiles because we know we will see them again. We will feast with them at God's table! And in those days, death will be no more!

## Discussion and Prayer

1. Talk to your kids about death and grieving. What strategies do we have for coping with sadness and loss? Remind them that though we won't see our loved one for a while, we believe that we will all be together with God one day.

2. Imagine who will be at that feast in heaven. Talk about what it might look like.

3. Talk about ways your loved ones who have died trusted in God.

4. Pray, thanking God that we will see our loved ones again. Ask for help in trusting God.

# Second Week of November
# Mark 12:38-44—"Giving Generously"

## Your Story

Has there been a time when you didn't have much, but you still gave to the church or to someone else? Talk about that sacrifice: how it felt, how you had to step out in faith, etc.

## My Story and the Bible Story

If you are ever around someone who doesn't have much, you'll notice something. Most of the time, such people are a lot more generous than others who have much more. There is story after story of people experiencing homelessness who share what little they have with others. In fact, in Charlotte, North Carolina, one man gave 18 cents to a church as his tithe because that's all he had.[12] Even though it was a small amount, he still wanted to give to God. Something similar happened in Jesus' day.

Read Mark 12:38-44.

The widow in Jesus' time gave all she had. She gave generously, and, according to Jesus, she gave much more than those who gave what they would never miss. The homeless man who gave 18 cents gave more than CEOs who can give thousands of dollars, because his gift forced him to step out in faith. He had to trust that God would take care of him. Giving is about trusting God to take care of us. God doesn't need our money; without it, God would still find a way to make things happen. But we need God, and in order to grow in our faith, we have to trust that God is always with us and knows what we need. God wants us to give so we will trust that God can provide. For most of us, that doesn't mean giving all we have. It does mean listening and obeying when God asks us to give.

## Discussion and Prayer

1. Talk about the different ways that you and your family give: time, money, talents, etc.

---

12. Dominique Mosbergen, "Please Don't Be Mad, I Don't Have Much': Homeless Person Donates 18 Cents To North Carolina Church," 30 April 2015, www.huffingtonpost.com/2015/04/30/homeless-donation-church-18-cents_n_7177352.html.

2. Pray about how God wants you and your family to give this week; then, follow through with what God says.

3. Pray, asking God for help in trusting God more. Pray to be aware of ways to give this week.

# Third Week of November
# Psalm 126—"Thanksgiving"

## Your Story

Talk about what you are thankful for this year. Then, tell your family about some of the big things you've been thankful for in the past.

## My Story and the Bible Story

Thanksgiving is this week. It's a time when families gather together around a table filled with food and remember all of the things for which they are thankful. Some years it is easy to remember our blessings. It's easy to be thankful. But other years, it seems as if nothing has gone right. Sometimes it seems like we've gone from one problem to the next, and it doesn't seem like there is much for which to be thankful. For kids, that may mean they don't like a class at school, they have a hard time understanding something, or they feel left out. Or it could mean deeper and more difficult problems. For adults, it may mean work is hard, they are dealing with health issues, or there are even larger problems to face. For whatever reason, some years it is hard to be thankful. When we read Psalm 126, we learn that the Israelites dealt with something similar.

Read Psalm 126.

At the beginning of Psalm 126, the writer talks about the good fortune of his people. God brought them back to their land and everything went well. But now their crops are dying from lack of rain and they are struggling. That doesn't sound like much to be thankful for. Even so, they remember a time when God rescued them, when God showered blessings down on them, so they pray for that time to come again. They are thankful for the past, and they look with hope to a future in which God will once again rescue them and shower down blessings.

If it is hard to find reasons to be thankful this year, remember Psalm 126. Like the Israelites, think about the ways God has blessed you in the past. Remember all the things throughout the last few years for which you are thankful. Then say a prayer, asking God to rain down blessings once again. Ask for help with the things happening in your life, and ask God to help you remember the blessings from the past.

## Discussion and Prayer

1. Ask your family to talk about the reasons they are thankful.

2. Talk about any hard situations that are happening with your family members right now. As you talk through them, help your children find God's blessings in the midst of those situations.

3. Take time this week to tell people who have been a blessing to you and your family that you are thankful for them.

4. Pray, asking God to help you and your family through whatever is happening in your lives. Ask for help in remembering your blessings.

# Fourth Week of November
# Psalm 93—"Who Is the Lord?"

## Your Story

Talk about a time when you felt God's majesty. Where were you? How did you feel?

## My Story and the Bible Story

I tend to feel God's majesty most when I am in the midst of His creation. I feel awestruck when I stand next to the crashing waves of the ocean. When I look out at those waters, I am amazed at the beauty that God has created.

I find myself feeling the same way when I stand at the top of a mountain. As I gaze out into the distance, I feel small. I realize what a small part I play in all of creation. And I remember that God is the One who created everything we see.

Read Psalm 93.

Who is the Lord? The Lord is full of majesty and strength. He established the world to be firm and secure. God has always been and will be forevermore. The seas lift their voices to God because He is mighty. He is mightier than the thunder of the waves crashing to shore. His statutes, the rules He has given us to live by, stand firm. The Lord is holy.

When you think about God, what characteristics come to mind? I think about God's love first, and how it is never-ending. I think about how God loves us no matter what happens. And I think about His holiness. God is perfect, and we are not. And it is only because of Jesus that we can be in God's presence. And yet, even though God is holy, even though He is perfect and we sin, He still wants to spend time with us. I think of how mighty God is, how much bigger and better God is than anything else in this world. And I think of God as Creator. I love seeing all the wonderful things God has created. Seeing a beautiful sunset reminds me that our God is a painter. Seeing the stars in the sky reminds me that God knows each of us by name because He knows each of them by name. Hearing the laughter of a child reminds me that our God loves joy.

Who is the Lord? He is Creator, Sustainer, Redeemer, and Friend. He is holy, He is mighty and perfect. We cannot comprehend His love. God is so much bigger than anything else in this world. He has been here since the beginning and will be with us until the end. Let us praise the Lord for who He is and for what He has done for us.

## Discussion and Prayer

1. Ask your children to share who God is for them. Ask them to talk about the names of God that are most important to them, and the characteristics they think about when they think of God.

2. As a family, discuss ways that each of you can share God with others.

3. Explore some of God's names in the Bible. Choose one to use when you talk to God this week.

4. Pray, thanking God for who He is and for how much He loves us.

# Year C

# December

## First Week of Advent
### First Week of December
### Psalm 25:1-10—"My Hope Is in the Lord"

**Your Story**

How has God come through for you? How has your hope in God been proven true?

**My Story and the Bible Story**

We sang a song at Vacation Bible School a few years ago called "My Hope Is in the Lord." Here are the lyrics:

> I can't help but feel a little down
> a little worried when I look around
> That's why my hope is in
> My hope is in the Lord
> I fix my eyes upon the God who gives
> 'cause all I need is what I have in Him
> that's why my hope is in
> my hope is in the Lord
> My hope is in the Lord
> I belong to Him
> He will never let me go
> My hope is in the Lord
> I can count on him
> My hope is in the Lord[13]

Sometimes this world seems hopeless. There are times when it feels like God has left us and nothing will get better. There are times when we worry that our hope in God is for nothing. As the song says, there are times when

---

13. Sanctus Real, "My Hope Is in the Lord," *Changed*, 2018.

we feel down and worried when we look around. But, like the psalmist, we realize that our hope is in the Lord and we can count on God.

Read Psalm 25:1-10.

We can put our hope in God because we can trust that God is there for us. God is our Savior who knows what's best for us. God is fair and just and will lead us step by step. When the world tells us that God isn't real, we can trust that God is. We know this through all the things God has done. God created us and our world. God made the leaves so that they change in the fall and come back every spring. God made the flowers to bloom and the grass to grow. God made animals to adapt to their environments and made us to worship God. The God who made us and redeems us is the God who is with us. We can count on God. Don't worry that God will desert you. Don't worry that your hope is for nothing. God is always there and will never leave us. Our hope is in the right place: the Lord!

## Discussion and Prayer

1. Talk about ways you have been shown that God is real.

2. Talk about times when God has shown you that you can trust God.

3. How can we share our hope in God with others?

4. Pray, thanking God that we can always have hope. Ask for help in sharing God's love and hope with others.

# Second Week of Advent
## Second Week of December
## Luke 1:68-79—"Peace"

### Your Story

Talk about a time when God gave you peace. Did your situation change or simply your attitude?

## My Story and the Bible Story

Peace is a funny thing. We pray for peace in a world full of violence. We pray for peace in times of trouble. We pray for peace in times of stress. We pray for peace in times of worry. At first glance, we think peace means that our situation changes. The world puts down its weapons. Trouble ceases. Stress disappears. The things that worry us change. Yet most of the time this isn't what happens. Trouble continues. The circumstances that worry us don't change. Our stress remains a constant. But something happens. We still have peace. We have peace from God that reminds us God is there and will use whatever happens to make something good come from it. It is the peace of knowing that we don't have to be in control because God is so much bigger than we are.

I am a worrier. I worry about small things, like being late or missing something. I worry about big things, and when I worry, I think of all the things that could go wrong. Then I worry even more. I get stuck in a cycle, and I find myself worrying about everything. But if I let go of my worries and pray for peace, something amazing happens. The things I was worried about don't change, but my attitude does. God gives me peace. God helps me see that everything is going to be okay because God's love is bigger than anything else. God reminds me that I'm not in control and that's okay. God calms my worries and sets me on the path of peace.

Read Luke 1:68-79.

This is the prophecy of Zechariah, the father of John the Baptist. He knew that salvation was coming and that his son, John, would prepare the way for the Lord. John would go on to teach the people about their need for salvation, assuring them that one was coming who would save them. The one who was coming would forgive their sins because of the mercy of God and would guide their feet into the path of peace. We know that the one who was coming was Jesus. Through Jesus, our sins are forgiven. Through Jesus, we see God's mercy. God guides our feet onto the path of peace. So when you worry, remember that Jesus came to save us. He also came to bring us peace. God's peace doesn't mean our situations will change, but it does mean that God changes our attitudes. God reminds us that mercy will guide us on the path of peace.

## Discussion and Prayer

1. Give each family member time to talk about the things that worry them.

2. Talk about how God can help us when we are worried.

3. Practice asking God for peace whenever you are worried this week.

4. Pray, asking God for peace in the midst of your worries.

# Third Week of Advent
## Third Week of December
## Zephaniah 3:14-20— "Rejoice!"

## Your Story

Talk about a time when you were so joyful that you started singing. What made you so filled with joy? How did you feel?

## My Story and the Bible Story

I love singing praises to God. When I was a kid, I used to make up songs to sing in praise. Wherever I went, I was singing to God. God's joy was in my heart, and it overflowed into singing. Sometimes it's hard to sing praises to God. There are times when we don't feel like singing. There are times when we have really bad days. There are times when we are worried and anxious and afraid, when we are stressed about tests and projects, when we are worried about what's happening in our lives. In those times, it's hard to sing. It's hard to feel joyful. But in the times when we struggle to find joy, Zephaniah reminds us that God rejoices over us. We bring God joy, and God takes great delight in us.

Read Zephaniah 3:14-20.

"The LORD your God is with you, he is mighty to save. He will take great delight in you, he will quiet you with his love, he will rejoice over you with singing." The Lord takes great delight in you. Let that sink in. The God who created the universe takes great delight in you. In fact, you make God smile! Zephaniah reminds us that God not only takes delight in us but also rejoices over us with song. God sings over us! Can you imagine the heavenly tune when you accepted Jesus? How about God's song when you help someone else? Or God's tune when you did what God asked you to, even though it was hard? God sings over us! When we don't feel joyful, when we struggle and we go through tough times, God is with us and saves us. We have no need to fear. When we feel anxious and afraid, God quiets us with love.

These verses are life changing because they remind us of God's joy. I first heard these verses as a teenager. I was a little awkward and didn't always feel like I fit in. But these verses reminded me that God created me, that God is always with me, and that God's love is enough. God knows what we need and will help us. God created us to be exactly who we are and is happy with our creation! God is full of joy about you and sings over you. Think about God's heavenly song for you this week. How do you think it sounds?

## Discussion and Prayer

1. What are some things you have done to make God sing? As a family, talk about at least one thing each person has done that you think made God sing.

2. What are some things we can do to make God sing?

3. When you have a bad day, what are some ways you can remember the joy God put in your spirit?

4. Pray, giving thanks for how God has created you. Ask for help in quieting your anxiety or fear. Ask for help in remembering your joy.

# Fourth Week of Advent
## Fourth Week of December
## Luke 1:46b-55— "Mary's Song"

### Your Story

Talk about a time when you shared God's peace with others. What did you say? What stories from your own life did you use?

### My Story and the Bible Story

Since I'm a worrier, I have to ask God for peace a lot. So when someone I know is having a hard time, I tell them about God's peace. My sister was recently going through a tough time. Every time we talked, I reminded her of how much we loved her and that we are always there for her. And I also reminded her that God is always by her side and that God would help her. I told her that God would give her peace. All she had to do was ask!

Read Luke 1:46b-55.

Mary has great news! God has sent the Savior, and Mary wants everyone to know, so she sings a song. Mary sings, "His mercy flows in wave after wave on those who are in awe before him." God's mercy doesn't just come to us once. It continues to flow, over and over again. Mercy is compassion and kindness. It is grace, something we don't deserve and haven't earned. Mercy sees us where we are, sees the things we have done wrong, and forgives us. And God forgives us not once but over and over again. But God does much more than that: God takes care of us, pulls the victims from the mud, feeds the starving poor. God does exactly as promised. God promised that the Messiah would come, and Jesus not only came to this world but also did something completely unexpected: he died for us so that we could be free. Jesus came and brought with him hope, love, joy, and peace. Like Mary, when we experience the things Jesus brought to us, we should share them! Mary sings of God's mercy. We, too, can tell others of the mercy and peace God brings to us.

## Discussion and Prayer

1. Think about God's peace. How has God brought you peace? How has God shown you mercy?

2. How can you share God's peace and mercy with others? What are some ways you can share Jesus with those around you?

3. If you were singing a song of joy to God, what would it contain? This week, as a family, write a song of joy to God. Use Mary's song for inspiration.

4. Pray, giving thanks for God's mercy. Ask for help in sharing God's mercy and peace with others.

# Christmas Day
## John 1:1-18—"The Christ Candle"

### The Christ Candle

If you have been lighting candles to remember the Advent season, today you will light them all! If you haven't been lighting candles, then you can say: Today, Christians around the world who use Advent wreaths will be lighting all of the candles. They will light the candles of hope, love, joy, and peace. They will also light the Christ candle as we celebrate the birth of Jesus. The other candles remind us that Jesus brought hope, love, joy, and peace to our world.

Read John 1:1-18.

"In the beginning was the Word . . . ." Jesus is the Word, and he has been around since the beginning of time. And yet he waited until the time was right for him to come into the world, to jump-start God's rescue plan and to save us because we couldn't save ourselves. Have you ever thought about how long Jesus waited? Since Jesus has been with God since the very beginning, he watched Adam and Eve turn their backs on God. He watched the people make bad choices and fall further and further from God. He watched some people choose God and some people turn from God. I sometimes wonder if Jesus was like a child who has woken early on Christmas morning, asking "is it time yet?" every five minutes. Maybe every so often Jesus looked at God and asked "is it time yet? Can we rescue them yet? Can we interrupt the messiness and save them yet?" Or perhaps Jesus waited patiently, until he felt it in the depths of himself that finally it was time. However he felt, Jesus waited until just the right moment to come into the world as a baby.

Once again, God did something unexpected. The people were expecting a king to come—but they got a baby instead. In that perfect moment, Jesus chose to come down to the world, the people received a far better gift than they could know or understand. The Gospel of John reminds us that the world didn't recognize Jesus. The world didn't understand that a Messiah had come in the form of a baby to change our lives forever. But those who recognized Jesus and believed received a far better gift than they expected.

We have been patiently waiting (or not so patiently waiting) to celebrate Jesus' birth. And on this day of celebration, remember that Jesus waited until just the right time to come to our world. As we pray and present requests to God, may we remember that God waits until just the right time to answer us.

## Discussion

1. As a family, talk about times when you have had to wait until a certain moment to do something. Perhaps for your children, it was this morning when they had to wait to open presents. How did it feel to have to wait? How does it sometimes feel to have to wait on God?

2. Remind your family that even though it can be hard to wait, we can have peace knowing that God waits until His perfect time to answer us.

3. Pray and thank God for sending Jesus to rescue us. Thank God for God's overwhelming love and perfect timing.

# Last Week of December
# Luke 2:41-52—"Jesus as a Boy"

## Your Story

Did you ever get lost because you were so engrossed in something that you were left behind? Did you panic? Did those who were with you panic? What happened?

## My Story and the Bible Story

I love the Eiffel Tower. I'm not sure what it is about that tower, but it has always fascinated me. When I went to Paris for the first time as a teenager, I was determined to see it. In fact, I told the tour guide that if we didn't go see it, I would stay behind until I did! He must have known that I was serious because we went to see it the day before we left. I could have stayed in the Eiffel Tower for hours. I might have been left behind if my mother hadn't been with me. I was so excited to be there, and I knew it was an important place for me. I wanted to stay for a long time.

Jesus knew that the temple was an important place for him. After all, it was his Father's house! Because it was an important place, he wanted to stay there.

### Read Luke 2:41-52.

Before we judge Mary and Joseph too harshly for not realizing Jesus was missing for a whole day, we need to understand that this wasn't like a modern-day road trip. It wasn't that Jesus didn't get in the car and they failed to notice. They were traveling with a large group of relatives and friends, including other children. Most likely, Mary and Joseph thought that Jesus was playing with someone else in the group, so they didn't worry. They knew members of their group would take care of each other and that Jesus was safe. We can imagine what happened next. That evening, as they set up camp, they started looking for Jesus. It was dinner time and getting close to bedtime. It was then that they discovered he was missing! They set out as quickly as they could back to Jerusalem, where they anxiously searched for Jesus for three days.

When they finally found him, Jesus was surprised that they didn't immediately look for him in the temple. The temple was his Father's house. Jesus loved the temple because it was a place for him to meet with God. This story reminds us that as we grow closer to Jesus, we should love being in God's presence. As we grow closer to Jesus, we should want to spend more time with God, like Jesus did.

Even though we don't always feel a burning desire to spend time with God (staying in the temple for three days is a long time!), we should still make time for God in our lives. Jesus knew how important it was to spend time with God. It was so important to him that he lost track of time and didn't even care that his parents had left without him. As we enter a new year, find ways to spend time with God each day. When you do, you will find yourself growing closer to God and to Jesus, becoming more like Jesus every day.

## Discussion and Prayer

1. As a family, talk about ways you can spend time with God (through prayer, reading your Bible, reading the Bible as a family, time at church, singing songs to God, serving God, etc.).

2. Make a New Year's Resolution together to spend more time with God. Be specific about when and how you want to spend time with God. Write it down and put it on the refrigerator or another place where it can be easily seen.

3. Pray, asking for help in spending more time with God.

# January

## Epiphany
### First week of January
### Ephesians 3:1-12—"The Mystery of God"

**Your Story**

Describe something you discovered about God that helped you understand some of God's mysteries. Share any epiphanies you had about God.

**My Story and the Bible Story**

I love mysteries. And I, like most others, would love to figure out the mysteries of God. I would love to know exactly how God makes decisions, how God knows what's best, why God chooses not to interfere, and the list goes on. But one mystery that I find easier to understand is that we all stand on the same ground before God. It doesn't matter if you grew up in the church or if you are just beginning to explore faith. It doesn't matter if you are a Jew or a Gentile. It doesn't matter where you have been or what you have done, we are all on the same ground. This mystery of God is a welcome one for us all. Paul talks about this in Ephesians.

Read Ephesians 3:1-12.

Today we celebrate the Epiphany. It's the time when the wise men found Jesus. Epiphany means the appearance of God (which makes sense, since we are celebrating the wise men finding Jesus). It also means a sudden insight into the meaning of something. As we celebrate Epiphany, we remember the mystery of God. We also remember the insight into the mystery that every one of us is a child of God, that we all are on equal ground with God. God doesn't play favorites and He loves each of us. Once Jesus came and taught and died, the people discovered that they didn't have to be Jews to be part of God's kingdom. All they had to do is believe! There are some mysteries of God that we may never understand, but this one we know is true: God created each one of us and we are all equal in His eyes.

## Discussion and Prayer

1. Ask your children to name some things they don't understand about God.

2. As a family, talk about some of the things your children named. Share your insights.

3. Talk to your family about ways you can find out more about the mysteries of God (read the Bible, ask a minister, etc.), and talk about how there are some things about God that we will never understand.

4. Pray, thanking God for loving us no matter what and for loving us all equally. Ask for help in finding peace with God's mysteries.

# Second Week of January
# Luke 3:15-17, 21-22—"Why We Baptize"

## Your Story

Tell your children your story of accepting Jesus and being baptized. How did you feel when you came out of the water (or, if you were sprinkled, how did you feel after that experience)?

## My Story and the Bible Story

I have loved Jesus for practically my whole life. I grew up in church, and we were there pretty much every time the church was open. At seven years old, I told Jesus that I wanted him to be my Savior and I was baptized. At 16, I was baptized again because I didn't really remember the first one. I was worried that it must not have been important to me since I couldn't remember it, and I wanted to make sure that Jesus was, in fact, my Savior. Looking back, I'd like to tell my 16-year-old that I didn't need to be baptized again, that Jesus was already my Savior and that baptism is a small, though important, part of the Christian journey.

But why do we baptize? For Baptists, why do we get into a pool of water and go completely under only to be pulled back up?

Read Luke 3:15-17, 21-22.

Baptism is a symbol. Water makes us clean, and the waters of baptism remind us that Jesus makes us clean. He clears away the sin from our lives. We are baptized because Jesus was baptized. Baptism reminds us that we cannot fix ourselves. And even though someone else baptizes us, that person cannot fix us either. Only God can take away the things we do wrong. Only God can make us more like Jesus. But in order for us to be more like Jesus, we have to do what God wants us to do, even when we want to do something different. We have to ignore ourselves and what we want (which is sometimes called dying to self) and do what God wants us to do instead. Being a Christian is a lifelong journey. For all of us, it begins with accepting Jesus, which is usually followed by baptism. Baptism reminds us that Jesus has made us clean. What a wonderful thing to remember!

## Discussion and Prayer

1. If your children have been baptized, have them share their stories of accepting Jesus as their Savior and being baptized. How did it feel to be baptized?

2. If they haven't yet accepted Jesus, talk about what it means to accept and follow Jesus.

3. Thank God for sending Jesus to make us clean from our sins. Thank God for the sacrifice Jesus made so that we could always be friends with him.

# Third Week of January
## Psalm 36:5-10—
## "How Big Is God's Love?"

## Your Story

Talk about a time when you felt how much God loves you. Perhaps you felt surrounded by God's love during a difficult time in your life. Or perhaps you realized how much God loves you when your children were born.

## My Story and the Bible Story

I can remember saying as a child, "I love you *this* much!" with my arms open wide. I'm sure you've seen children do this before. Or they give you a bear hug and squeeze and say the same thing. Whatever it is, you can see the depth of their love. And then you open your arms to them as well, as wide as you can, and say, "I love you *this* much!" As a parent, you deeply love your children. As your children, they deeply love you. How much more, then, must our Heavenly Parent love us?

### Read Psalm 36:5-10.

How big God's love must be! God's love reaches all the way to the heavens. Think about the tallest skyscraper you know of. The tallest skyscraper in the United States is the One World Trade Center at a gigantic 1,776 feet tall. The Empire State Building is 1,250 feet tall.[14] These are huge buildings, and yet they cannot compare to God's love. Psalm 36 tells us that God's love reaches all the way to the heavens. God's love is bigger than the tallest skyscraper in the world (the Burj Khalifa in Dubai is 2,717 feet tall with 163 floors). If God's arms were open wide to show us how much God loves us, they would be bigger than the tallest skyscraper in the world! Isn't it amazing to think that God's love is bigger than the biggest building we have?

Psalm 36 goes on to tell us that God not only loves us but also provides us refuge. When things are going wrong in our lives, when it seems like nothing good ever happens, we can hide in the shadow of God's wings. We can go to God and ask for help and God will give us peace. God never stops being our refuge and loving us. The next time you wonder how big God's

---

14. "List of Tallest Buildings," Wikipedia.org/wiki/List_of_tallest_buildings.

love is for you, remember that it is bigger than the tallest building in the world, and it is deeper than the deepest part of the ocean (which is almost 36,000 feet deep!).[15] What an amazing God we serve!

## Discussion and Prayer

1. Ask your children how they know that God loves them.

2. Google pictures of the tallest buildings in the world and the Mariana Trench in the ocean to show your children a visual example of how big God's love is.

3. Talk about ways to show God's love to others this week.

4. Pray, giving thanks for how much God loves us. Ask for help in sharing God's love with others.

# Fourth week of January
# 1 Corinthians 12:12-31a—
# "The Body of Christ"

### Your Story

Talk about a time in your life when you had to work in a team with others. Talk about what your role was and how each person had a different role. Did working as a team help you accomplish something? Was it easy to work together or difficult?

### My Story and the Bible Story

In our team of ministers at church, everyone has a different role. I work with children and their families. Our youth minister works with youth and their families. Our minister of spiritual development works with adults. Our music minister works with the choir and the orchestra (and leads

---

15. National Oceanic and Atmospheric Administration, oceanservice.noaa.gov/facts/ oceandepth.html.

music for the entire church), and our pastor works with everyone. And each of our roles is very important. Without one of our roles, our church would suffer. If we didn't work together, our church would suffer. It's the same way with the body of Christ. In order for us to fully be the church that God has called us to be, we need everyone working together to share Jesus with the world.

Read 1 Corinthians 12:12-31a.

We all have a part to play in the body of Christ. When we say "the body of Christ," we mean the church. The church is made up of people who are following Jesus and doing what Jesus wants them to do. Because of that, we are the body of Christ since he is no longer physically on this Earth. It doesn't matter if you are a child or an adult, a minister or a volunteer, a teacher or a singer. Whoever you are, you are important. You matter in the body of Christ. There are things you can do better than anyone else. God has created you with gifts, and God wants you to use them to show others who Jesus is.

## Discussion and Prayer

1. As a family, talk about the gifts of each person in the family. Talk about ways these can be used in the body of Christ.

2. If you are not already using your gifts for the body of Christ, find ways this week to use them. For instance, if you are a great encourager, find someone who is having a hard day and encourage them. Or, if you like to help, ask others how you can help them this week.

3. Thank our Creator for granting our gifts and ask God for help in knowing how to use them.

# February

## First Week of February
## Jeremiah 1:4-10—
## "God's Great Plan for You"

### Your Story

If you have known God since you were a child, talk about ways God worked in your life when you were young. If you remember them, talk about ways God worked through you to show love to others. If you became a Christian later in life, think back on your childhood and talk about ways that you realize God was working in you or through you.

### My Story and the Bible Story

As a child, I never liked to see people unhappy. I always wanted to do what I could to help. When I was about five years old, we went to a local nursing home to sing for the residents. While we were there, we met a lady in a wheelchair who really wanted to go home. I wanted her to be happy, so I decided we could take her home with us. My mom said I tried to wheel her out the door before she saw me and stopped us. Looking back, I can see that my calling to ministry was present at a young age—I just didn't know it yet.

Read Jeremiah 1:4-10.

God had a plan for Jeremiah. God knew all about Jeremiah before Jeremiah was even born. God knows all about us too. Before God created you, God knew about you. God knew what color your hair would be and how your eyes would be shaped. God knew what you would be good at and the things you wouldn't do as well. God knew about your talents and your sense of humor. God knows everything about you, including what you can do best in this world. Like Jeremiah, God has plans for you. If you listen to God as Jeremiah did, God will share those plans with you. You will know what God wants you to do.

## Discussion and Prayer

1. As a family, talk about how you all may hear God's call in your lives (a feeling, a voice, from family or friends, at church, etc.).

2. If they aren't sure, talk about ways they can already use the gifts God has given them.

3. Pray, thanking God for knowing everything about us and loving us anyway. Ask God to help you and your family to understand God's calling in each of your lives.

# Second Week of February
# Luke 5:1-11—"When God Asks"

## Your Story

Talk about a time when God asked you to do something and it turned out better than you could have imagined.

## My Story and the Bible Story

During my freshman year of college, my campus minister told me about a summer job he thought I was perfect for: the children's intern at a church in Macon. I laughed and told him I didn't really work with children, but I said I would pray about it and see what God wanted me to do. I really wanted to work at the bookstore, and that's what I planned to do. But the next week, a friend of mine brought me a flyer for the same job at the church. I felt those nudges were from God, so I called and set up an interview. A few days after the interview, the preschool and children's ministers called to tell me that they thought I was the right person for the job. I was shocked, but I felt like it was what God wanted me to do. Even though I was nervous, I said yes. I had no idea at the time how much that would change my life. God used that job to show me what God wanted me to do as a career. I have been blessed in ways that I couldn't imagine back then.

Read Luke 5:1-11.

Simon, James, and John were fishermen when Jesus met them. They had just come in after a long night of fishing, but they hadn't caught anything. They were probably upset and maybe even worried. No fish meant they couldn't feed their families and had nothing to sell at the market. They were tired, too, because they had been out on the water all night. But then came Jesus. The people were crowding around him, so he asked Simon to take his boat out to a distance where he could preach to everyone. Simon was tired but he agreed, and what happened next changed his life. When Jesus finished preaching, he told Simon to go further out and put his nets in the water. Simon had been fishing all night and knew the fish weren't biting, but he did as Jesus said, and something amazing happened: the nets were so full that they started to break! They had so many fish that the boats began to sink! They could feed their families and have a lot of fish to sell at the market. They couldn't believe it! They knew Jesus had done this miracle for them, and they left everything to follow him.

Jesus did so much more than they ever expected! He gave them far more than what they needed, and he showed them that they could trust him. God does the same for us. If we listen to God, follow God, and do what God asks us to do, God can do far greater things than we could ever imagine. God is generous. When we do as God says, God not only helps us but also blesses us in ways we couldn't imagine.

## Discussion and Prayer

1. Think about the things God has asked you to do. What was the outcome?

2. Think about what God may be asking you to do. Talk about it as a family. Do you need help doing what God wants you to do?

3. How did Peter, James, and John show their faith in Jesus? How can we show our faith in Jesus?

4. Pray, thanking God for being so generous to us. Ask for help in doing what God wants you to do.

# Third Week of February
# Luke 6:17-26—"Blessed Are You"

## Your Story

Talk about a time when you were jealous of someone because it seemed like everything was going their way. How did you work through your jealousy?

## My Story and the Bible Story

We all have tough times in our lives. Your pet is missing. A parent lost their job. Something scary happened, and it's been bothering you. Your friends haven't been acting like friends. A family member is sick. Whatever it is, we face difficult times. And when we do, there's usually someone whose life seems perfect. In a world of social media, it's easy to look at other people's pictures on Facebook and Instagram and think that everybody else's lives are perfect. There are times when I scroll through Facebook and it seems like great things are happening to everyone else. When you are going through something difficult, it's hard not to feel jealous when you see such pictures. In Jesus' day, it was even worse. If things were going wrong in your life in Jesus' day, people assumed that you had done something wrong. If you were sick, it meant that you had sinned. If you were poor, it meant that God didn't bless you. But Jesus showed the people a different way.

Read Luke 6:17-26.

Jesus taught that the kingdom of God is what is most important. In God's kingdom, no longer will anyone be hungry or poor or weep or be hated. Instead, they will be treated as God sees them: beloved. Jesus changed the people's beliefs. Before, the people believed that the rich would get everything—that if you were rich you were blessed by God, and if you were poor you had done something wrong. But Jesus showed them that God loved them all and that there would be an end to their suffering. Even though it seemed like some people would continue to get everything, the kingdom of God was different. The kingdom of God was for everyone. God would change their lives.

It sometimes seems as if some people have perfect lives. It can seem like they never have any problems, and nothing ever goes wrong. It can seem like God has blessed them and hasn't blessed us. But when you feel jealous, read this and remember that the kingdom of God is for everyone. Instead of saying that the rich are blessed, Jesus said the poor will be blessed. Those who are hungry will be blessed. Those who weep will be blessed. Those who are insulted because they follow Jesus will be blessed. The people who go through tough times will be blessed. God is with us and promises to help us through whatever we face. One day, in the kingdom of God, our tears will turn into laughter. Hunger will be satisfied. Take heart, because in God's kingdom it doesn't matter how much money you have. What matters most is that you follow God.

## Discussion and Prayer

1. What are some ways that hard times can be a blessing? (For example, your faith grows stronger when you have to trust God to help you through.)

2. How can we help bring the kingdom of God to Earth?

3. How can you encourage others?

4. Pray, giving thanks that God doesn't care about how much money or stuff we have. Ask for help in seeing others the way God sees them.

# Fourth Week of February
# Genesis 45:3-11, 15—
# "God Can Use Anything"

## Your Story

Talk about a time in your life when something difficult happened and God used it for good.

## My Story and the Bible Story

My parents got a divorce when I was really young. It was tough growing up without my dad close by. I was jealous of other kids who had both parents living with them. It was tough trying to spend time with both of my parents. But even though it was a hard thing that happened, good things came from it too. I'm really close to my mom. I can encourage and empathize with other kids whose parents are also divorced. I have a better appreciation for dads who are a big part of their children's lives. I even plan events that help strengthen marriages because I know how important it is to have both parents at home. God used something hard in my life to do good things. Romans 8:28 says, "And we know that in all things God works for the good of those who love him, who have been called according to his purpose" (NIV). We see this very clearly in Joseph's life.

## Read Genesis 45:3-11, 15.

God doesn't make bad things happen. God didn't make my parents get a divorce, didn't throw Joseph into a well to be kidnapped and sold into Egypt, and doesn't make hard things happen in your life either. But God does use these times. God uses hard things in our lives to do good. God uses difficult times to teach us, to grow us, and to do good things through us. God used Joseph in mighty ways. Joseph's brothers kidnapped him, threw him in a well, and sold him to traders—but then God took over. When Joseph went to Egypt, God helped him. God helped him interpret dreams for Pharaoh, and Pharaoh then made Joseph a leader. God showed Joseph what he needed to do to help the people during the famine. And then, when Joseph's brothers came looking for food, God used Joseph to help his family. Even though Joseph's brothers had done a terrible thing, God used what happened to Joseph to help others and to do big things through Joseph. God helped Joseph forgive his brothers as well. Joseph knew how God had used the bad things that happened to him. When he confronted his brothers, it wasn't out of hatred but out of forgiveness and thankfulness that God had done something great through him.

Bad things happen. Sometimes people hurt us, and many circumstances are out of our control. Painful situations can happen in our lives. But no matter what happens, good or bad, remember that God is with you. God can do great things with you. God can use everything that happens in our lives to do good things. God took Joseph's bad situation and turned it into something good, and God promises to do that for us too. So when something difficult happens, pay attention. See how God uses it to do something good. Then tell others about it. Spread the word that God takes painful things and makes something good out of them!

# Discussion and Prayer

1. Ask your children to talk about bad or hard things that have happened in their lives.

2. Help your children see how God has used those things to do something good.

3. How can we share about those things with others? When can we share with others what God has done?

4. Pray, asking God for help in seeing the ways God turns hard things that happen into something good.

# March

## Transfiguration Sunday
### First Week of March
### Luke 9:28-36—"Jesus Is Transformed"

### Your Story

Talk about how Jesus transformed your life. Did you undergo a big change when you accepted Jesus, or was it more gradual?

### My Story and the Bible Story

I became a Christian when I was seven years old. I loved going to church, and I loved Jesus when I was a kid (and I still do!). For me, salvation wasn't a major change. I had loved Jesus for as long as I could remember, so asking Jesus to be my friend forever and being baptized felt natural to me. Not much changed in my life after I became a Christian. But as I grew up, I started to look at things differently. I slowly started to see the parts of my life that needed to change to be more like Jesus. God started showing me what needed to be transformed. My walk with Christ has been all about gradual changes. There hasn't been a giant transformation, and that's OK. I still find myself more like the disciples at the Transfiguration than like Jesus.

### Read Luke 9:28-36.

Every time someone in the Bible comes face to face with God, they are changed. For Moses, being on top of Mount Sinai and talking to God to get the Ten Commandments meant that his face was radiant and the people were afraid (Exod 34:29-35). When Jesus talked to God in Luke, we read that his appearance was changed as well.

In our Scripture, Moses and Elijah appear with Jesus in glorious splendor. Can you imagine this scene? Jesus' clothes were as bright as a flash of lightning, and there stood Moses and Elijah, who had long been dead but were now radiant and alive. What once had been an ordinary day was transformed into extraordinary! The disciples knew that God had done something amazing, and they wanted to stay there, to build shelters for Jesus, Moses, and Elijah, and to remain in the midst of the presence of God. But the mystery of the presence of God is this: it's not just in one place. God is everywhere. God is always with us, and we are to take God's presence to others. Moses came down the mountain to share God's presence with the Israelites through the Ten Commandments. Jesus, too, didn't want the disciples to stay where they were. Everything had been transformed, but they were still called to share God's presence with others. Later in the story, when Jesus and the disciples come down the mountain, a man begs Jesus to heal his son. Jesus' mission continued. He couldn't have stayed on the mountain.

We may not have been transformed in the same way Jesus was, but our mission is similar. God has called us to share love with others, and the only way to do that is to leave the mountaintop. It is great to spend time worshiping God. We need to spend time with God so that God can slowly transform us to be more like Jesus. At the same time, we can't just stay in God's presence. God has called us to help others. God continues to work to transform us when we are helping others, and when we help others, we can help God transform our world.

## Discussion and Prayer

1. Talk about how God has changed your life.

2. Ask your children to talk about how God is changing them. Encourage them by sharing ways you see God working in their lives.

3. What are some ways that your family can help others and participate in God's work to transform our world?

4. Pray, thanking God for transformations, big and small. Ask for courage in working to help transform the world.

# Ash Wednesday
## First Wednesday in March
## 2 Corinthians 5:20b–6:10–
## "Being Right with God"

## Your Story

Talk about a time when you paid off a debt. How did you feel? Or, talk about a time when you owed a debt that was forgiven. How did that feel?

## My Story and the Bible Story

I don't like to borrow money. When I ask someone for a loan, I do my best to pay it back as quickly as I can. I don't want to owe them money any longer than I have to. I don't feel right buying anything else when I have a debt to a friend hanging over my head. I don't feel right with my friend until my debt is paid. Here's the thing about owing money: it sometimes spirals out of control. We sometimes borrow a lot more money than we can pay back, and we get into a lot of trouble. Sin is the same way. We can't seem to stop sinning. We know what we should do and yet there are times when we choose to do the wrong thing. And if it were up to us, we could never be right with God. But thankfully, God sent Jesus so that we could be square with God. Our debt is paid by Jesus so that we can be right with God.

### Read 2 Corinthians 5:20b–6:10.

God put the wrong on Jesus, who never did anything wrong, so that we could be put right with God. Jesus took our punishment, our debt, so that we could always be friends with God. On Ash Wednesday, we remember our sin. We remember that we aren't perfect and that we choose to do wrong. And we remember that our sin is what led to the cross. God is friend to us before we ever choose to be His friend, because He sent Jesus so that we could always be close to Him. God heard the people crying out for their Messiah, and he sent Jesus. Today we remember that we are human, that we make mistakes, that God created us and that someday, we will no longer be in this world. But we also remember that Jesus took our sins, so that we could be put right with God. When you do something wrong, ask God for forgiveness. God promises to always forgive you, to always be with you, and to always love you. Jesus took on all our sin so that we no longer bear it alone. We can always be right with God.

## Discussion and Prayer

1. Ask each member of your family to write down something they have done wrong. Then, when everyone is finished, tell each member of your family that God promises to forgive their sins, that Jesus took all our sins so that we could always be close to God. Tell each person to pray, asking God for forgiveness. Then, have each person tear up what they have written and throw it in the trash. Say "God promises to forgive our sins. Jesus has made you clean. Your sins are forgiven."

2. Talk about ways to share the good news of Jesus with others, that Jesus took on all the things we do wrong so that we could always be close to God.

3. Pray, thanking God for Jesus and asking for forgiveness of your sins.

# First Week of Lent
## Second Week of March
## Romans 10:8b-13—"Everyone"

### Your Story

Talk about a time when you and everyone else won a trophy. How did it feel knowing that everyone was getting a trophy? Conversely, if this hasn't happened to you, talk about a time when you saw someone who perhaps didn't deserve a trophy or award receive one anyway. What was their reaction? What was yours?

## My Story and the Bible Story

My granddad loved to fish, but I wasn't a fan. In fact, I thought fishing was pretty boring. One day, though, he talked me into going fishing with him for a tournament. We have pictures to prove that I caught a fish that day (that I wouldn't touch!), but the best thing about that day was getting a tackle box that included a big sleeve of about ten huge gum balls. I was so excited to get them. Every child got a tackle box that day with gum in it. It didn't matter whether or not we caught a fish; we were all considered winners.

In the book of Romans, we find that everyone can be a winner in God's eyes too.

Read Romans 10:8b-13.

"Everyone who calls on the name of the Lord will be saved." In God's eyes, everyone can be a winner. It doesn't matter if you are the fastest or the slowest. If you are the best speller or the worst. If you are a liar or a thief. If you do great things or terrible things. No matter who you are, if you call on the name of the Lord, you will be saved.

That's both great news and not so great news. It's great news because all of us do things that are wrong. We all make mistakes. We all sin. But God says that anyone who believes will be saved. It doesn't matter what you have done; God will forgive you and God will save you. But that also means that people we don't think deserve God's love, people who have done really bad things, can still be saved. Sometimes it's hard to accept the truth that none of us really deserve God's love, but all of us can be saved. The good news of God is that everyone who calls on the Lord will be saved. Everybody can be a winner with God. All we have to do is call out to God. The God who made us will also save us.

## Discussion and Prayer

1. Have your children talk about any bullies at school. Then talk about what it means that God loves everyone, even bullies.

2. Talk about ways to share God's love with others.

3. Thank God that the good news of Jesus is available for everyone. Ask God for help in remembering that God loves everybody, even bullies and people who constantly do the wrong thing.

# Second Week of Lent
## Third Week of March
## Psalm 27—"Waiting on the Lord"

## Your Story

Talk about a time when you've had to wait for something big, whether it was waiting until you were 16 to get your license, waiting to purchase a house, etc. How did you feel during that time of waiting? Excited? Anxious? Nervous?

## My Story and the Bible Story

I find myself feeling anxious a good bit of the time. I worry about what will happen, whether or not something will actually occur, and if things will turn out okay. It seems like Psalm 27 was written for worriers.

### Read Psalm 27.

"Wait for the LORD; be strong and take heart and wait for the LORD." We wait for many things. We wait in line at the store, we wait for the end of the school day or workday, we wait for summer vacation, we wait for Christmas, and the list goes on. Much of the time we wait impatiently, anxious to be at the head of the line. It's the same with God. Many times we have to wait on God. We have to wait for answers to our prayers. We have to wait for God to work in our world and in our lives. In David's time, waiting for God was scary because it meant that he was waiting for God to take care of his enemies before his enemies caught him. But in the midst of David's anxiety, he reminds us that we will see the goodness of the Lord. We can take heart because God will show up.

It's hard to wait on God. We want things as soon as we ask; praying to God is no different. We want things to happen immediately. But God does things in God's own perfect time. We can rest in the fact that God wants what's best for us and that we have no need to fear because God is always by our side. When you find yourself waiting this week, pray and ask God for help as you wait.

## Discussion and Prayer

1. Ask your kids to talk about ways they have to wait. How does it make them feel?

2. Talk about things we can do while we wait for God.

3. Pray, asking for help in waiting on God. Pray for God's peace in the midst of anxiety.

# Third Week of Lent
## Fourth Week of March
## Psalm 63:1-8—"Thirst"

### Your Story

Talk about a time when you were so thirsty that all you could think about was getting some water. How did you feel once you got something to drink?

### My Story and the Bible Story

We went to camp one summer in July in the middle of Alabama. It was so hot! The heat index was about 100 degrees every day. One day, after outdoor recreation, we were all dehydrated. All we could think about was finding a place to cool off. We went into the air-conditioned worship center, where we sat on the cool floor and took turns drinking from the water fountain. I was very grateful for water and air conditioning that day. Most of us take clean water and air conditioning for granted, but that day, my fellow campers and I were grateful for a place to recover and water to drink.

Think about the hottest you have ever felt. Chances are pretty good that you were looking for a place to cool off and water to drink.

Read Psalm 63:1-8.

"My soul thirsts for you." Have you ever thought about what that means? When we are thirsty, we long for something to drink. It's all we think about. We look and look until we find it. Our soul thirsts for God. It longs for God. God created us and God created our souls. We were created to worship God. Because of that, we long for God. There's something in us that looks for God. There's something in us that thirsts for God, like when we thirst for water on a really hot day. When we connect to God, worship God, pray to God, and feel God's love, our soul is satisfied. If you've ever been outside on a very hot day and then come in to get some cold water and eat an ice pop, you know what that satisfaction feels like. You are happy and content because you are no longer thirsty and you feel nice and cool. When we spend time with God, our soul is content.

But when we don't spend time with God, when we ignore God, when we're too busy for God, when we do our best to quench our soul's thirst on things other than God, what happens? Our soul becomes thirstier and thirstier. It's like trying to drink hot water or a hot soda on a hot day. It doesn't help. In fact, you may feel even thirstier after trying to drink that. Your mouth gets dry and you feel hot and you look around for something that will help. If you don't get water when you're hot and thirsty, then eventually, some scary things can start to happen to your body because you get dehydrated. Scary things may not happen when you ignore God, but when you don't quench your soul's thirst, you worry more. You are anxious. Things start to feel overwhelming. You feel like you're missing something. When you spend time with God, though, your soul is "satisfied as with the richest of foods." Your soul clings to God, and God's hand lifts you up. You remember that God's got you. God will never let you go. You can rest in God and know that everything is going to be okay. Like that cold water on a hot day, God's presence quenches the thirst of your soul. You feel satisfied. When you find yourself thirsty, think about your soul's thirst for God. Make sure you are quenching that thirst too!

# Discussion and Prayer

1. Ask your children to talk about a time when they were really hot and thirsty. How did it feel to get something to drink?

2. Talk about ways you can spend time with God. How can God quench your soul's thirst?

3. Talk about how our souls long for God. What are some ways you can share God with others?

4. Pray, thanking God for satisfying our souls. Ask for help in finding ways to spend time with God.

# April

## Fourth Week of Lent
### First Week of April
### Psalm 32—"Guilt and Forgiveness"

**Your Story**

Talk about a time when you felt guilty for something you had done. Did someone else forgive you for what you did? If so, did that make you feel better?

**My Story and the Bible Story**

Imagine that you've done something wrong—and instead of confessing and asking forgiveness, you try to cover up the mistake. Maybe you broke something you aren't supposed to play with, so you hid it under a sofa cushion and acted like nothing happened. Then, when your mom finds it and gets upset, maybe you blame it on your brother or sister, and they get in trouble. As the day goes on, you feel bad that you got them in trouble. You feel bad for breaking something your mom valued. You feel guilty because you know it was your fault and someone else was punished. Eventually, your guilt gets bigger and bigger. It gets so big that your stomach hurts and you can't eat your dinner. It gets so big that you finally tell. You blurt out to your mom that you broke it and you're so sorry. But then something happens: you may get in trouble, but your mom also gives you a hug. She thanks you for telling the truth and tells you that she forgives you, and you feel so much better. You're sad that you got in trouble, but your stomach doesn't hurt anymore and you don't feel guilty. You feel forgiven. That's the way it is with God.

Read Psalm 32.

When we hold on to our sins, to the things we do wrong, we feel guilty. We think about all the things we've done wrong, and we feel bad. We think about the people we've hurt and we start to think there's no way God can love us. That's what David means when he says, "Before I confessed my sins, my bones felt limp, and I groaned all day long." He felt bad because of what he had done. His sins were heavy. But then, when he told God everything he had done, God forgave him! Even better, God took away his guilt.

God not only forgives us and takes away our guilt but also protects us. We won't be swept away by things that happen because God is there. We sing to God because God has saved us. God shows us the way to go and what we should do. God's kindness shields us. We don't have to feel guilty anymore. All we have to do is ask God for forgiveness. No matter what we did, God will always forgive. We can celebrate because God loves and forgives us. God's grace covers us. Like David, we don't have to walk around with guilt and the weight of the things we do wrong. Does this mean we won't get in trouble for doing something wrong? No. There are always consequences to our actions. You will still get in trouble for breaking your mom's figurine or hitting your sibling. But you can know that you are forgiven. You don't have to feel guilty, because God forgives us. Since we are forgiven, God wants us to forgive others too. So if someone does something to you, forgive them. You don't have to be their friend, but you need to forgive them. God forgives us no matter what and wants us to forgive others too.

## Discussion and Prayer

1. As a family, talk about things you've done wrong that made you feel guilty. If you have young children, explain to them what it means to feel guilty.

2. Write down something you want God to forgive. Then, as a family, say a prayer asking God for forgiveness.

3. Pray, thanking God for always forgiving us. Give thanks for God's kindness to us. Ask for help in forgiving others.

# Fifth Week of Lent
## Second Week of April
## Psalm 126—
## "The Lord Has Done Great Things"

## Your Story

Talk about a time when God did something great in your life.

## My Story and the Bible Story

"The LORD has done great things for us, and we are filled with joy" (Ps 126:3). I can name many times when God has done great things for me. When I was in the sixth grade and I didn't have any friends, God sent me one. God gave me a wonderful family that has always been there for me and supported me. God showed me what I was to do with my life, and I am so thankful to be a children's minister. Life has not always been great; there have been difficult times, but through it all, God has done great things.

### Read Psalm 126.

The Israelites had difficult lives. They had times when things were good, but they also spent a lot of time being held captive by others who conquered them. They were taken to a different country and forced to work very hard. They were not free. There were times when other countries attacked them and they had to fight for their lives. There were times when they wandered around in the desert for years and years, sometimes trusting God and sometimes not. But then they were set free! God brought them back to where they belonged. Their hope had come true! Suddenly, they were filled with joy. They could laugh again. God had rescued them. Other nations saw this and said, "The LORD has done great things for them." The Israelites knew what God had done for them, and they celebrated. Looking back, they could see how the Lord had been doing great things for them throughout their lives.

The Lord does great things for us as well. God created us and redeemed us. God saves us and loves us unconditionally (no matter what). God forgives us. On top of all that, God blesses us, giving us a family to take care of us and friends to help us, talents and abilities, safe places to go, and people who listen to us. Even when things are hard, the Lord is there. Psalm

126 reminds us that those who "sow in tears will reap with songs of joy." God turns our tears into songs of joy. There will be times when we will be sad. There will be times when we are upset, angry, and frustrated. There will be times when we are hurting. But we can trust that God is there and will do great things. God will turn our tears into songs of joy. The Lord has done great things for us and will continue to do great things!

## Discussion and Prayer

1. Talk about some of the great things God has done for your family. Be specific.

2. Talk about ways to celebrate what God has done for you and your family. How can you remember what God has done for you?

3. If your family is going through a difficult time, talk about how God will see you through. Look for ways to share with your family how God has turned your tears into songs of joy.

4. Pray, giving thanks for the great things God has done for you and your family. Ask for help in recognizing the great things God does.

# Palm Sunday
# Sixth Week of Lent
# Third Week of April
# Luke 19:28-40—"Going to Jerusalem"

### Your Story

Talk about a time when you felt moved to praise the Lord. Talk about the circumstances and what you did to praise God.

## My Story and the Bible Story

I made up songs a lot when I was a kid. I wanted to sing to God, so I made up songs of praise. I felt like I just had to get my words of praise out to God. I can't remember the tune of those songs now, but I do remember how it felt to sing those praises to God. And now, I still sing praises. They have been written by someone else, but they still help me to praise God. There are times when I think of a song and I have to sing it to God. Jesus reminds us in Luke that we all have that part in us that wants to praise God. And if we don't sing those praises, the stones will cry out. We are made to worship God.

### Read Luke 19:28-40.

Jesus was going to Jerusalem. He told the disciples where they could find a colt. They brought it back to him, and Jesus rode that colt into Jerusalem. As he went along, the people celebrated that Jesus was finally coming to see them. They spread their cloaks on the ground and began to praise God. Luke tells us the whole crowd of disciples began praising God for everything that Jesus had done. The disciples knew who Jesus was, and their love for God spilled out, coming out in praises to God. But the Pharisees were irritated that the disciples were making such a fuss. They didn't believe, and they wanted the people quiet. But when they said something to Jesus, he told them that if the people were silent, the stones would still cry out praises to God.

We were created to praise God. The people were excited about what God was doing, so they praised God. But there are some people who try to keep us quiet. There are people, like the Pharisees, who are so threatened by Jesus that they do their best to keep everyone quiet. But the disciples didn't listen. They still praised God.

There are countries where Christians can be punished for praising God, but still they sing praises to God. Why? Because God is the God of the universe. God created each one of us. And God loves us so much that He sent Jesus (who was God and human together) to Earth to show us how to live but also to die for us, so that we could always be close to God. When Jesus entered Jerusalem that day, he knew what was going to happen, but he was obedient to his Heavenly Father. He went because he loved us. So sing praises to God. Sing praises when it's easy and when it's hard. The disciples showed us what praising God looks like. So don't make the stones cry out. Sing praises to God!

## Discussion and Prayer

1. Ask your family about ways they praise God.

2. As a family, write a song, poem, skit, interpretative dance, etc., to show praise to God. Decide when and where you'd like to use it to show praise to God.

3. Talk about how it was dangerous for the disciples to sing praises to God when Jesus was going to Jerusalem. Talk about why they did it anyway.

4. Pray, thanking God for the ability to praise Him. Ask God for courage to always praise Him.

# Good Friday
## Luke 23:1-25, 38-49—
## "The Trial of Jesus"

### Your Story

Have you ever been accused of something you didn't do? Talk about how that felt and what happened afterwards.

### My Story and the Bible Story

As the older child, I was sometimes accused of doing things that my little sister had done. It didn't matter how much I protested, I still got in trouble. It wasn't fair, but it's what happened. Being punished for something I didn't do made me angry and upset. Eventually, I convinced my mom that I hadn't done what she thought I did—but I had still been punished for it. My punishment doesn't compare to the punishment that Jesus took for us. Luke makes it clear that Jesus was innocent, and that the people in charge knew it. But Jesus was still put to death on a cross.

Read Luke 23:1-49.

Jesus didn't do anything wrong. It's the Jewish leaders, the chief priests, and the rulers who kept shouting, "Crucify him!" They asked for Barabbas, the man who was guilty of insurrection and murder, to be freed instead of Jesus. Pilate knew Jesus was innocent. Herod knew Jesus was innocent. The criminal on the cross knew that Jesus was innocent. And the centurion at the foot of the cross knew he was innocent too. But still, Jesus was crucified. Jesus' death on the cross was terrible. But Jesus died on that cross so our sins could be forgiven, once and for all. No longer would the people have to sacrifice in hopes of being forgiven. Now, the veil between God and humanity had been torn. Because Jesus died, we can be close to God. Our sins have been forgiven and we have been made clean; this is why we call today Good Friday. Here's the thing: we all sin. Jesus died for us, for our sins, so that we could be forgiven. Remember that terrible day and thank God that Jesus died for us so that we could always be close to Him.

## Discussion and Prayer

1. Ask your family to talk about a time when they were unfairly accused of something. What happened?

2. Talk about how sometimes people make mistakes and they accuse us when we did nothing wrong. How can we still show God's love in that situation?

3. Pray, thanking God that Jesus died for us and asking for forgiveness of your sins.

# Easter
## Fourth Week of April
## Luke 24:1-12—"The Empty Tomb"

### Your Story

Talk about the first time you heard about Jesus. Did Jesus' resurrection sound unbelievable? How did you come to believe?

## My Story and the Bible Story

I've believed in Jesus for as long as I can remember. I was in church almost from the moment I was born, and I don't remember believing anything different. I have always believed that Jesus died but that Jesus also rose again. But, as I have thought more about it over the years, it does sound fantastic. After all, nobody else has ever risen from the dead—only Jesus. In *Surprised by Hope*, scholar N.T. Wright talks about how we know that Jesus rose from the dead. One of his reasons is that the women were the ones who witnessed it. In those days, women's voices and opinions weren't valued. If you were making up a story you wanted others to believe, you wouldn't make women the primary witnesses. In addition to this evidence, we also have evidence that is less tangible but no less real. Jesus changes people. When we believe in Jesus, it changes us. Jesus' death was important, but his resurrection was even more so. He died for us, but by rising, he also defeated death so that we could always be close to God. As you read through this Easter passage, think through how you might have felt if you were one of the women who discovered that Jesus was gone. Think through how you might have felt if you were Peter.

Read Luke 24:1-12.

Jesus was alive! This had never happened before, and it was hard for the apostles to believe. But, in Luke's Gospel, the women believed. They saw that Jesus' body was gone, they heard from the angels that Jesus had risen, and they believed. They told these things to the apostles, but the apostles thought it was nonsense.

How many times do we think that the things God does are nonsense? How often do we say, "that's impossible" or "that couldn't have happened"? How many times do we find ourselves later saying "wow, I didn't think God could do that"? God is bigger than anything we can understand. We try to put God in a box and God refuses to go. We try to say God can't do something and God does it. And when the people killed God's Son, God raised Him from the dead. There's nothing that God can't do! When you hear about something that God is doing that seems unbelievable, remember that first Easter morning. And remember that, "what is impossible with man is possible with God" (Luke 18:27).

# Discussion and Prayer

1. As a family, talk about any things God has done that are hard for you to believe. Remind your children of how much bigger God is than we think.

2. Talk about that first Easter morning and how the women must have felt. How do you think the apostles felt when they heard the news?

3. How can you share the good news that Jesus rose from the dead?

4. Pray, thanking God that He is bigger than any of the boxes we try to put Him in. Thank God that nothing is impossible with Him.

# End of April/Beginning of May
# John 20:19-31—"Seeing Is Believing"

## Your Story

Has something ever seemed too good to be true? Was it? Talk about a time when you didn't believe something someone said until they showed you proof. Why didn't you believe? Did the proof change your thinking?

## My Story and the Bible Story

In the movie *Big Fish*, Edward Bloom has told his son Will fantastical tall tales about his life. Now Edward is dying and Will, as an adult, no longer believes his father's stories. All he wants is the truth from Edward, yet Edward continues to tell the same stories of giants, conjoined twins, the circus, and an amazing town called Spectre. After Edward dies, Will is surprised to find the people from his father's stories at his funeral. The giant isn't a giant, but he is a very tall man. The conjoined twins are not actually conjoined, but they are identical. Will begins to see that in many ways, his father was telling him the truth all along.

Like in *Big Fish*, sometimes things seem too outlandish to be true. In the Gospel of John, Thomas feels the same way about Jesus' resurrection.

Read John 20:19-31.

The disciples saw an amazing sight: Jesus, risen from the dead, walking into the room even though the doors were locked. Can you imagine if you were there? How would you feel seeing Jesus walk through the wall? The disciples were probably confused and amazed. Some of them may have even been a little afraid. But then Jesus speaks words of comfort: "peace be with you." He proves to them that he is actually Jesus who has risen from the dead. It's no wonder that Thomas didn't believe the disciples when they told him about this. After all, people didn't come back to life after they were dead, and people certainly couldn't walk through locked doors. The disciples' story of seeing Jesus seemed too strange for Thomas to believe.

But it was true. Eight days later, Jesus appeared again, walking through the locked door and showing his hands and side to Thomas. Finally, Thomas saw the truth. Thomas believed that Jesus had risen from the dead, just as Jesus said he would. Jesus went on to say that those who don't see Jesus but believe are blessed. They have a bigger faith because they didn't have to see Jesus to believe in him.

Have you ever thought that maybe we have a bigger faith than the disciples because we've never seen Jesus and yet we believe? Thomas had to have proof that Jesus had risen from the dead. Two thousand years later, there's not really any proof for us to see, and yet we believe because we see evidence of Jesus all around us. We see evidence that God is real everywhere in creation, from how our organs work together, to how intricate DNA is and how it makes us who we are, to sunsets and the flowers that bloom every spring. We know that Jesus is real because we feel it deep in our souls, and we see how Jesus has changed others and changed us.

The disciples' story of a risen Jesus sounded pretty far-fetched, but we know it was true. That story has changed our world, giving us hope, peace, and the strength we need to work with God to make our world a better place.

## Discussion and Prayer

1. Ask your children if they've ever heard a story that sounded too good or too strange to be true. Was it?

2. Talk about ways to respond if people say Jesus sounds too good to be true.

3. Pray, thanking God that Jesus isn't too good to be true. Ask God to help us believe in the miracles that happen in our world.

# May

## First Week of May
## John 21:1-14—"Recognizing Jesus"

### Your Story

Talk about a time when you were surprised by a friend or relative whom you didn't recognize initially, but who recognized you. Was it a time when you got lost and that person found you? Was it a time when you were upset and that person comforted you? What happened?

### My Story and the Bible Story

A few years ago, I ran into a friend from college at a Mercer University football game. I was with some other friends and didn't expect to see him there, so I actually walked right past him. All of a sudden, someone grabbed me into a hug, and when I looked up, I was overjoyed to see my friend! We were able to catch up on life and spend some time together. I'm so glad he recognized me when I didn't recognize him.

Read John 21:1-14.

The disciples weren't expecting to see Jesus on the shoreline. Jesus had risen from the dead and done many miraculous signs in the disciples' presence, but they still weren't expecting him that day. They had gone fishing, doing what they used to do to make money. Perhaps they were going back to this career, or maybe they just needed something to eat. They fished all night but didn't catch anything. Then, suddenly, they saw a man on the shore. The man asked if they had caught anything. At this point, they still didn't know it was Jesus. Maybe they thought the person on the beach was hungry, looking for others willing to share their food. Then the man made an odd suggestion. He told them to cast their net on the right side of the boat, and they would catch some fish. At this point, the disciples were probably a bit desperate, since they had fished all night and caught nothing. They figured, "What could it hurt?" and followed the man's instructions. They got much more than they had bargained for! Instead of a few fish, there were so many fish that they couldn't haul the net back into the boat!

It was too heavy. Suddenly, they realized that this man was Jesus. Jesus once again performed a miracle, and they recognized him by his actions.

Like me with my friend, we don't always recognize the people we know. Sometimes we are thinking about other things and walk right past people we care about. But hopefully that person recognizes us and shows us who they are.

Sometimes, like the disciples, we don't recognize Jesus. Jesus may not be standing on a shoreline, like in this story, but we can see Jesus in others. Sometimes we are so focused on how someone else is different from us that we miss seeing that Jesus is part of them too, just like he is part of us.

## Discussion and Prayer

1. Ask your children to tell you about a time when someone recognized them before they recognized that person, or about a time when they recognized someone who didn't recognize them. What happened?

2. Talk about ways we can see Jesus in others (through their actions, how they treat others, etc.).

3. This week, play a game as a family where you try to find a quality of Jesus in every person you meet. Share the results with each other.

4. Pray, thanking God that Jesus always recognizes us. Ask for help in recognizing Jesus in others.

# Second Week of May
# John 10:22-30—"God's Sheep"

## Your Story

Talk about a time when you felt that God was speaking to you. What was the situation? What was God speaking to you about? Did you follow God's leading?

## My Story and the Bible Story

Last week I got to see some sheep up close and personal, and I learned a few things. Sheep will "baa" at you when they think you've got something to eat. It doesn't matter if they have just eaten; they will still complain. Sheep will follow the voice they recognize. My uncle Keith raises sheep, and right now he has about twenty lambs (baby sheep). One lamb, called Nine, drinks from a bottle. When he hears Uncle Keith's voice, he comes running. Last week, Nine followed Uncle Keith until he settled in to give him the bottle. It didn't matter who else was talking to Nine; he followed his shepherd's voice.

Read John 10:22-30.

The Jews wanted to know for certain if Jesus was the Messiah—the Savior they had been promised for so long. But instead of saying yes and moving on, Jesus reminded them that he had told them who he was over and over again, but they still didn't believe. He used an example that was familiar to everyone at the time: sheep. The people knew that sheep follow their shepherd. They knew that sheep listen to their shepherd's voice. And God's sheep listen to Jesus. Those "sheep" knew that Jesus was the Messiah, and they followed him. It didn't matter what others were saying about Jesus; these people knew that they belonged to him and that no one could take them away. No one could keep them away from God.

It seems harsh that Jesus told this group of Jews that they weren't his sheep, but the only way they could be his sheep was to believe in him. It is clear that they didn't believe Jesus was the Messiah. It didn't matter how many times he told them; they still didn't believe. When we believe Jesus, we become his sheep. When we choose to follow Jesus, he shows us the way. He speaks to us, and even though we may not hear a voice with our ears, we hear him with our hearts. Like a shepherd, Jesus guides us, and if we listen for his voice, we know where to go.

Thanks be to God that no one can snatch us out of God's hands. Jesus and the Father (God) are one. Jesus is our shepherd and we are his sheep. If we follow him, we will have eternal life. Listen for the voice of your shepherd. He will tell you what to do. And then follow him. If you follow Jesus, you will have eternal life. How can you be like a sheep today?

## Discussion and Prayer

1. Ask your children to talk about times when they felt God speaking to them. Have them describe the situation and share whether or not they did what God told them to do.

2. Talk about ways we can listen for Jesus' voice (through prayer, reading our Bibles, listening in Sunday school, etc.).

3. How can you help others also become Jesus' sheep?

4. Pray, thanking God for leading you in the way you should go. Ask for help hearing God's voice.

# Third Week of May
# John 13:31-35—
# "The Command that Jesus Gave"

## Your Story

Talk about a time when you were intentional about loving others. What did you do? How did you feel? What were the results?

## My Story and the Bible Story

Every year, our church has a service day called Beyond Our Walls. On this day, more than 300 people go out into the community to serve. Some of our families and children spend time with senior adults at assisted living facilities. They play bingo, do a craft, and get to know the older people. I love seeing the faces of these senior adults light up as they spend time with our kids. Some of them may not get many visitors, and they love having our group come. Other groups serve at various charities around our community. Some work on homes of the elderly, doing yard work, roof repair, and more for seniors who cannot do these things themselves. One group works with the city, helping keep our city parks safe and beautiful. It's amazing to see the difference love can make. Showing love to others helps them, but it also changes us. It reminds us that we are all God's children and that we are all loved by God.

In the Gospel of John, Jesus gave his disciples and us a command.

Read John 13:31-35.

Jesus knew that he was leaving soon, and he wanted to make sure his disciples knew what to do when he was gone. There were so many things he could have told them. He could have given them a list of things to cover when they taught others. He could have given them places to travel to spread the good news about him. There are many things Jesus could have told them, but his focus was love. He gave the disciples a new commandment: to love one another. The most important thing Jesus wanted them to know was that they should love others. In fact, he said everyone would know they were followers of Jesus if they showed love.

More than 2,000 years later, not much has changed when it comes to Jesus' commands. Like the disciples, we too are called to love one another. The best way people can know that we are followers of Jesus is by seeing our love. In our world, many people are focused on themselves and what is best for them. They will do anything to get what they want. But Jesus gives us another way. Instead of only looking out for ourselves, we are called to love others. Instead of ignoring someone who needs help, Jesus wants us to help them. Instead of sleeping late every Saturday and always doing what we want to do, sometimes Jesus wants us to get up early and help others. Instead of spending all of our money on ourselves, Jesus calls us to be generous. Loving others means we think about what they need, how we can help them, and what God would want us to do. When we show others God's love, we are showing them that we are followers of Jesus. How might you show love to others in your life?

## Discussion and Prayer

1. As a family, talk about ways you have shown love to others.

2. What are some ways you can show love to others this week? This month?

3. How can you show love to others at your school? At work? In your community?

4. Pray, giving thanks for how much God loves us and asking for help in knowing how to love one another.

# Fourth Week of May
# John 5:1-9—"Jesus Gives Us Hope"

## Your Story

Talk about a time when things seemed hopeless. Did God give you hope? How did God's hope come to you?

## My Story and the Bible Story

When I was in the sixth grade, it felt like my life was falling apart. I didn't have any friends, there was a lot of bad stuff happening at my church, and my mom and my stepdad were getting a divorce. Things seemed hopeless, and it didn't seem like things would ever get better. But I knew that God was always with me and would never leave. I prayed and prayed, and eventually things started to get better. God sent me a friend at school. We found a new church that I loved and I found a place to belong. There was peace in our home. When things seemed hopeless, God gave me hope. I was reminded that God was there and that I could have hope in God. I knew that eventually things would change because God gives us hope!

There are people in the Bible whose lives seemed pretty hopeless: the paralytic whose friends cut a hole in a roof so they could lower him to Jesus, the woman who had been bleeding for years and years, the Israelites when they were captured by other people groups. And yet God was there with them. God promised never to leave. In the case of the paralytic and the bleeding woman, Jesus healed them. He gave them hope. There are many stories in the Gospels about Jesus healing others. In the Gospel of John, we find another sick and hurting man. But this time, Jesus asks him what he wants.

## Read John 5:1-9.

This man had been an invalid for a long time. He was sick and had a hard time walking. He needed help even to get into the pool quickly. He felt like things were hopeless and that he would never get better. But then Jesus came. Jesus saw the man and asked him if he wanted to get well. After all, the man could earn money as a beggar. The man told Jesus why he couldn't get into the pool, and Jesus healed him! The man got up and walked away, praising God that he had been healed.

Jesus healed this man's body, but he also gave him something else: hope. Before, the man was hopeless. He knew what his life would be, and there was no way for him to get better. But after Jesus, he had hope again. Suddenly, his life changed! Jesus gives us that hope as well. When we meet Jesus, when we learn about Jesus and what he did for us and how much God loves us, we discover something amazing: we find hope. Without Jesus, we are stuck. There's no way for us to be friends with God. We aren't perfect and we choose to do the wrong thing sometimes. Without God's love and grace, there's no way we could be friends with God. But Jesus gives shows us God's love and grace. He helps us be friends with God. He can heal our lives. That doesn't mean Jesus is always going to heal our bodies. Sometimes we get sick, and sometimes bad things happen. But Jesus can heal our lives. He can help us take bad things that happen and turn them into something good. He can help us choose the right thing. He can help us forgive others. Even though Jesus is no longer walking on Earth where we can see him, he can still heal our lives. All we have to do is ask!

## Discussion and Prayer

1. Ask your children about times when they feel hopeless and think that nothing will ever change.

2. Remind your family that God gives us hope, even when it seems like things won't change. Talk to them about how God can take the bad things that happen and make something good out of them (for example, when a bad storm happens, people help each other).

3. Talk about ways you can share God's hope with others.

4. Pray with your family, asking God to remind each of you that God is always there and that our hope comes from God.

# June

## Ascension
### First Week of June
### Ephesians 1:15-23—"Jesus Is in Charge"

### Your Story

Talk about a time when you were given a promotion. How did you feel?

### My Story and the Bible Story

As a teenager, I loved volunteering for Vacation Bible School. It felt like a promotion to be able to help. Suddenly, I was in charge (sort of). Instead of listening to what I was supposed to do, I was the one giving direction. I like to be in charge. But, when someone else knows what's going on and gives direction, I'm comfortable following, too. While it can be hard for some of us (like me) to know that we aren't in charge of everything, it can also be helpful. We aren't in charge of keeping this world under control; we don't have to take everyone's burdens. Jesus does that.

Read Ephesians 1:15-23.

When Jesus ascended into heaven, God gave him a spot at His right hand, far above everything else. Jesus is above us, above the powers of this world, above presidents and royal families, above even the angels. God also made Jesus the head of the church. When we think of who's in charge of our churches, we may think about the pastor first. But Jesus is the head of the church. On Ascension Sunday, we remember and celebrate that when Jesus ascended, he became in charge of everything. Instead of us feeling the weight of the world on our shoulders, we can give our burdens to Jesus. And in our churches, when we struggle with a decision, we should remember that Jesus is the head of the church. And may we listen to him when he asks us to do something. May we always remember that Jesus is in charge. And may that give us peace.

## Discussion and Prayer

1. Ask your children how their responsibilities have changed as they've gotten older.

2. Remind your family of the importance of listening to Jesus, especially when they are in charge of something.

3. Talk about how we can give our burdens over to Jesus and he will give us peace.

4. Pray, thanking God that Jesus is in charge of everything, and ask for help in remembering that we don't have the weight of the world on our shoulders.

# Pentecost
## Second Week of June
## Genesis 11:1-9—
## "Understanding Each Other"

### Your Story

Talk about a time when you had a difficult time understanding someone else's language or point of view. How did you work together so that you could understand?

### My Story and the Bible Story

I've always loved the French language, and when I got into French classes in high school, I had the opportunity to travel to Paris. I was so excited! But my first few days in Paris, it was tough to understand native French speakers. They spoke so fast that it was hard for me to translate in my head. And boy, did my head hurt from trying to understand! But after a few days, I started to get better at understanding what they were saying. My French grew stronger, and I was able to better communicate.

Read Genesis 11:1-9.

In Genesis, the people understood one another. They all spoke the same language, and they began to work together to build a tower that would reach to the heavens. They wanted to make a name for themselves, to prove what they could do. They wanted to be like God, so God gave them different languages to keep them from planning even bigger things. Then God scattered them over the face of the Earth.

There are many languages spoken across the world. Wherever you go, chances are good that you will hear another language. There are times when those barriers make it hard for us to understand one another. The miracle of Pentecost was that everyone understood what the disciples were saying. The Bible tells us that every nation under heaven was represented in Jerusalem, and that each person in the crowd heard their own language spoken. Although the people were given different languages and scattered after the Tower of Babel, the Holy Spirit brought the people together, helping them understand one another.

When we can't understand one another, trying to communicate can be frustrating. Fortunately, the Holy Spirit can help us. The Holy Spirit may not translate things for us like Google Translate, but it can help us understand the heart of another person. After all, we are all created by God. When you don't understand someone, instead of getting frustrated, brainstorm. Use hand gestures, pictures, or the internet. Find ways to work together. God created us all, and the Holy Spirit can help us understand each other. It's clear from what happened at Pentecost that God wants everyone to understand about Jesus. If we work together, we can find ways to share Jesus with everyone we meet.

## Discussion and Prayer

1. As a family, brainstorm ways to share the love of God with people who don't speak the same language as you.

2. If there is someone in your life who speaks a different language, talk about ways that you can work together to understand one another.

3. Commit to learning a few words in a different language so that you are better able to communicate with someone else.

4. Pray, thanking God that the Holy Spirit can help us understand each other. Ask for help in understanding someone in your own life.

# Third Week of June
# Romans 5:1-5—"Don't Give Up!"

## Your Story

Talk about a time when you struggled with something. Do you feel like God taught you anything through that experience? Did you grow stronger in your faith?

## My Story and the Bible Story

When we were kids, my sister hated school. She didn't want to do her homework or study, so there were many times when she didn't understand the material. When she was in middle school, though, she had an especially hard time with math. I was in college by that time, and my college room-mate tutored her. Once she understood, it was like a light bulb came on. All of a sudden, she got it, and she (somewhat) wanted to do her work because she finally understood it. She grew stronger in math and realized that she could actually do well in the subject.

Read Romans 5:1-5.

When we have a hard time, like my sister did with math, it sometimes feels easier to give up. It can feel that way as a Christian too. There are times when being a Christian is hard—maybe when your friends are trying to get you to do something you know you shouldn't do, or you know you should stand up for someone but you're afraid everyone will make fun of you. For some Christians around the world, there are times when someone threatens to put them in jail because of their beliefs. There are times when it feels easier to give up. Paul reminds us in Romans that if we continue to follow God even when it's hard, our troubles will give us patience. That patience can turn into good character or perseverance.

How do we keep going? Thankfully, we don't have to try to keep going alone. God helps us. When we become a Christian, God fills our lives with the Holy Spirit. We can't see the Holy Spirit, but the Holy Spirit helps us know what is right. The Holy Spirit also helps us know what we should do and can give us the strength we need to keep going. When you are having a hard time with school or someone is bullying you, remember that God can use the Holy Spirit to help you. Don't give up!

## Discussion and Prayer

1. Ask your children about times when school has been hard or they have had a difficult time dealing with other people. What did they want to do? What did they do? Did they ask for help from God?

2. Talk about how we can always ask God for help. Share examples of times when God has helped you.

3. Talk about ways we can know that God is with us.

4. Pray, thanking God for always being there for us and for helping us when things are hard. Ask God to help you and your family remember that God is always there!

# Fourth Week of June
# Galatians 3:23-29—"We Are Free"

### Your Story

Talk about a time when you felt free. What was that like?

### My Story and the Bible Story

When I was a teenager, there was a popular praise and worship song by the Newsboys called "I Am Free." Here are the lyrics:

Through you the blind will see, Through you the mute will sing
Through you the dead will rise, Through you all hearts will praise
Through you the darkness flees. Through you my heart screams,
I am free, Yes, I am free
I am free to run, I am free to dance, I am free to live for you
I am free, Yes, I am free
Through you the kingdom comes, Through you the battle's won
Through you I'm not afraid, Through you the price is paid
Through you there's victory, Because of you my heart sings
I am free, Yes, I am free[16]

When I think of Jesus, I think of freedom. I think of the freedom grace gives us—the freedom to be ourselves, to be human, to mess up sometimes and to know that God will love us no matter what. No matter what happens, there's nothing we can do to make God stop loving us. It is comforting to know that we are free in Christ, even when our world tries to tell us what we should do, what we should wear, what we should eat, and even who we should be.

## Read Galatians 3:23-29.

Before Jesus came, the Jewish people had tons of laws that they had to follow. According to the Pharisees, they had to follow them all even to think about getting into heaven. No one could ever measure up. They were prisoners of the law because nobody did everything exactly right.

Then Jesus came and set us free from those expectations. Jesus wants us to do good things, to love others, and to love God, but we don't have to memorize and follow every single rule to be loved by God. There are times when we still do the wrong thing, but now, thanks to Jesus, we are free. Not only are we free; we are also equal. When Jesus came to Earth, people's importance was based on whether or not they were slaves or free, whether they were Jews or Greeks, and whether they were men or women, it was a big deal for Paul to say that everyone is equal in Christ Jesus. It doesn't matter how much or how little you have, whether you are a man or a woman, or whether you are Jewish or a Gentile. Everyone can be free in Jesus. When you feel like you are stuck in a box that's too small, like you have to do everything everybody else says, that you have to dress a certain way or wear your hair a certain way or act a certain way, remember that you are free. Thanks to Jesus, you are free to be who you are, and you are free

---

16. Newsboys, "I Am Free," *Go*, 2006.

to accept God's love. God gave us freedom and grace through Jesus, and that is great news!

## Discussion and Prayer

1. Ask your family if they ever feel pressure to dress a certain way, act a certain way, or be a certain way. Talk about their responses.

2. Talk about how God's freedom through Jesus means that we have grace no matter what. Remind your children that it's okay to make mistakes and mess up. God wants us to do what we are asked to do in the Bible, but God always loves us no matter what.

3. Pray, thanking God for our freedom in Jesus and asking for help in listening to what God asks us to do.

# July

## First Week of July
## Galatians 5:1, 13-18, 22-25—
## "The Fruit of the Spirit"

### Your Story

How do you see the fruit of the Spirit in your own life?

### My Story and the Bible Story

I am a terrible liar. I'm bad at it. I tried to lie about not talking during the fire drill when I was in the first grade (I definitely talked during the fire drill), and I got in trouble for lying. I know that even if I could do something wrong without anyone knowing it, I would try my best not to because I would probably tell on myself. For instance, if nobody was around and there were delicious cookies sitting on the table right before dinner, if I took one and ate it I would probably tell my mom. Paul would say that type of honesty is a good thing. Last week, we learned about how we are free in Christ. We are no longer under the law. This is great news! But does it mean we can do whatever we want? Let's find out what Paul has to say.

Read Galatians 5:1, 13-18, 22-25
(for older children, feel free to read all of verses 13-25).

Paul reminds us that we are free in Christ. But just because Christ has set us free, that doesn't mean we can do whatever we want to do. It doesn't mean we should go up to someone at school, push them down, and say, "Christ made me free so I can do what I want." It doesn't mean you should be mean to your parents or rude to your siblings. Christ gave us freedom, and we are free to do all of those things, but God wants us to love our neighbor as ourselves. When Jesus came, he taught us to love God with everything we've got (our hearts, our minds, our souls, and our strength) and to love our neighbor as ourselves. So instead of being mean to others because we can be, we should love others as we love ourselves. When we do that, when we follow God and do what God wants us to do, it's like we are a tree that blooms. Instead of flowers or apples, we have the fruit of the Spirit, which is love, joy, peace, patience, kindness, goodness, faithfulness, gentleness, and self-control. When we follow God, we are free, but God wants us to choose to love, to be joyful, to offer peace instead of fighting with others, to be patient instead of rude, to be kind, to be good, to be faithful to God, to be gentle with others, and to practice self-control. We are free in Christ, and when we live the fruit of the Spirit, we can help others find their freedom in Christ too.

## Discussion and Prayer

1. Ask your children how they can show the fruit of the Spirit at school and in their neighborhood. How can they show God's love to others?

2. Talk about how freedom is a wonderful gift, but it's also a responsibility. Help your children understand that when you trust them with freedom, you still expect and want them to do the right thing. Explain that God is the same way.

3. Talk about how sometimes we make mistakes, but God's grace is always there for us. Make sure your children understand that none of us is perfect and that freedom in Christ means that God doesn't expect us to be perfect.

4. Pray, thanking God for freedom in Christ and asking for help in living the fruit of the Spirit.

# Second Week of July
# Psalm 66:1-9—"Sing Praises to God"

## Your Story

Talk to your family about a few times when God has answered your prayers. What were you praying for and how did God answer you?

## My Story and the Bible Story

God has answered many of my prayers over the years. Some of God's answers have been yes, some no, and some that it wasn't the time and I needed to wait. But I know that God always hears my prayers. When I was in high school, I prayed that God would show me which college I should go to. I worried that I would choose the wrong one and somehow wouldn't still be in God's plan. But I was worried for no reason, because God answers our prayers. When I walked on Mercer's campus, I knew that it was home. It was the right place for me. Sometimes, our answers aren't as clear. Sometimes we aren't sure what God wants us to do, but the psalm reminds us that God helps us. Our lives are in God's hands and He will never leave us. God answers our prayers.

The Israelites knew that God answered prayers. In Psalm 66, we are reminded of some of the things God had done for the people.

Read Psalm 66:1-9.

God not only answers prayers but also holds our very lives in God's hands. God keeps our feet from stumbling, knows what we need, and helps us. There's no person on Earth who is any match for God. God is more powerful than anything and anyone else, and God cares about us! I am clumsy, and there are plenty of times when I trip and fall, but the psalmist means that God helps us know which way to go. God helps us avoid hurtful things if we listen. God shows us the way, just as God made a way for the Hebrew people through the Red Sea. There are times when it seems as if there's no way things will get better. The Hebrew people struggled in Egypt, and they cried out to God. It seemed as if they would always be stuck in Egypt, working for a pharaoh who continued to make them work harder. It seemed as if it would always be that way. But God made a way. God sent Moses to set them free. When it seemed as if all hope was lost, when they were stuck between Pharaoh's army and the Red Sea, God made a way for the people then too, creating a dry path for them to walk across.

God knows what we need and keeps us from stumbling. We can trust that God is there for us and will help us. Sing praises to God, because God is our Creator and our Redeemer who listens to our cries for help. Remember that God will answer our prayers. God is always by our side!

# Discussion and Prayer

1. Have each person in your family share how God has answered their prayers.

2. Ask everyone to talk about something for which they are praying.

3. Brainstorm ways to track when God answers prayers. You may create a prayer board for your family, moving each prayer to an "answered" column, or have a "prayer" jar and an "answered prayers" jar. Choose a way that helps your family see how often God answers their prayers.

4. Pray, giving thanks that God always answers us. Offer praise for all the things that God has done.

# Third Week of July
# Luke 10:25-37—"The Good Samaritan"

## Your Story

Tell your children about a time when you tried to justify your behavior to God or when someone you didn't expect showed compassion to you. You can also talk about a time when you were the "good Samaritan," or perhaps the person who needed help, or even one of the people who walked on by. Talk about what happened and what you learned.

## My Story and the Bible Story

At just over five feet tall, I sometimes have a hard time reaching things on the top shelf. It's even worse in grocery stores, when there's nothing for me to stand on. There was a time in the grocery store when I was trying to reach a box of cereal on the top shelf. I kept stretching, trying my best to reach it. I touched it, but I also knocked the other ones behind it. Just before a cereal box avalanche landed on top of me, a stranger steadied them and handed me the box of cereal. This man had no reason to help me, but he was walking by and saved me from disaster. He helped me when he didn't have to, when no one else had.

*For preschoolers and younger elementary students:* Because the story of the good Samaritan is violent, this version (from *God's Story for Me: Bible*

*Storybook*) leaves most of the violence out and is appropriate for younger children. Tell them that this is a story that Jesus shared.

A man was walking a long way. While he walked, some men grabbed him, hurt him and took all his money. The man lay hurting on the ground. He couldn't even get up! But soon, an important leader walked by! The hurt man lay there, waiting for help. But the leader didn't help! He hurried away. The hurt man groaned. He hurt all over! But now another man came near. He stopped and looked at the hurt man. The hurt man lay there, waiting for help. But the second man hurried away, too! The hurt man could only lie on the ground. But then he heard a clippety-clop sound. A donkey stopped. Another man got off. This man put medicine on the man's sores. He bandaged the man's cuts. He put the hurt man on the donkey and brought him to a safe place. He paid money to be sure the hurt man would be taken care of. The man on the donkey showed God's love. He was kind to the hurt man!

Read Luke 10:25-37.

## Discussion and Prayer

1. Ask your children to think of a time when they made fun of someone because of what the person wore, where the person lived, or how the person looked. Variation: You may also want to ask if there was a time when someone made fun of them because of these things.

2. Talk about a time when you knew you should be nice to someone, but you decided not to be.

3. Talk about a time when, instead of admitting you did something wrong, you tried to get away with it.

4. Find ways for your family to show kindness to others this week. Do something nice for the neighbor whom nobody likes to talk to, seek out others who seem to be on the fringes of life,

invite a new family over for dinner, volunteer at a homeless shelter or food pantry, etc.

5. Pray, asking God to help you and your family see that everyone is our "neighbor." Ask God for courage to help you reach out to outcasts or those on the fringes of life.

# Fourth Week of July
# Luke 10:38-42—"Being Busy"

## Your Story

Talk to your family about a time when you were so busy that you missed something important. What did you miss?

## My Story and the Bible Story

I like to be busy. If I'm watching TV or even a movie, I want to do something else at the same time so I don't feel like I'm wasting time. So when I watch a movie or TV show at home, I also find myself looking at Facebook, checking email, or even playing an online game like "Candy Crush." Sometimes a few minutes will go by and I will realize that I wasn't paying attention to what I was watching. Something important happened and I missed it because I was too busy.

In the Gospel of Luke, Martha, Lazarus's sister, is that way too. She likes to be busy, and she is a worrier. She always wants to make sure everything gets done.

### Read Luke 10:38-42.

Mary and Martha had Jesus and the disciples over for a meal. There was a lot of work to do. When people come over to your house, your parents want to make sure everything is clean. This usually means you get put to work, too. It was the same way for Martha: she wanted to make sure everything was perfect for the Lord and his disciples. But she didn't get a phone call beforehand. Instead, they were passing through and Martha invited them in. Preparations had to be done while Jesus and the disciples were already there, and Mary wasn't helping! Instead, Martha had to do everything by herself. She was busy, and she was missing what Jesus had to say. She got angry and asked Jesus to tell Mary to help her get things ready. Jesus did something surprising. He told Martha that Mary was doing exactly what she should be doing. Instead of being busy, Mary was listening to Jesus.

That's a big lesson for us. Sometimes we get so caught up in wanting to be busy that we miss what Jesus says. We go from school to soccer or tennis practice, to piano lessons, or to some other obligation, rush home for a quick dinner and homework, and then all of a sudden it's time for bed. All of these are good things, but they are things that can get in the way of listening to Jesus. Does that mean you shouldn't go to school? Of course not. But it means we all have to take time in our busy days to stop and pray, asking God to show us what to do and then sit and listen quietly until we have heard from God. Is this hard when there are so many other things we want to do? Yes, it can be very hard to sit still and listen quietly for God. But if we do, then we will spend our lives doing what God wants us to do. We will discover purpose in our lives. Like Mary, we will be doing the one thing that is needed.

## Discussion and Prayer

1. Ask your children to name the things that keep them busy. As a family, talk about ways you can each take time to sit and listen to God.

2. Is your family too busy? Take a hard look at your family schedule and see if you need to say no to something so that your family can spend time listening to God. Are there important things your family is missing out on (like family time) because you all are so busy?

3. Talk about ways you can build family time into your schedule (if it's not already there), and then work to make room for it.

4. Pray, asking God to help you say no to things that keep you too busy to listen to God.

# Fifth Week of July
## Luke 11:1-13—"Prayer"

## Your Story

Have you ever gotten something you asked for but weren't expecting to get? What was it? Who did you ask? Were you surprised when you received it?

## My Story and the Bible Story

When I was 10, my father asked me where I wanted to go on vacation for my 13th birthday. Turning 13 was a big deal, so I got to pick our vacation spot. I thought of the craziest place I could imagine, sure that we wouldn't get to go. I picked Hawaii. Sure enough, when I turned 13, we went to Hawaii on our vacation. I didn't think we would get to go, but because that was what I asked for and wanted, my dad made it happen.

In the book of Luke, Jesus says God does the same thing.

### Read Luke 11:1-13.

Jesus says to ask God for what we need. He tells us to be bold and ask! Here's the thing: it never hurts to ask for something. You may ask your parents for a new gaming system and they may say no. Or you may ask to eat cookies for dinner and they say no too. But it never hurts to ask, because sometimes the answer may be yes. Jesus says to ask and it will be given to you. Does he mean that if you ask God for a pony, one is going to drop out of the sky? Probably not. But it never hurts to ask God for help, to ask God to show you the way, to ask God to heal someone, etc. Sometimes the answer will be no, but sometimes it will be yes. Your parents love you and want what's best for you. They want to give you good things. Sometimes they can give you what you want and sometimes they can't.

As much as your parents love you, God loves you even more and also wants to give you good things! God wants you to talk to God, to ask for what you want and what you need. God may not always give you what you want, because what you want may not be the best thing for you. But God will always give you what you need. In Jesus' prayer that he taught the disciples, which we call the Lord's Prayer, he tells the disciples to talk to God and ask God for help. In the beginning of the prayer, he reminds the disciples how great God is and says they should praise God. Then he tells them to ask God for what they need ("give us our daily bread"). After that, we are to ask God to forgive us. Finally, we are to ask God to help us do the right thing. God wants what is best for us. God wants us to have amazing lives that we use to do what God wants us to do. And God is ready and waiting to help us. All we have to do is ask!

## Discussion and Prayer

1. Is there something you need to ask God for right now? Are you afraid to ask? Why?

2. Talk about the different ways that God has provided for your family.

3. Ask your children about times when they feel like God said yes to them. What did they ask for? What did God give?

4. Pray, thanking God for giving us what we need. Take this time to ask God for something you really need.

# August

## First Week of August
## Luke 12:13-21—"Greed"

**Your Story**

Talk about a time when you were greedy. How did you feel when you realized how you were acting?

**My Story and the Bible Story**

As an only child for seven years, I wasn't always great at sharing. Even now, I want to make sure someone is going to take good care of my stuff before I lend it. I didn't like to share as a child because I was afraid that my stuff would get broken. Eventually, though, I outgrew all of my toys. They were still in great condition, but I no longer wanted to play with them. Instead of giving my friends a chance to play with them, there were times when I kept my toys to myself, out of fear that something would happen to them. I still have some of my old Barbies, but all they do is collect dust. Instead of being played with by other children, they are sitting in my grandmother's attic.

Greed is part of us because we are human. It's hard not to want to keep our stuff. But listen to Jesus talk about greed.

### Read Luke 12:13-21.

Jesus points out that it does us no good to store up everything we have, because eventually we will be gone from this world, and we don't get to take our stuff with us. The Egyptians used to bury gold, treasures, and even favorite pets with their leaders when they died. Thousands of years later, archaeologists found those treasures, still intact, in their tombs. The gold didn't do those leaders any good. Instead of being used to help people, it was left to get dusty in the tombs. We cannot take our stuff with us. Jesus calls us to use the things we have been given to help others.

Part of being greedy is thinking that you deserve the stuff you have, that you've earned the stuff you have, and that other people need to earn their things too. While this is what our culture says, it isn't what Jesus says. Instead, Jesus calls us to have compassion on others. Yes, we may have earned what we have, but none of us have earned God's grace and love. We could never do enough to earn that. God gives it to us freely because we could not earn it. God wants us to show love to others too, which means sharing what we have with those who don't have enough. It means doing the unexpected and being generous when others are storing everything they have like the rich man in this story. It's hard not to be greedy, but Jesus reminds us that "life is not defined by what you have, even when you have a lot." Instead, life is defined by how much we show God's love to others and how we show others who Jesus is. We cannot show God's love if we aren't willing to be generous the way God is generous.

## Discussion and Prayer

1. As a family, talk about why it's sometimes hard to share with others. Ask your kids why they sometimes don't like to share.

2. Brainstorm ways each of you can be more generous. Ask your kids what ideas they have.

3. Pick a few of these ideas and implement them this week. Find ways to be more generous as a family.

4. Pray, giving thanks that God is never greedy and instead lovingly gives us grace even when we mess up. Ask God for help in being more generous and less greedy.

# Second Week of August
# Hebrews 11:1-3, 8-16—"By Faith, Part 1"

### Your Story

Talk about something you did that required a leap of faith. Perhaps it was moving to a new place or quitting your job. Talk to your family about how you knew what God wanted you to do.

## My Story and the Bible Story

As Christians, we believe in what we cannot see. We cannot see God, but we know God is there. Believing in God and becoming a Christian makes us a take a leap of faith; we cannot see God but we believe anyway. We have faith in a lot of things. We have faith that our cars will work when we turn them on and that the lights will come on when we flip the switch. We believe these things, and although we can't see how our cars work and how our lights work, we know that they are true. It's the same with God. Someone asked me why I believed in God and I told them it's because when I look at the leaves changing in the fall, I know someone had to create that. There's no way it's an accident, so I have faith in my Creator. I know that faith doesn't mean I will always get my way and everything will go exactly right. But faith does mean we can trust God. We can trust that God is there and God's promises are true. We know that the promises God makes are true because of what we read in the Bible.

Read Hebrews 11:1-3, 8-16.

Hebrews 11 is often called the "Faith Hall of Fame." This is because the writer of Hebrews talks about many important people in the Old Testament who had faith in God. Even though they didn't always see God's promises come true while they were alive, they knew that God could be trusted. They could put their faith in God because God's promises were true. God promised Abraham that he would have as many descendants as there were stars in the sky, and when God made that promise, Abraham and Sarah didn't even have a child! But they trusted God to keep the promise, and God did. Even when they couldn't see what God was doing, they trusted God to keep the promises.

God makes promises to us too. There are times when we have to walk by faith, because we can't see what God is doing. Sometimes that means God wants us to move to a new town where we don't know anyone. We have to trust that God will be with us and help us. Sometimes that means God tells us to do something that seems too hard. Then we must trust that God will be with us and help us do it. We can put our faith in God because God always keeps promises. Trust in God and follow God. Live by faith and see what God can do!

## Discussion and Prayer

1. Talk about times when you and your family trusted in God's promises. What were they, and how did it work out?

2. Ask your children if they have ever had to trust God. How did they trust God to help them?

3. Talk about things we put our faith in and how earthly things will always let us down (sometimes the power doesn't work, the car runs out of gas, etc.), but how we can always put our faith in God because God will never let us down.

4. Pray, giving thanks that we can trust God and asking for help in taking a leap of faith.

# Third Week of August
# Hebrews 11:29–12:2—"By Faith, Part 2"

## Your Story

Tell your family's story of faith. If your ancestors were immigrants, the story may begin with something like this: "By faith my great-great-great-grandparents left the home and land they knew and came to America in search of a better life. By faith they looked for work, believing that God would provide . . . ." Whatever your story looks like, tell it to your family. If your parents or grandparents don't know Jesus, then you can simply talk about your own faith journey.

## My Story and the Bible Story

By faith, my grandmother and grandfather raised their children. By faith, my grandmother stretched the budget so that everyone had enough to eat. They trusted that God would provide for them, and God did. By faith, my mother moved back to Macon to raise me. By faith, she took me to church, believing that God would call to me just as God had called to her as a child. By faith (and a lot of prayer), my mom raised us. By faith, I stepped out to be a minister. Sometimes we do things by faith, not knowing what's going to happen but trusting that God is with us.

Read Hebrews 11:29-12:2.

"God had a better plan for us: that their faith and our faith would come together to make one completed whole, their lives of faith not completely apart from ours" (11:40-41, *The Message*). All of our stories of faith have two things in common: God and other people. Without other people listening to and following God, I would not have been able to step out in faith. The faith of others helps us and holds us up, giving us the courage we need to step out in faith. These stories we find in Hebrews are stories of faith, and our own faith is built on them. Without these stories, without the faith of people like Moses and Israel, Rahab, Samson, David, Samuel, the prophets, and others, Jesus' story might have been different. Each person played a role in preparing the world for Jesus, and because of their faith, because of how much they trusted that God would send a Messiah to deliver them, we can trust that God saves us too. Because we know their stories, we can step out in faith when God asks us to. We know that God can be trusted because others have stepped out in faith and shown us how to follow God. Don't lose sight of the finish line, which is spending eternity with God. Step out in faith and join the others throughout history who have done the same.

## Discussion and Prayer

1. Ask your children if they feel like God is nudging them to do something. What is it? How can they step out in faith and follow?

2. Is God calling you as a family to step out in faith and do something?

3. Talk about ways to trust God this week—for example, trusting that God will give you the courage to make new friends at school, to talk to people who are lonely, to do the right thing even if others don't like you because of it.

4. Pray, thanking God for the many people who have shown us how to step out in faith. Ask for help in trusting God and following where God wants us to go.

# Fourth Week of August
# Isaiah 58:9b-14—
# "How Can We Find Joy in the Lord?"

## Your Story

Talk about a time when you felt joy in the Lord—that is, when you knew you were doing what God wanted you to do and you were satisfied in the Lord. What were the circumstances? How did it change your perspective?

## My Story and the Bible Story

There are days when I feel close to God and days when I don't. There are days when I absolutely know that I am following God and doing what God wants me to do, and there are days when I'm a bit unsure. But every summer, I find my joy in the Lord during Vacation Bible School. Seeing the excitement on the faces of the children as they sing praises to God reminds me of my own joy and excitement in the Lord. Seeing how generous our children are toward others who need help reminds me of how generous God is to every one of us. Seeing the Bible stories come to the life for these kids reminds me of how the stories have come to life for me. Many times, I find my joy in the Lord by serving others. I find my joy when I help others, when I teach them about God, and when I share God's love with them. As I read Isaiah 58, it makes sense that I find my joy in the Lord when I am serving others.

## Read Isaiah 58:9b-14.

How can we find joy in the Lord? According to Isaiah, we find it by helping the hungry and oppressed and by honoring the Lord. Simply put, we find it by loving God and by loving others (the two greatest commandments according to Jesus). When we do these things, Isaiah tells us that the Lord will guide us always. God will satisfy our needs and help us rebuild. We find our joy by following the Lord. We discover a joy greater than ourselves when we commit to loving the Lord. When we talk to God and when we listen, when we follow and honor God, then we will find joy.

Joy isn't the same thing as happiness. We are happy when something good happens to us or around us. But joy, especially the joy of the Lord, is deeper. It happens when our souls are satisfied. The joy of the Lord means that no matter what happens, we know that God is with us. In tough times, we may not have a smile on our faces, but we have a smile in our souls because we know that God will take care of us. We know that God will guide us and will satisfy our needs. This week, focus on the joy of the Lord. Find ways to love God and to love others. When you do, Isaiah promises that you will find your joy in the Lord!

## Discussion and Prayer

1. Ask your family to talk about times when they feel close to God. When are the times that they feel closest to God?

2. Talk about ways that you can help the needy this week. (Maybe you can help serve food to homeless people. Perhaps you can donate clothes to a shelter. Maybe you can volunteer at a senior center. Think of creative ways that you can help.)

3. Choose one way to help others this week. Afterward, debrief with your family. Talk about what you learned and how you felt.

4. Pray, thanking God for giving us joy. Ask for help in following God and finding ways to honor God.

# September

## First Week of September
## Hebrews 13:1-3, 6-8—"Entertaining Strangers"

### Your Story

Have you ever helped someone you didn't know? Or has someone come into your life at just the right time and it felt like they were sent from God? Pick one of these times to talk about with your family.

### My Story and the Bible Story

Sixth grade was a hard year for me. I had a falling out with my best friends at school, and I felt like I didn't have any friends. Our church was going through some conflict as well, and I felt alone. I leaned on God a lot in those times. And something amazing happened. A new girl transferred to our school, and all of a sudden I had a friend again. Her name was also Jessica, and she and I were inseparable. I had a friend just when I needed it. After that year, we went to different middle schools and I never saw her again. I've tried to find her and haven't been able to, so I wonder if God sent me an angel in the form of a sixth-grade stranger who was there for me just when I needed it.

Read Hebrews 13:1-3, 6-8.

God promises never to leave us or forsake us. God is always there for us. Sometimes God sends us people when we need them. As in my story, God can send people who help us keep going. Those people are there for us when we need them, and many times they eventually fade away from our lives. The point is that they were there to help us through. Sometimes we get to be that person for someone else. God promises never to leave any of us. Sometimes we are the ones who need help, but other times it may be a stranger who needs it. We may feel a nudge from God to help someone else. We may not understand it at the time, but we may be God's presence for others. Listen for God's nudges. Follow when God nudges you to help someone else. And when you are having a hard time, be on the lookout for

God's presence in the eyes of a stranger. God is all around us and always there for us. So be kind to strangers—you never know where you'll find God's presence next.

## Discussion and Prayer

1. Ask your children if someone has come into their lives at the right time (like a Sunday school teacher, a friend at school, or even a pet).

2. Talk about what it means that God never leaves us and that God is the same yesterday, today, and forever.

3. Talk about ways you can show hospitality to strangers as a family.

4. Pray, asking God to keep your eyes open to God's presence. Ask for help in following God, particularly when it comes to helping others.

# Second Week of September
# Jeremiah 18:1-11—
# "God Makes Beautiful Things"

### Your Story

Talk about a time in your life when you made a wrong decision and God brought something good out of it, or when a tragedy happened and God made something good happen through it.

### My Story and the Bible Story

I'm very clumsy, and sometimes I break things. There have been times when I have broken dishes as I was washing them, or I have broken things by knocking them over. Usually, when I break something I have to throw it away. It's broken so it's no good. It doesn't seem fixable, so I throw it out.

But the Japanese have another solution. When a piece of pottery is broken, they use a precious metal, like gold or silver, to fix it. It is an art called *kintsugi*, and it takes something broken and turns it into something beautiful. The ceramic bowl or vase or plate has "scars" where you can see gold or silver, but it is beautiful. It is celebrated. They take something broken and make it beautiful again.[17]

God does the same thing in our lives. We all make mistakes. We all do things that are wrong sometimes. Sometimes we really mess up and it seems like God should just throw us away. But God doesn't. God makes us into something beautiful again.

Read Jeremiah 18:1-11.

The Israelites made a lot of mistakes. They were constantly turning away from God, and they even ended up wandering around the desert for forty years. But, when they turned back to God, when they followed God, God used them to do great things. It didn't matter that they had made mistakes. They were God's people and God could use them. God uses all of us. None of us is perfect, and we all make mistakes. But God can take the things we do wrong and turn them into something beautiful. No matter what you do, God loves you, and God can always work in your life. Our lives are like clay and God is the potter. Even if the vase falls apart on the potter's wheel, God can reshape it into something else. God uses each and every one of us and can make something beautiful out of something broken.

What about when tragedy and disasters happen? What about when hurricanes and tornadoes destroy? God can make something beautiful out of that too. When bad things happen, God sends others to help us. God sends others to help us rebuild and to remind us that we are never alone. God helps us no matter what, and God can take mistakes and tragedies and bring something good out of them.

# Discussion and Prayer

1. If your kids are artistic, ask them about things they have made that didn't end up the way they hoped. How did it turn out?

2. Remind your children that God used people in the Bible who made a lot of mistakes: Paul killed Christians before he became one. Moses killed an Egyptian. Abraham lied that his wife was

---

17. For more information about this, see Stefano Carnazzi, "Kintsugi: The Art of Precious Scars," *Lifegate*, www.lifegate.com/people/lifestyle/kintsugi.

his sister because he was afraid. Talk to them about how God used each of these biblical figures.

3. Talk about how God uses us in big and small ways.

4. Pray, asking God to make something good out of a bad situation and asking for help to remember that God can always use us.

# Third Week of September
# 1 Corinthians 1:18-25—
# "Our Wisdom vs. God's Wisdom"

## Your Story

Do you pride yourself on being a logical person? Is it hard for you to lean on God instead of your own wisdom? Talk about a time when you had to have faith in God, when you could not depend on your own wisdom to get you through. Talk about a leap of faith you had to take. How did it feel? What was the outcome?

## My Story and the Bible Story

There are many instances in my childhood when logic got me into trouble. It usually began with me saying, "I told you so," which never ended well. Many times I irritated my whole family by saying, "You know, you're just going to have to . . . ." In my defense, I was generally right. A plus B equaled C, and my logic was sound. But of course, that generally wasn't the point. Sometimes it's hard to make the leap from logic/wisdom to faith.

If, as Christians, we think about what we believe, we see that it doesn't make logical sense. God came down in the form of Jesus, who was both human and divine and completely sinless. But instead of taking complete control, Jesus taught, allowed the people to arrest him, and died on a cross between two thieves. If that were the end of the story, it would truly seem like a complete failure. Thank goodness it's not the end, though. What happened next defied logic, wisdom, and the laws of nature. Jesus rose from the dead and left us with the Holy Spirit. Everything about Jesus' ministry, including his miracles, his spending time with outcasts, his caring for the poor, and his refusal to take military power, defied the conventional wisdom of the day. Jesus respected women, recognized the importance of children, and touched the people considered unclean. From the moment he set foot on Earth, he turned wisdom and logic on its side.

Read 1 Corinthians 1:18-25.

It's easy to lean on our own wisdom. After all, we don't like to ask for help. With this brand of wisdom, it can be difficult to accept God's wisdom. As this passage of Scripture states, God's wisdom can at times look ridiculous. We know and accept the story of Christ, but for many, it seems too absurd to be true. It doesn't make sense, and with their conventional wisdom they simply cannot understand how it could happen. Rather than taking a leap of faith, they choose to rely on their own logic and come away empty-handed. But those of us who follow Christ see the power of God in the story. God chose to become like creation in order to experience life as we do, walk beside us, and allow humanity to do our worst while still accepting us as God's own. Jesus laid down his own life for us so that we might live. Conventional wisdom tells us to save ourselves in times like that, but Jesus chose to save us instead of himself. When others see your faith and tell you that you are foolish to believe, remember that "the foolishness of God is wiser than man's wisdom, and the weakness of God is stronger than man's strength" (1 Cor 1:25).

## Discussion and Prayer

1. If your children have accepted Jesus, ask them if anyone has made fun of them for being a Christian.

2. Talk about ways they might respond.

3. Talk to your children about times when you've had to rely on God.

4. Ask your children if there are times when they've had to take a leap of faith and rely on God.

5. Pray, giving thanks that God's wisdom is so much better than ours. Ask God to help you listen as you make decisions and for help in following God's wisdom instead of your own.

# Fourth Week of September
# 1 Timothy 2:1-7—"Pray for Everyone"

## Your Story

Who do you pray for? How do you pray? Talk to your kids about the different ways you pray and the people you pray for. If you pray specifically for your kids, tell them.

## My Story and the Bible Story

When I was a kid, I wanted to pray for everyone. Every night as we said prayers at bedtime, I always added, "God bless the whole world." Every time we had prayer request time at Girls in Action at church, one of my requests was for "the whole world." Looking back, I realize that it may be a little silly to pray for the whole world. At the same time, though, the world needs our prayers. Our lives are better when we have God in them. Our lives are better when we take time to talk to God. The lives of others are different because we (and others) pray for them. Prayer is important, and my young self knew that the whole world needed it.

### Read 1 Timothy 2:1-7.

"The first thing I want you to do is pray. Pray every way you know how, for everyone you know" (v. 1). Prayer is so important that Paul told Timothy it needed to be the first thing he did. Paul didn't just tell Timothy to pray for the people he liked or only for other Christians. Instead, Paul told Timothy to pray for *everyone he knew*, including the rulers. In the time of the New Testament, the government didn't always treat Christians very well. In fact, there were times when rulers went out of their way to punish Christians simply because they believed in Jesus. There were times when it was hard to like the government because they were the ones punishing and hurting people. But Paul tells Timothy to pray for them. Paul tells Timothy to pray for everyone, including the people with whom Timothy disagreed. If Paul were writing to us today, he would tell us to pray for everyone, including friends *and* bullies, people in desperate situations, people who have a lot less or a lot more than we do. He would also tell us to pray for our govern-ment. It doesn't matter if we agree with their decisions; Paul would tell us to pray for them. He would tell us to pray for teachers and the principal, even when they make decisions we don't like.

Prayer is powerful. Prayer has the power to change the world. Prayer is our conversation with the God of the universe, and we know that God listens to us. Prayer can change the heart of a bully so that they stop hurting others. It can change the lives of people in jail. Prayer can change anyone, and it also changes us. When we pray for others, it is harder to hate them. When we pray for those who bully us or disagree with us, we remind ourselves that God created them just like God created us. Prayer can change their hearts and it also can change ours. We pray for everyone so that our world can change. We pray that others will see God so that their hearts can be changed like ours were changed. As you pray this week, pray for your friends and for your family. Also pray for everyone you know, the people you like and the people you don't. Pray for our leaders, that they will know what is best for our country.

## Discussion and Prayer

1. Talk about different ways to pray. (If you need ideas, look online.) Ask your children which idea they like best and why.

2. Pick a different way to pray this week and practice praying in that way. At the end of the week, ask your family if their prayers felt different because they were praying differently.

3. Ask your kids who they pray for. Then talk about other people they can pray for.

4. Pray, asking God for help in praying for people you don't like. Pray for everyone you know. Pray for our leaders. Thank God for always hearing our prayers.

# End of September/ Beginning of October Psalm 146—"The Lord Is Faithful"

## Your Story

Talk about a time when you placed your trust in someone and you were disappointed.

## My Story and the Bible Story

When I was a kid, my stepdad promised he would take us to Europe. Years went by and eventually he and my mom got a divorce. In that whole time, he never took us to Europe. He didn't keep his promise. He meant well when he promised to take us, but he couldn't make it happen. That happens to all of us. People promise to do things or to give us things. We get excited about it, but sometimes, for whatever reason, they never do those things or give us what they promised. Maybe your parents promised you a puppy but it turns out that your brother is allergic, or maybe someone promised to give you their favorite toy and they didn't. Sometimes people promise us things and it just doesn't happen.

Read Psalm 146.

Psalm 146 reminds us that while people can promise things, they can't always follow through. But God is faithful, all the time. God reigns forever and always follows through with promises. Eventually, every single one of us will die, but God will not. God has been and will always be there, through the generations. God remembers what was promised to Noah and Abraham, to Moses and Joshua, to Deborah and Ruth, to Paul and Lazarus. And God remembers what was promised to us. We can cling to the promises in the Bible because we know that God is faithful and does what God promises. We can't always do what we promise others, but God can and God does. What great news that is! No wonder the psalmist says that he will sing praise to God for as long as he lives. We can trust God!

## Discussion and Prayer

1. Ask your children about broken promises. Has anyone broken a promise to them? Have they broken promises to others?

2. Talk about how we all break promises. You might talk about a promise you made to your children that you had to break. Share your reasons for doing so.

3. Talk about the things that God has promised us: God will take care of us, will never leave us, will never destroy the Earth again by flood, will forgive us, etc.

4. Pray, thanking God for always being faithful. Ask for help in remembering God's promises.

# October

## First Week of October
## 2 Timothy 1:1-14—
## "I Know Whom I Have Believed"

### Your Story

Talk about how you have seen God's power at work in your life. What has God done in your life?

### My Story and the Bible Story

When we ask Jesus to be our friend forever, when we tell God that we know Jesus died for us and we want to follow him, we are committing our lives to God. We are saying that God knows better than we do and that we will listen to God and obey. We will act like Christ by following God. We can trust that God will hold on to us. God will treat our lives as precious and will walk beside us.

Read 2 Timothy 1:1-14.

Paul reminds Timothy that God has saved us not because of what we have done but because of who God is. We don't know why God has chosen to save us, but thank goodness God has! Our lives are precious to God, and God will guard them. We can trust God with everything, even our lives, because God destroyed death and offered love, a love that is the most powerful force in the world. Paul reminds Timothy to keep believing no matter what happens, because God gives us power.

### Discussion and Prayer

1. If past generations of your family were Christians, tell your children how God worked in their lives. If they weren't Christians, talk about how you can see God working in your children's lives.

2. Talk about ways you can share with others about God's power. How can you share your own stories of God's power?

3. Pray, giving thanks that God holds on to us and never lets us go. Ask for help in seeing God's power at work in our lives.

# Second Week of October
# 2 Kings 5:1-3, 7-15c—"Easy vs. Difficult"

## Your Story

Talk about a time in your life when you thought something would be difficult but it turned out to be easy. It could be a school project, work project, or simply something you dreaded doing that ended up being easy.

## My Story and the Bible Story

There have been many times when I have put off doing something because I either thought it was going to take a while or would be hard to do. A few years ago I got a new dining room table and chairs. Putting the table together took forever, so I didn't put the chairs together that night because I thought they would take a while too. The next day, I discovered it took about twenty minutes to put together all four chairs! I also tend to put off washing pots and pans after I cook because I think it's going to take forever. When I finally wash them, it usually only takes about five minutes. Sometimes we don't want to do something because we think it's going to take a while or will be hard. And sometimes, we think something sounds so easy that there's no way it could be worthwhile.

### Read 2 Kings 5:1-3, 7-15c.

Naaman got upset with Elisha because Elisha told him to do something easy. All Naaman had to do was wash in the Jordan River and his leprosy would be gone. But Naaman thought he surely needed to do something harder in order to be cured. Sometimes we fall into that trap too. We think we need to do something to earn God's grace. We think the only way we can be saved is to do difficult things to prove our worth to God. But all we have to do is accept God's grace. There's nothing we can do to earn it, and yet it's sometimes hard for us to trust that it's so easy.

On the flip side, there are times when we give up before we ever start because we think something's going to be so hard that we won't be able to do it. There are times that those things are hard, but many times they are easier than we think. The truth is this: if what we think is too hard is something God has asked us to do, then God will help us through it. We may not be strong enough to do it on our own, but if we trust in God, God will help us. There are going to be times in our lives when, as with Naaman, something seems too good or easy to be true. When that happens, listen to God. God will tell you what's true. There will also be times when things seem too hard. Listen to God then, too. If it's something God wants you to do, God will help you make it through. That is great news!

## Discussion and Prayer

1. Ask your kids if there have been times when something seemed too good (or too easy) to be true. Also have them talk about times when they thought something would be too hard. What happened? Did they ask for help?

2. Why do you think Naaman eventually did what Elisha told him to do? What should we do if it seems like God is telling us to do something really easy or something really hard?

3. Pray, thanking God that all we have to do to be saved is accept God's grace. Ask for help in doing things that are hard.

# Third Week of October
# Psalm 121—"The Lord Watches Over You"

### Your Story

Talk about a time when you knew God was watching over you. Talk about the peace you felt.

## My Story and the Bible Story

It's almost Halloween, and this time of year tends to be a bit scarier than normal. People decorate their houses to look frightening, scary movies come on TV, and some people wear scary costumes on Halloween. Sometimes there's even spooky Halloween music, like the song "Somebody's Watching Me." This song is about how it feels like someone is watching the singer, no matter what he does. It sounds scary to think that someone is watching us. In fact, we have someone who watches us all the time, but it's not scary. It's an amazing thing!

Read Psalm 121.

The Lord watches over you. God doesn't sleep, get tired, or get bored. God keeps us safe and watches over us. We don't need to be afraid of monsters under the bed or monsters in the closet or people dressed up in scary costumes, because the Lord watches over us. Halloween may be a scary time, but we don't have to worry, because the Lord never leaves us. God is right there with us, watching us and keeping us safe. We can rest assured that God sees us wherever we go, and if we get scared, God is there, ready to offer us comfort. Instead of being scared at Halloween, remember that God watches you. The God of the universe cares about what happens to you. There's no need to be afraid.

# Discussion and Prayer

1. Ask your children what they are afraid of. Talk about how God can help them face their fears and what it means that God is watching over them.

2. If there are specific things that they are afraid of at this time of year, talk about ways they can face their fears, reminding them that God gives us courage.

3. Ask your children if there has been a time in their lives when it felt like God was watching over them and that everything would be okay. What happened?

4. Pray, thanking God for always being there for us and for watching over us. Ask God for help in facing your fears and ask God to give you courage.

# Fourth Week of October
# Luke 18:9-14—"You're Not Perfect"

## Your Story

Talk about a time when you were a kid and you knew you had done something wrong. How did you feel? Did you ask for forgiveness? How did you feel after that?

## My Story and the Bible Story

When thinking about the things I've done wrong, I sometimes compare my sins to other people's sins. Unsurprisingly, when imagined this way, my sins seem to be the less serious ones! I think about white lies I have told or other minor transgressions. Then, when I hear about a terrible thing that someone else did, I feel better, thinking that at least I didn't do something like that.

It's easy to forget that we make mistakes, that we sometimes make the wrong choice, especially when we see someone who has done something that we think is worse.

### Read Luke 18:9-14.

If we're honest with ourselves, most of the time we are like the Pharisee. We say things like, "Well, I may have done this, but at least I didn't do *that*." We judge others for the wrong that they have done. "I was mean to someone, but at least I'm not like the kid who stole from someone." But here's the thing: God sees all of our sin the same. Whether you lied, stole, hurt, or even killed someone, God sees all sin the same. That means we are no better than a bully, because we've done wrong things too. Instead, Jesus says we should be more like the tax collector, who didn't look at others and think he was better or worse than them. Instead, he focused on asking for God's forgiveness because he did something wrong. God is ready and waiting to forgive us. God is eager to forgive, but forgiveness requires something of us too. It requires that we recognize that we did something wrong. The Pharisee didn't see that he had done anything wrong. He even thanked God that he wasn't like those sinners. But the tax collector knew that he had made mistakes and that he needed God's forgiveness. We all do things that are wrong sometimes, and we all need God's forgiveness. God is pleased with us when we don't compare ourselves to others but recognize that we do wrong too. When we ask, God is quick to forgive.

## Discussion and Prayer

1. Ask your kids about times when they have done something wrong. How did they feel? Did they ask for forgiveness? How did they feel after that?

2. Give some examples of things that people do wrong. Talk about how we all make the wrong choice sometimes. Assure your children that God's love is so great that God is able to forgive anything, even things that we cannot forgive.

3. Remind your children that Jesus never did anything wrong but that he took on all of our wrongs so that we could always be forgiven.

4. Pray, asking God for help in not judging others. Ask for help in recognizing the things you have done wrong. Ask for forgiveness for specific things. Thank God for loving us no matter what.

# November

## First Week of November
## Luke 6:20-31—"Remembering the Saints"

### Your Story

Talk about someone who was an important part of your faith who has passed away. Alternatively, you can talk about someone in your family who had strong faith, or someone in your church or throughout history whose faith you admired.

### My Story and the Bible Story

On All Saints' Day, we remember the important people in our faith. We remember people like Abraham and Moses. We remember David. We remember Peter and the disciples. We remember Paul. We remember the people who died for being a Christian. We remember Martin Luther, who led the Protestant Reformation. We remember Mother Teresa, how much she loved and cared for the poor. We remember these important people, but we also remember people whom the world may not know but who have been important in our faith journeys. We remember people who began our churches, perhaps long ago. We remember family members who taught us about faith. I remember my great-grandmother and her strong faith in the face of adversity and obstacles. I remember my grandfather and how his faith got him through the Korean War, then passed that faith on to us. I remember my great-uncle and how much he loved God and the church. We remember people who believed and who are now with God in heaven, and we also think about the way they lived. They lived to serve others. They followed the way that Jesus told us to live.

### Read Luke 6:20-31.

The NIV version of verse 31 says, "Do to others as you would have them do to you." On All Saints' Day, we remember people of faith. They all lived by this verse. They lived knowing how God wanted them to treat others, even when others did not treat them the same way. Jesus reminds us that what the world thinks is wrong: when you have everything, that doesn't mean you are blessed. When you have God, you are blessed even when everything has fallen apart. We may have all the stuff in the world and not be happy if we don't have God. We are to give God away to others too. God wants us to live a life that shows others God's love. Jesus tells us to love our enemies and pray for them. He tells us to be generous with others and to do what we want others to do for us. When we do this, we share God with them. We are blessed. All the saints, both those who are well known and those who are only important to us, knew that. Let us live as they did, sharing God with those around us.

## Discussion and Prayer

1. As a family, spend a few minutes finding information about some of the saints of the church. Talk about the ways they served God. Then talk about some of the people in your own lives who serve God.

2. Talk about ways you each can be more like these saints. What are some ways you can serve God together?

3. Talk about ways that you can remember the "saints" of your family for All Saints' Day.

4. Pray, thanking God for these people of faith and the people who have been important in your own faith journey. Ask God for help in being more like them.

# Second Week of November
# 2 Thessalonians 2:13-17—"Stand Strong"

## Your Story

Talk about a time when you felt like you stood firm in your faith. You might have trusted God when things seemed uncertain or been confident when someone made fun of your faith.

## My Story and the Bible Story

A few years ago, we sang a song in Vacation Bible School called "Stand Strong." Here are the lyrics:

Stand strong when life changes
Stand strong through the ups and downs
Stand strong for you know that God is in control

The storms of life will push and pull
But we are standing on the Rock that never rolls
The storms of life will push and pull
We will keep standing
God is in control[18]

Sometimes bad things happen in our lives. A loved one dies. Someone gets sick. You have to move and leave your friends behind. Parents sometimes divorce. There's a bully at school or on the bus. You start a new school and you don't understand what you're trying to learn. These are hard times. There are also times in life when things are good, but this song reminds us to stand strong through the ups and downs. We can stand strong because we know that God is in control. Second Thessalonians encourages us to stand strong.

Read 2 Thessalonians 2:13-17.

"God picked you out as his from the very start." Have you ever thought about that? You are God's. God picked you out from the very start. You are God's child, and God loves you. God created you to be who you are and included you in the plan of salvation. So stand strong and keep your head high, because the Creator of the universe picked you from the very start! When people make fun of you, remember that you are God's. When things are uncertain, like when you go to a new school, remember that God is with you. When your friends try to get you to do something you know isn't right, take a stand because you are God's and God will show you what's right. Whenever anything happens, you can stand strong because God is always beside you. But even if you stumble and fall, even if you don't stand strong, remember what we learned a few weeks ago: God can take our mistakes and turn them into something beautiful. So stand strong, because you are God's.

---

18. "Stand Strong," Kingdom Rock VBS, Group Publishing, 2013.

## Discussion and Prayer

1. Invite your children to share ways they have been standing strong. Celebrate what they have done.

2. Talk about things that help us stand strong: making sure we have friends who believe in what we do, going to church, reading our Bibles, praying to God, etc.

3. Brainstorm ways to encourage one another to stand strong (sticky notes on the mirror, lunch box notes, texts, etc.).

4. Pray, asking God for help in standing strong. Give thanks that God chose all of you from the very start!

# Third Week of November
# Psalm 98—"Music"

## Your Story

Talk about a time when music has helped you feel closer to God. What music do you love to listen to when you want to praise God?

## My Story and the Bible Story

A dear friend once gave me a great piece of advice: when life feels out of control, listen to praise music. As you praise God through song, you start to realize that God is in control and is bigger than anything happening to you. As I write, the presidential election is this week, and for the past several months life has felt out of control. It's hard to turn the TV on without hearing news about rude comments made by candidates, reasons we can't trust either of them, and the candidates treating one another badly. It's hard to log on to Facebook without seeing post after post about the election and why neither candidate can be trusted. In the midst of all of the name-calling, mudslinging, and other awful behavior, the world is at war. People are fleeing their homes as bombs fall in Syria. Hurricanes have left people without food, water, and shelter. Life feels out of control.

And yet we remember that God has done marvelous things. God came down into our mess when life was out of control and saved us. This is why we sing praises to God even when life is out of control. God never leaves us and always loves us. We can trust God. We can trust that God is our helper, our friend, and our Savior. We know that no matter what happens in our country or on Earth, God's love is bigger than any of it.

Read Psalm 98.

What a beautiful picture of praise! Can you imagine the seas and rivers praising God? When the waves of the sea clap together, they are praising God. When the river hits the rocks, it too praises God. If creation can praise God in this way, how much more should we praise God? God has done marvelous things for us. God has created us, saved us, and loved us unconditionally. There's never anything we could do to make God stop loving us. When the world feels out of control, we can rest in God's love.

Life is busy. Maybe your world feels a bit out of control as well. No matter what happens in this election or any other big decision, one thing will not change: God loves you. God wants to talk to you. And God loves to hear your praises. Take time to sing praises to God. If life feels out of control, listen to praise music whenever you can. As you sing, remember that God sees the bigger picture. At the end of everything, it's all going to be okay because God is in control!

## Discussion and Prayer

1. Ask your family if life feels out of control for them. In what ways does it feel out of control?

2. Talk about how you can have God's peace even when life feels out of control (all you have to do is ask for it!).

3. Ask your children (if they are at least elementary age) how you can help them feel like life isn't so hectic. Maybe they need more time to do their homework, or maybe they need an evening where everyone unplugs and spends time together.

4. Pray, asking God for help in praising God no matter what happens. Ask for God's peace.

# Fourth Week of November
# Philippians 4:4-9—"Count Your Blessings"

## Your Story

Tell your family about some things for which you are thankful. Include ways that God has answered your prayers this year.

## My Story and the Bible Story

This is the time of year when we stuff our faces with turkey, dumplings (my grandmother makes the best!), mashed potatoes and gravy, green bean casserole, and a lot more dessert than we need. But it's also a time when we gather with our families and remember the things for which we are thankful. This year I am thankful that my sister got into a program to train her to live out her calling. I'm thankful for another year at a wonderful church, and I am thankful to know so many caring people here. I am thankful for the smiles and hugs from the kids at church, and I am grateful that I get to teach them each week. I am thankful for my family and my friends, both near and far.

It can be easy to forget our blessings. During moments of pain, anger, or sadness, it can be easy to forget all the good things we have. That's why this passage from Philippians is so important.

Read Philippians 4:4-9.

This is one of my favorite passages of Scripture because it reminds me not to worry. Worrying doesn't get us anywhere. All it does is upset us and make us feel bad. Worrying doesn't change what's going to happen. God doesn't want us to worry; God wants us to talk about it. Tell God what's going on, what we're worried about, and what we need. But God also wants us to come with thankful hearts. When we worry, we tend to forget how big God is. We forget that God created the universe, knows everything about everyone, and, no matter how many people God has created, still wants to talk to us. When we come to God with thankful hearts, it means that we remember the things God has done. We remember how God has been there for us, helped us, and loves us. When we thank God for things, we remember that God is in control and we are not, and that no matter what happens, God will never leave us.

Thanksgiving is a time of remembering the good things and being thankful for them. It's also a time when we can remember everything God has done for us and be thankful for God. When we remember the things God has done, we receive God's peace. We see that in those times, God showed up for us, and we know God will always be there and will always love us. So whether you are worried or full of thankfulness, present your requests to God with a thankful heart, because God will always be there for you. And when you do, you will find God's peace.

## Discussion and Prayer

1. Ask your family about things for which they are thankful. Talk about these things as a family.

2. Ask your family if they are worried about anything.

3. Pray, presenting your requests to God. If you are worried or upset, give your concerns to God. Give thanks for specific things God has done in your life and in the lives of your family members. Ask for God's peace.

# Extra Devotions

## Psalm 34:1-8, 19-22— "God Is Good, All the Time!"

### Your Story

Talk about a time when God delivered you from your fears or used troubles in your life to make something good happen.

### My Story and the Bible Story

When I was a teenager, our youth group used a certain saying to end our meetings each week: "God is good, all the time! All the time, God is good!" Good is good all the time. Regardless of what's happening in our lives, good or bad, God is always good. Psalm 34 reminds us of that.

### Read Psalm 34:1-8, 19-22.

David, who likely wrote this psalm, reminds us to bless God every chance we get. David's life wasn't perfect by any means. His best friend's dad, Saul, was like a father to him but tried to kill him because he knew that David was destined to be king. David had to run from Saul to stay alive. David made some big mistakes in his life, and several of David's children died. But still David says he will praise the Lord every chance he gets because God is always good. David reminds us that we can run to God no matter what happens. God will be there every time. God doesn't expect us to get ourselves out of our own messes. Instead, God is right there beside us, helping us up and making something good out of our troubles. God has saved us and redeemed us and continues to help us. Because of this, like David, we are called to praise God every chance we get. No matter what is happening, the God of the universe is there. We don't have to hide what we feel or what we have done, because God knows all of it. God will calm our fears and pick us up when we fall. Our God is always there. Praise the Lord!

## Discussion and Prayer

1. Talk about ways to praise God this week. What does it mean to bless God every chance we get?

2. Ask your children to talk about their fears. As a family, talk about how God can calm our fears.

3. Praise the Lord for who God is! Thank God for always being there and for helping us.

# Psalm 111—"Praise the Lord!"

## Your Story

Talk about a time when you felt like you praised the Lord with your whole heart. How did it feel?

## My Story and the Bible Story

I love going to conferences and retreats. Conferences mean long days of learning from lots of different speakers. They mean being around thousands and thousands of people, which for me is pretty tiring. But they also mean worship. They mean singing praises to God with thousands of other people. They mean taking a break from regular life and spending time focused on God. It is during these times when we are singing to God that I most feel like I am praising the Lord with my whole heart. I am focused only on God in those moments, and no matter what is happening in my life, it is easier to praise God.

Have you ever sung a song as loudly as you could? When you sing a song like that, you let go of everything else. Your only focus is that song. It makes you feel great. God wants us to do that too. When we praise the Lord with our whole hearts, it feels great because it reminds us of all that God has done.

Read Psalm 111.

"To him belongs eternal praise." We praise God because God deserves it. Praise belongs to God. Great are the works of the Lord, whose deeds are majestic. God remembers the people and is faithful and just. We can trust God. God provides for us and walks beside us. God is gracious and compassionate. When we worship God with our whole hearts, we remember all that God has done for us. When we focus on God, we realize that things like video games or trophies don't really matter much. The Creator of the universe made us, and we get to worship the Lord. We get to sing praise to God's name. When we focus on God, everything else becomes clearer. It is easier to understand what we are to do when we are focused on God. It's easier to be nice to others or to help others when we are focused on God. It's easier to serve others when we are focused on God. So sing a song of praise to God. Sing it as loudly as you can and focus on God. You'll be glad you did!

## Discussion and Prayer

1. What are your favorite songs of praise to God?

2. As a family, talk about how you can incorporate songs of praise into your everyday lives. Maybe that means singing worship songs while you do the dishes or playing them as everyone gets ready in the morning.

3. How can you worship God this week?

4. Pray, giving thanks for who God is and what God has done. Offer praise for God's mighty deeds. Thank God for always being there for us and that we can always trust God.

# Isaiah 40:26-31—"Everlasting"

## Your Story

Talk with your family about a time in your life when God has given you strength.

## My Story and the Bible Story

"Everlasting God," a Chris Tomlin song, is inspired by this passage of Scripture. Here are the lyrics:

> Strength will rise as we wait upon the Lord,
> wait upon the Lord, we will wait upon the Lord.
> Strength will rise as we wait upon the Lord,
> wait upon the Lord, we will wait upon the Lord.
> Our God, You reign forever
> Our hope, our strong deliverer.
> You are the everlasting God,
> The everlasting God.
> You do not faint,
> You won't grow weary.
> You're the defender of the weak,
> You comfort those in need,
> You lift us up on wings like eagles.[19]

I love this song because it reminds me that we don't have to do everything on our own. There are days when it seems as if I can't keep going. There are days when I feel too sad or too worried or too stressed, and all I want to do is hide under the covers. Yet, when I grow weary, God doesn't. When I am weak, God isn't. When I wait on God, when I hope in God, and when I trust that God is there, God gives me the strength I need.

Read Isaiah 40:26-31.

Isaiah reminds us that God is our strength. When it's hard for us to keep going, God is there, holding us up. Maybe you're having a tough time at school. Maybe there's a bully who keeps picking on you and you don't know what to do anymore. Or maybe you're worried about every test you take. Maybe you're sad because someone you loved just died. Parents, maybe you feel like all you ever do is run from one thing to the next, and you are tired of running. Whatever is going on in your life, God knows it. Whenever you are tired and feel like you can't keep going, God will give you the strength you need. God will help you focus so that you can study. God will help you know what to do about a bully (and maybe what God tells you to do is tell a grownup). God will give you the strength you need to go from one thing to the next. God is everlasting, which means that God never ends. God

---

19. "Everlasting God," by Chris Tomlin.

doesn't have a beginning or an ending. God is God, and God has always been and will always be there. God never gets tired and never wants to give up. God always knows when we are tired and when we want to give up. If we tell God about it, we will receive the strength we need to keep going. Strength will rise as we wait upon the Lord!

## Discussion and Prayer

1. Ask your family to talk about times when they needed strength (or courage) from God. Have there been times when they wanted to give up? What did they do?

2. Make sure your children understand what "everlasting" means.

3. Talk about what to do when you feel like you want to give up (pray to God, talk to someone, talk to a grownup, etc.).

4. Pray, thanking God for never leaving us. Ask God for strength for specific things. Give praise that God never grows weary.

# Matthew 5:38-48—"Love Your Enemy"

## Your Story

Have you ever experienced an unexpected good deed from someone you considered an enemy? If so, talk about that experience. If not, talk about a time when you chose to show love instead of hate to someone you felt had wronged you.

## My Story and the Bible Story

"You have heard that it was said, 'Eye for an eye, and tooth for tooth'" (Matt 5:38). Many of us live our lives in this way. All we have to do is watch the news to see people responding like this. Someone is attacked, and their country responds with war. Someone is made fun of, and they respond by making fun of others. This way of living leads to violence and fear. When we strike back at someone, all we do is continue the cycle. Imagine this: Someone makes a hateful comment on a picture on your

Instagram or Facebook. It makes you angry, so you respond back with a hateful comment. Then that person responds again, and suddenly, you are arguing about a picture. Or maybe someone steals your favorite toy. You finally get it back, but you are angry and you want that person to hurt like you did, so you take something of theirs. Then maybe they push you down for taking it, and suddenly you are fighting. There's a better but harder way to live.

Read Matthew 5:38-48.

"But Jesus," we want to say, "surely you don't mean that I can't defend myself? That person hurt me and I want to make sure they don't do it again." There are times when we have to stand up for ourselves, but here's the difference: we are called to love everyone, not just the people we like. Think about God: God loves every single one of us. It does not matter what you have done or not done, God loves you. And God loved the people who put Jesus on the cross. Jesus died asking God to forgive the people who killed him. God gives his best to every single one of us, whether we are lovable or not.

One of the hardest parts about being a Christian is loving our enemies. It is hard to love someone who is mean to us. In fact, we can't do it by ourselves. But Jesus isn't telling us to. He says, "When someone gives you a hard time, respond with the energies of prayer, for then you are working out of your true selves, your God-created selves." God created us to be who we are and created us for love, not for hate. So the next time someone seems unlovable or does something that makes you angry, pray for that person. Ask God for help in loving them. When you do, you will be doing what God wants you to do: "[living] generously and graciously toward others, the way God lives toward you."

## Discussion and Prayer

1. Ask your children to talk about times when they felt like someone was their enemy. How did they respond? Role-play ways to respond differently, ways that show love to our "enemies."

2. Talk about ways we can show love to others when they aren't very lovable.

3. Who do you know who isn't lovable?

4. Pray, asking God for help in loving everyone. Ask for help in seeing God's face in others.

# Matthew 6:25-33–"Do Not Worry"

## Your Story

Talk to your children about various (age-appropriate) things you have worried about. Has God given you a reminder that God will take care of you? What has that looked like?

## My Story and the Bible Story

I'm a worrier. I worry about all kinds of things, and I have done this ever since I was a child. As a child, I worried about tests at school, but I also worried about safety. I even had an escape plan in case of fire or a burglar. I worried that there was something under my bed or in my closet. When I worried, I would pray and ask God for help. I still do the same thing: when I worry, I pray. God reminds me that God will take care of me.

Read Matthew 6:25-33.

These are life-giving words from Jesus because they remind us that God knows what we need. God knows when we need a friend. God knows when we need encouragement. God knows when we are upset or afraid and need comfort. God knows when we need food. God knows exactly what we need and cares for us. God will provide for us. Jesus pushes back on our worry in this passage when he asks if any of us can add a single moment to our lives by worrying. Worry doesn't add anything to our lives; instead, it takes away our joy and peace. When you worry, trust that God will take care of you. Pray about those worries and ask God to take your worries away. God will give you peace.

## Discussion and Prayer

1. Ask your children about what they are worried about.

2. Remind them that God sees them and knows everything about them. God knows about their worries and wants to give them peace.

3. Talk about ways that God has provided for your family.

4. This week, be intentional about having your whole family pray about what each person is worried about. At the end of the week, talk about ways that taking your worries to God helped.

5. Pray, asking God to take away your worries (name them specifically). Ask God for peace.

# Mark 1:14-20—"Fishers of People"

## Your Story

Tell your family about someone who told you about Jesus. How did they do so? Were they happy, sad, or mad? Did they yell at you on a street corner, or did they sit with you and talk about what Jesus had done in their lives? Did they make you want to know Jesus better, or did they push you farther away?

## My Story and the Bible Story

Going fishing takes patience. You have to wait a while (sometimes a very long while) before the fish start biting. First, you put something on your hook that you hope the fish will want to eat. Then you plop the hook into the water and wait. Sometimes you may move it around some, but you have to wait for the fish. I'm not good at the waiting part. I've never liked to fish because it seems like a waste of time to sit and wait. But my granddad loved to fish. He never minded the waiting. The waiting was a time to catch up, to read, to talk to one another. Or a time to simply sit and be. To spend time with God. To sit in quiet wonder.

Read Mark 1:14-20.

Simon (Peter) and Andrew were fishermen. They knew what it was like to sit and wait for the fish to come. Every day, that's what they did, until Jesus came along. When Jesus invited them to follow him, to become fishers of people, they immediately left their nets and followed. As fishers of people, their job was different. Instead of casting a net off the side of a boat, they were telling others about Jesus. They were there to witness Jesus' miracles. But there were still times when they had to wait. They weren't waiting for fish anymore; they were waiting for people. They had to wait for the people to come and to follow Jesus. They had to wait for transformation. It didn't matter how many times they told people about Jesus, God still had to do the transforming. In order for God to change the people, they had to want God to.

Like Simon and Andrew, we are fishers of people. We don't walk around with fishing poles and hooks like most fishermen do. Instead, we tell people about Jesus. Then we wait for God to touch their hearts and transform their lives. Our job is to tell others about Jesus. God's job is to transform them. Sometimes people don't want God to change them. Sometimes people are afraid of what God will do in their lives, or they simply don't want to change. In that case, we have told them about Jesus, and then it's up to them. But never forget that we are fishers of people, called to tell others about Jesus. God is a God of transformation: God can change people's lives in a way that we can't. So be a fisher of people like Simon and Andrew. Tell others about Jesus, and then wait for God to change their lives.

## Discussion and Prayer

1. How can we help others learn about Jesus?

2. How has Jesus changed you?

3. Pray, asking God to help you be a fisher of people. Ask for help in sharing Jesus with others.

# About the Author

Rev. Jessica Asbell is the Minister to Children and Families at First Baptist Roswell, where she has been serving since 2012. She has written the children's curriculum for Smyth & Helwys Publishing's Annual Bible Study for the books of Daniel; Ezekiel; Luke; Jonah; 1 Corinthians; 1, 2, 3 John and Jude; Colossians; and *The Story of Israel's Ancestors: Living toward a Promise*. She has also written for CBF's Spark and Form and for Affect in CBF's *fellowship!* magazine. Married to Jonathan Oravec, Jessica reads every chance she gets.